SMALL BOAT IN SOUTHERN FRANCE

SMALL BOAT IN
SOUTHERN FRANCE

BY

ROGER PILKINGTON

Illustrated by David Knight

MACMILLAN
London · Melbourne · Toronto

ST MARTIN'S PRESS
New York
1965

MACMILLAN AND COMPANY LIMITED
St Martin's Street London WC 2
also Bombay Calcutta Madras Melbourne

THE MACMILLAN COMPANY OF CANADA LIMITED
70 Bond Street Toronto 2

ST MARTIN'S PRESS INC
175 Fifth Avenue New York 10010 NY

Library of Congress Catalog Card No. 65–13564

PRINTED IN GREAT BRITAIN

Tant qué lé moundé durara,
Toun noum, Riquet, brounzinara!

As long as the world shall last,
your name, Riquet, shall resound!

DAVEAU: Epigraph to an ode on
the Canal du Midi

FOREWORD

This is not the first book to have come out of the travels of the *Commodore*. It is the twenty-first, and with it she retires both from literary effort and from her role as the flagship of the unregistered Pilkington line.

Not that I or any other among her friends are going back to the land. It is just that boats, like dogs and parrots, age. There comes a time when their movements are not so brisk as once they were, and they want nothing so much as a basket by the fire, or a heavier table-cloth over the cage, or a nice quiet slipway according to their taste and genus. That she is to be replaced by another younger and more active than herself may worry a female parrot. Or it may not. But I like to think that the old *Commodore* does not bear any grudge in knowing that whilst I am writing the opening pages of her last venture some skilled men down at a Greenwich shipyard are actually setting up the frames of *Commodore II*. Indeed, although she has never had a deep analysis, emotions of envy and jealousy are so foreign to the *Commodore*'s nature that I am sure she does not even begrudge her successor the distinction of being built on the meridian and thus being by birth neither east nor west.

The *Commodore* herself is built of wood, and is stout enough only to shake slightly when run down by a Belgian barge steered by a man with side-whiskers, a rakish nautical cap, and a lady's black corselet worn over his trousers to improve his figure. Her frame is rigid enough to take the shock of bare rocks which rear up overnight beneath the surface of Swedish lakes, and her bottom is so beautifully rounded as not in any way to restrict her rolling, which she does from sheer exuberance. Structurally she might be termed a gastrula, for she has a double skin — an ectoderm and endoderm as it were — the outer one of planks running horizontally and the other slanting. This construction has never failed to impress continental bargees, and their amazement is still further increased when I tell them that the hull was actually built at Pwllheli in Wales. The skippers of French 38·5-metre barges often express satisfaction at meeting a boat which originated in that fabled country, a land for which they still have profound respect because of the ex-*Prince-de-Galles* who once heroically abandoned all for the love of a *belle dame* and so may be regarded as *un homme formidable*, the lustre of whom is yet reflected upon Wales itself and anything of Welsh origin, including the *Commodore*.

It is easy to be romantic about Wales if you have never been there, but more difficult if one has seen it at first hand. Fortunately the *Commodore*'s Welshness is limited to her having slipped down one of their slipways, and she has nothing Welsh in her character. She is reliable, and does not burst into tears whatever. Indeed, her place of origin is purely accidental. During the Second World War the British had a navy, and an admiral to run it, and this man needed some kind of barge to barge about in and make sure his ships were properly fixed. Somebody in the Admiralty thought it would be nice to build him a new one, all bright and shining from the keel up. The idea of having it built at Pwllheli was so that it might bamboozle Admiral Raeder, who wouldn't be quite sure which side it was on, and couldn't ask his only superior because he dared not try to say Pwllheli for fear of being thought insubordinate and offensive.

The grand scheme actually came to naught, because the admiral's *petit bateau* was not completed until the week the war was over and the admiral himself was due for cocooning. Eventually they decided to sell her as a sort of wreck, and that was how her real life began. When we bought her we little expected that for fifteen years she was to take us on voyages through the whole of western Europe and to rivers and lakes and valleys beautiful beyond imagination, and unknown to us even from the map.

Not every reader will have met the *Commodore* before, so perhaps a little should be said about her to supplement the detail in David Knight's charming sketches. She is, as I have said, of wood. She has a motor on one side amidships and a galley on the other. This motor has anything from 30 to 195 horse-power, *hästkraft,*

Pferdestärke, paardekracht or *chevaux* according to what system of rating the natives use and whether or not the dues are charged on engine-power and modesty is therefore economical. Underneath, near the blunt end, is a propeller, and on the sharp end she wears a nose-bag of rope and canvas to help her push resistant lock gates on the more peaceful and sleepy waterways. Her stays, like those of a duchess, are elastic, and so her mast will tip back of its own accord when entangled in overhanging branches. The steersman stands out in the open, in sun and hail and horsefly alike, and this feature is being repeated on *Commodore II*. One can sail the Atlantic without needing to be able to see very much, for there is little enough to see; but inland waterways call for quick decisions and accurate navigation. It has always been our belief that it is better to get wet and see where we are going than stay dry and collide with a Rhine tanker. Besides, it is a rule of the ship that the steersman may have a glass of hot rum hourly when it is raining. A hatch is provided through which it can be handed up.

There are six berths, and heating when necessary. I believe the *Commodore* is unique in having an open wood fire within four and a half feet of the petrol carburetter. Under the floor is a bilge, inhabited by a bilge dragon which emits sucking noises and scraping sounds at dead of night. There is a collapsible cycle in the hold, and a medicine chest with everything but a bone-saw. Otherwise the inventory is very much as one might expect — a few cushions, a tin of mothballs, enough china to entertain parties of visitors who want to see how '*le five-au-clock*' is really done, an assortment of ropes, pails, fender-tyres, cats-o'-nine-tails and soap. There was once a compass, but when we found it always pointed the same way we threw it overboard and took to using the sun instead, just as bees do. There is no echo-sounder, for we follow the tradition of the Rhine tugs that it is better not to know just how little water there really is beneath the keel.

One can become very fond of a ship, and I believe that the *Commodore* in turn has taken quite a liking to us. However that may be, the earlier books of her voyages have always brought comments from reviewers about this 'us'. Some are relieved that readers do not have to endure a lot of chitchat about people in whom they are not interested. They are quite happy that the story is left to the *Commodore*, the canal engineers, and the villains and heroines of medieval history. I entirely share this view, for nothing annoys me more in books of travel than a recital of the author's friends and relatives and any slight acquaintances who happen to have titles. Of course I realize these people are only mentioned in the hope they will buy copies for their own friends and relatives, and will recommend the book to any slight acquaintances of their own who happen to have titles, but they bore me just the same. So do the author's immediate family. I once read a book in which the man's wife laddered her sixty-deniers every time she went up the companion way. Either that, or she snagged her tailor-made skirt on a marline-spike or a breeches-buoy. Soft soul that he was, her husband would set off into the town and buy her another pair, or have the marline-spike made blunt, and the tale was halted every few pages while he fixed her hosiery or did a bit of haberdashing. I couldn't imagine why he didn't push the woman off the dock and get on with the tale, and it worries me still.

Besides, I just don't like writing about people I know in any personal context. Once a writer takes the easy step of regarding his family and friends as press-fodder he is, I think, finished. He may go on writing, but he can never again have a genuine and honest relationship with others if they are always suspecting — and rightly — that everything they do or say will be taken down and used in evidence against them, that even the simplest remarks will be carefully noted and stored, later to be sifted into the banal and the usable. As an author I am used to being thought a bit queer, but I would not like to be suspected of flogging the intimate thoughts and feelings of people who trust me with their confidence, and even risk themselves under my pilotage aboard the *Commodore*.

On the other hand, there are reviewers who regret what they regard as omissions. A few think it a pity I do not always give the depths of water, the dues, the tidal constants if any, and a lot of other hydrological data. These should take to reading nautical almanacks instead. But several seem worried by the 'we' and 'us' aboard the *Commodore*. Who, they ask, *are* these people included under the pronominal umbrella? Why may the reader not know?

Certainly there is nothing to hide, for the *Commodore* was in no way involved in the Great Train Robbery, which occurred while she was in the canal basin at Toulouse. But if I still think that I am the better judge of the matter and decline to interrupt the narrative with such personalia as would be the life-blood of radio and television magazines but would sink a ship and wreck a story, I realize that this present occasion is not an ordinary one. The *Commodore* is here relating the story of her final voyage, and if this is to be the end of her act it is only right that she should have a chance to express her thanks, rather in the way that an annual social must end with thanks to the ladies who made the tea and heaven help the vicar if he leaves out the ones who brought the flowers. Besides, her friends have always had to work strenuously, and in her journey across France there were nine hundred pairs of lock-gates to be swung to let her pass. Not all of these were on the Canal du Midi, for the voyage began near Leiden, but the first half of it has already been told in *Small Boat through France*.

My wife, Miriam, was aboard all the way. From Leiden we had the help of our son Hugh, a classicist, as far as Reims, and my nephew Brian Dodds, now a curate, all the way to Château-Thierry on the Marne. At Paris we took aboard four deck-hands: our daughter Cynthia for the whole run to Sète, and her fiancé John Silvester Horne as far as Mâcon on the Saône; Michael Hocking, Rector of Guildford, and his wife Gillian were aboard from Paris to Lyon. On the Canal du Midi the crew consisted of Hugh and a fellow King's man and scholar, Stephen Bann.

If these ladies and gentlemen will be so kind as to bow we can now get on with the story, taking up our position between the damp walls of the *écluse* No. 8 of the River Saône, downstream of Trévoux and 26·530 kilometres above the confluence with that spectacular but difficult river, the Rhône. It is the morning of 21 October, but there is little point in our attempting to run up the signal appropriate to Trafalgar Day. We happen not to carry a set of flags. And even if we did, the fog is lying so thick over the river that our display of flagmanship would be seen by none.

ROGER PILKINGTON

Highgate, 1965

I

The sleepy Saône — Lyon of Gaul — the frail slave-girl —
low water in the Rhône — strategy of departure — Rhône
pilotage — shipping of the Rhône — La Mulatière — the
first hurdle

The Saône is a sleepy river. Its somnolence is not that of a sleeping princess or a troubadour dreaming of his fair mistress, but a sluggish, lazy, heavy, torpid, soporific inertia. The Saône is not sure where it is going, or why, and it really has little idea of how a river ought to behave. As a watercourse it is dull, and such few ducks as are willing to sit upon its surface in comatose postures must, I think, be the real dullards of the duck world. Grey-green and greasy like the Limpopo, its water is soupy, opaque with algae and slightly flavoured with the sewage of those cities of France which find it a suitable receptacle for ordure.

The reader may be beginning to suspect that I do not like the Saône. But all the water routes from northern Europe to the Mediterranean converge upon its upper reaches, and so the Saône is inescapable. At Tournus and Trévoux it flows past little towns of extraordinary beauty, but the charm is theirs and is in no way increased by the proximity of the broad river except in so far as the presence of its waters prevents the view from being obstructed by trees. Outside these places the river hangs apparently motionless between high banks piled up to contain the winter floods, its current so slight that when we anchored off Mâcon the stern hung the wrong way in the stream and we were obliged to push the *Commodore* round by poling, in order to satisfy convention.

There is a legend along the higher reaches of the Saône that further downstream its passage is dangerous. So perilous are its rapids, so hazardous the shoals and hidden rocks, so risky is it even for a native to attempt to steer through its tickling and tortuous

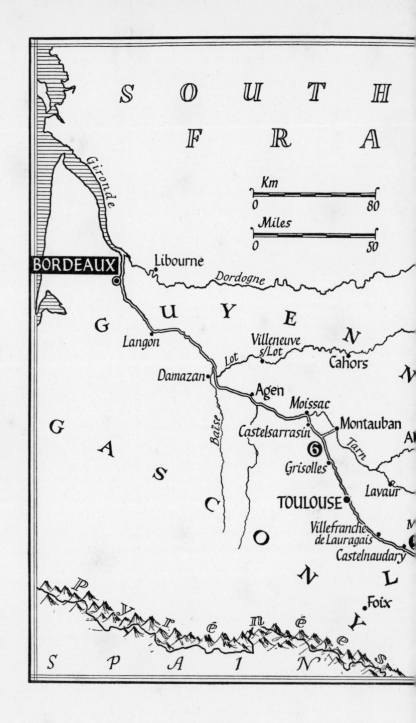

TRÉVOUX

1 Saône
2 Rhône
3 Canal du
    Rhône à Sète
4 Robine
5 Canal du
    Midi
6 Canal
    latéral à
    la Garonne

LYON

Rhône

Vienne

Valence

Montélimar

Ardèche

Aygues

Gard

Avignon

Beaucaire

Aigues-
Mortes

Arles

Montpellier

Hérault

Orb

SÈTE

MARSEILLE

Béziers

Agde

NE NOIRE

Aude

rcassonne

Narbonne

la Nouvelle

Perpignan

M e d i t e r r a n e a n

S e a

WBromage

channels that the stranger is sure to be wrecked, sunk, split, drowned and irrevocably lost and damned if he does not take aboard his ship a pilot — a highly skilled man whose time will inevitably be somewhat expensive. This tale is for consumption only by visiting yachtsmen, or by those of them who are so unobservant that they have not noticed that the French bargee is quite prepared to leave the navigation in the hands of his aged and half blind grandma whilst he reclines in his chair with a bottle of wine beside him and a newspaper pulled down over his face. The *Commodore* rightly assimilated the story as an interesting and profitable piece of folklore, but so as not to appear offensively unbelieving she merely indicated that she did not understand what was being said, and set off down the river. And it would be difficult to find a stream less obstructed by any kind of hazard — except, that is, for the fog.

There is no reason for the Saône to be occulted by fog. The air on either side is clear, the winds can rage in the Alps and the summer sun beat upon the russet vineyard hills of the Côte-d'Or, but between its banks the river is likely to be hidden away in a damp, dark vapour which smells of cabbage stalks. It is not a heat haze, nor a cold haze, but just a fog for no reason at all unless perhaps to delay shipping. This it does with good effect, for however willing one may be to proceed by hoot and by toot the lock-keepers refuse to open the gates until they can see from the cabin window some particular and traditional object such as the third fence post beyond the apple tree which old Jules was going to chop down if it went another season without yielding more than three kilos of fruit. It was for some such reason that the *Commodore* was obliged to lie for an hour or two on the morning of Trafalgar Day in the lock of Port Bernalin whilst we foraged among the dank grass of a thicket behind the bank for logs to chop with our axe.

Shortly after ten o'clock the wet mist disappeared so quickly that within a few minutes the sun was shining brightly and we could see right across the plain on either side. Under way again we headed downstream for Lyon, and by midday we were waiting at the head of the lock of St Rambert l'Île Barbe while the keepers worked the twelve low-geared and antiquated paddles on the gates. We had no objection to a slight delay, for we had already brought the *Commodore* through three hundred and sixty-eight locks from Holland, and only two remained between her and the wild water of the Rhône. Besides, there was no lack of interest, for at last the Saône was awakening to its responsibilities and putting on its best hat in order to curtsey to that great city of Gaul named in honour of the abundance conferred upon the country by the illustrious emperors of Rome.

Colonia Copia Claudie Augusta Lugdunum was founded by special order of the senate and set squarely upon the hill on the right bank of the Saône, a ridge which even today recalls by its name of Fourvière that it was formerly the *Forum vieux* of the Romans. A rich and flourishing city it soon became, a place of scores of thousands of inhabitants, with temples and aqueducts, baths, and the rich houses of traders and Roman officials. And the Saône, shaking off its dismal dampness, curves round the hill of la Fourvière between miles of quays which are no longer mere heaps of garbage and old boots and bedsteads as they were at Mâcon, but are fine solid walls of masonry which rival even those of the Seine at Paris.

The quays are no longer ranged by craft bringing goods from the Mediterranean lands, for Lyon now has the busy port sections of Rambaud and Édouard Herriot further downstream, but before the days of tugs and tow-trains the ships lay all through the city, and along the slower Saône rather than on the unbridled and unprincipled Rhône. And this activity of shipping, vigorous in the middle ages, was a feature of Lugdunum in Roman times. The corporation of boatmen was the most important of the many guilds of the city, and was not afraid of styling itself the *splendissimum corpus*. Its members were by no means the counterparts of the barge-skippers of today, but rich and influential merchants and contractors. They also provided services for the Roman authorities, and carried to Marseille the tribute levied in cash or kind upon the subject peoples.

The guild had three divisions. First there were the Rhône-shippers. Then came the boatmen of the Saône, and finally those who were engaged in transit and transhipment. Between them the

B

boatmen controlled a vast flow of imports and exports, and they were considered so important that some of the best seats in the theatre at Nîmes were permanently allocated to them.

This is recorded on a stone elbow-rest of the podium of the theatre in the mysterious shorthand D.D.D.N.N.RHOD. ET. ARAR. XL — meaning by decree of the decurions of Nîmes, these forty seats are reserved for the members of the corporation of shippers of the Rhône and Saône. And if they may have spent a pleasant evening watching the games and entertaining the vintners who provided them with a large proportion of their trade, the theatre at Lyon itself may have provided a grimmer scene to those who were among the spectators during the year 177.

The Christian community at Lyon was one of the oldest in Europe, a daughter foundation of the church at Smyrna, one of the seven churches in Asia for which John, exiled in 'preventive detention' in Patmos, wrote the *Book of Revelation* to strengthen them in the persecution which was about to break upon them. Under the leadership of Pothinus a group sailed for the Rhône and ascended it as far as Lyon. There they settled in the commercial quarter, among the traders who came from all the colonies of the Middle East, to many of whom the new faith could not have been entirely unknown. No doubt the absence of nationalism and racialism did much to commend Christianity to such a polyglot community, but the same characteristics made it a danger to imperial Rome. The church at Lyon was founded shortly before 150, and in 177 the blow fell. One of those who escaped wrote a detailed letter to the churches in Asia, and fragments of his eye-witness account have been preserved in Eusebius's *History of the Christian Church*, written about a century and a half after the events. Today, as one steers between the stone quays and through the arches of the Pont Clemenceau and the Pont de Serin, the Pont de l'Homme de la Roche and the Pont la Feuillée, one curves round the foot of the steep hill of Fourvière and has always in view not only the tall television mast but the spiky towers of the basilica of Notre-Dame on the hilltop. Close behind it lies the smaller church of St Irenaeus, the name of which reminds that Irenaeus somehow survived to lead and rebuild the shattered community of

Christians. Nearby, the cell is still preserved in which the life of the aged Pothinus ebbed away, and somewhere on that same hilltop Irenaeus was later martyred and the infamous Caligula was born. A little down the hill and nearer the river the amphitheatres are still to be seen. They looked romantic in the light of late October, but they reminded us grimly of the days when church membership was a highly dangerous activity, and persecution of Christians was not by the more modern means of disdain and contempt but was exercised with all the ingenuity which such experts in cruelty as the Romans could muster.

The Romans encouraged their subject peoples in Gaul to flock once a year to Lyon for an orgy of entertainment and celebration. It came to be noticed that a group of people absented themselves from these junkettings, and that these men and women were for the most part foreigners.

'At first they forbade us to use the public baths,' wrote the eyewitness to the congregations in Phrygia and Asia, strangely reminding a modern reader of the prohibitions imposed by the Nazis on the Jewish members of the community. The houses and goods of Christians could be plundered with impunity, and the believers themselves were dogged and pursued wherever they went. 'Finally, all the brutalities of a delirious population were unleashed upon us. Dragged to the market place, those who confessed their faith professed it publicly in front of an immense crowd.'

Appalled at this travesty of justice, Vettius Epagathus pushed his way to the front and demanded that the accused should be allowed a defence. He was a man who commanded great respect locally, but he was now howled down by the mob, and the governor ignored his objection and had him arrested.

The next step was to send soldiers to raid the houses of the Christians. Some of these had slaves who were not Christians, and these servants were tortured until they were ready from fear of death to confirm the wildest allegations. Yes, they said, the Christians always sacrificed children at the Eucharist. Certainly they were homosexuals, and bestials too. These things were all declared to the mob 'until even those who had relatives among the Christians ground their teeth in hatred'.

At last the people were ready for the real excitements. 'The first to be condemned to be torn by the beasts were Sanctus, the deacon of the Vienne congregation; Maturus, a new member who bore himself like a brave hero; Attalus of Pergamon, who had been a pillar of the church from the beginning, and Blandina. These were considered sufficient for one day's entertainment.' The first two were flogged with staves according to custom; and then the crowd demanded that they should be placed on the iron chair, heated red hot in the fire. Throughout the day until the evening the people did not cease to clamour for fresh tortures, but to all interrogation Sanctus answered only 'I am a Christian', refusing to reveal his status, his name, or his nationality in any other way. The governor ordered him to be squeezed between sheets of copper glowing red from the fire until his body was nothing but a mass of crushed limbs and burned flesh. Even then he was not dead, and he was carried back to prison to have the treatment repeated another day.

And so the frightful orgy continued. Alexander of Phrygia, a well-known doctor in the city, suffered the red-hot chair and all the other tortures without a word, after he had been seized upon for smiling encouragingly to the Christians brought before the governor. In all this horror, one figure above all others stood out, perhaps because such superhuman strength was not expected in such a person. This was the pale young slave girl nicknamed Blandina. 'Not only her mistress, who already lay in prison, but all of us feared that this particularly frail, gentle and delicate creature would give in to the tortures, and yet she was filled with such power that the torturers, who had to relieve each other in shifts from the exhaustion of working upon her from morning until evening, laid down their tools in astonishment that she was still alive after so many tortures, any one of which would have been — as they thought — enough to kill her. Yet all the while she only spoke softly the words, "I am a Christian. There is no evil done among us."'

Apart from her nickname, nothing is known of this gentle girl. She may have been a local maid, or perhaps from Smyrna. But the memory of her is still alive in the city which struggled so long to kill her, and where the exasperated officials next tied her to a cross in the arena for the beasts to attack. Every day while the tortures and burnings lasted, Blandina and a young lad named Ponticus were brought into the arena and forced to watch the end of their fellow-Christians. Each day they refused to recant, and the sympathy of the crowd for the two teenagers turned to fury. On the final day the fifteen-year-old Ponticus was tortured to death but died without a murmur of complaint, his courage continually sustained by Blandina. Last of the prisoners, the young girl was flogged, burned on the chair, wrapped in a net and tossed by a bull. Yet, like Stephen, 'she no longer felt what was done to her, living only in Christ. She was finally despatched by the sword.'

The Roman officials were thoroughly used to such scenes and watched them with the same casual detachment with which in our own day one might watch a football match on television. But to the people of Gaul gathered together for the public holiday this was something new. They had burned with lust for the blood of the Christians, and the forty thousand eyes which stared at Blandina as she suffered one frightful inhumanity after another were afire with murder and hate. Yet this girl above all the rest was to make the beginning of a transformation in these rough people. 'Even the pagans declared that they had never seen a maiden bear such sufferings with so much courage.' They talked and talked of the frail slave girl, and of the radiant serenity which surpassed anything in their experience. From her death the fame of the church grew, and even today her memory is alive in Lyon.

This all happened long, long ago. Nearly eighteen centuries have passed since the scores of mangled bodies of the Christians of Lyon and Vienne were exhibited for six days and exposed to every imaginable outrage before being burned and their ashes thrown into the Rhône so that their God could not recover them. In our own days we have Belsen and Auschwitz, horrors enough without need of recalling those of earlier times, and the reader may wonder why I should have brought out of the darkness of decent oblivion the tale of Blandina and her companions to cast a shadow of night-mare and terror over such a pleasant journey as a voyage down the Saône in such a well found ship as the *Commodore*. It is partly because I suspect that I am not alone in being unable to visit so prosperous and bustling an industrial city as Lyon without being curiously aware of that earlier age of trade and commerce and polyglot population, but it is also because the more I have voyaged through the waterways of Europe the more have I come to realize that all those things that are true and good in our modern mode of living are derived from those precious and eternal truths perceived by the early Christians and held in trust for later generations in the face of the worst that men could do. From Scandinavia and Scotland to the Mediterranean shores or the forests of Bavaria one continually crosses and recrosses the trail blazed by these fearless people, some of them simple but devoted, like Blandina and the youth Ponticus, as well as the more learned men like Irenaeus and Pothinus. Between them, these men and women held the fragile threads of the future of mankind. Whether they knew it or not, they were holding the world away from the abyss, and had they not been faithful to the vision which was theirs the world would probably long since have gone under in anarchy or have settled down to spiritual inertia in the anaesthesia of the religious traditions of the orient.

Notre-Dame is one of those churches best seen from a distance. It dates from the end of the nineteenth century, and contains the famous Black Virgin responsible, it is said, for delivering the city from the plague of 1643. At that time the statue was housed in a humbler chapel, but when in the course of the Franco-Prussian war the Germans were endeavouring to capture Lyon the clergy asked her assistance again and promised her a nice new basilica if she would oblige. Three Prussian attacks failed, and the Black Virgin won her magnificent hilltop home, where she is visited throughout the day by pilgrims, and penitents, and those with some particular concern to entrust to her. It is all very strange, this statue reigning over a curious mixture of extreme devotion and sincerity blended with superstition and golden calfery — but perhaps it is a strange statue.

On our way down the Saône we had passed a number of yachts from Britain and the Low Countries, temporarily laid up. There had been no rain for nearly two months, and the Rhône was at a lower level than had been known for a quarter of a century.

Already these craft had been waiting six weeks for enough water to float them in the Rhône, and when we saw the river itself in Lyon it appeared such a small and fleet stream compared with the sluggish Saône that it seemed impossible that a little further down it could really be navigable. The sight of it was so depressing that we preferred not to look at the great river at all, but to set out on foot to perform our various errands. One of these was to hunt up a cricket-pitch length of exotic material for the wedding dress of my daughter, who was with us. We had already secured the veil in Paris, and the possibility of a protracted stay in the city of silks and satins offered an excellent chance to set about the dress and train. While the bride and my wife set out to see what Lyon could provide, I sought out the office of the chief engineer of the Department of Bridges and Highways.

It is a general and very fair complaint of visitors that the French bureaucracy is enough to drive them to the edge of homicide. Yet by some means or other the men of the *Ponts et Chaussées* have escaped being trained in rudeness and obstinacy, and they invariably prove to be the most helpful and imaginative men one could wish to meet. At the same time they do not wish to have on their hands the wrecks of incompetent yachtsmen, and in the case of the Rhône they very wisely like to be sure that there is enough water for the draught of a particular boat before giving instructions to the lock-keeper at La Mulatière to let her pass through. For in most cases there can be no return. The Rhône flows faster than the top speed of all but the most powerful motor-yachts. Besides, wrecks are a nuisance. The Rhône rolls ahead of it such a quantity of shingle that the diversion of current by a stranded vessel can cause the channel to shift its position through all of the next few miles below the obstruction.

The yachts we had seen waiting above Lyon, and two others we had met heading regretfully home again, had in fact been stopped. Their crews had been asked by the helpful engineers to state their draught, and had done so. In a few cases a wish for self-aggrandizement or perhaps a tendency to slight exaggeration had led the owner to add a foot or so to the real depth of the ship — with the result that it had been declared to have too great a *tirant d'eau* for present conditions. It is a strange fact, however, that the *Commodore* has no fixed dimensions at all, and even her tonnage can range from four to sixty-five according to the motives inspiring the official who wishes to know it. I therefore had no doubt at all that she could adjust her bottom to suit the Rhône of the moment.

If the good engineers were in the habit of asking the skippers the draught of their craft and wisely pronouncing them too deep, it seemed to me more sensible that the questions should first be asked from the side of the *Commodore*. With this in mind I climbed the steps to the office which dealt with navigation, knocked, and entered.

'*Bonjour, messieurs!*' The men of the navigation were busy with plans of dykes and dredge-cuts and all manner of mysterious works, but one of them put down his ruler and came over to shake me by the hand.

'What is the minimum depth of water between Lyon and Beaucaire?' I enquired.

The engineer looked grave. Only one metre had been measured that very morning, it seemed. The level was still falling, too, and he calculated that by next day the figure would be down to ninety-five centimetres. '*Ce n'est pas beaucoup,*' he added sadly.

I then asked what would be the maximum *enfoncement* possible for a *bateau avalant*. In case the reader should think it odd that I should have stressed that the boat was going downstream I may add that in a swift river like the Rhône this makes a world of difference. A *bateau montant* would have to be forging so powerfully that the sheer thrust would sit the stern perhaps six inches deeper, whereas moving with the current a ship could float down with only enough power to keep steerage way.

The engineer said he considered that a boat of ninety centimetres might make the descent, provided she left on the following morning. She might be involved in one or two slight bumps on the gravel, but certainly she would be well clear of the rocks, provided she did not stray from the tortuous, but quite unmarked channel. He then asked what the *Commodore*'s draught was, and I told him eighty-five. This was the smallest figure to which her draught had ever been reduced, but I reckoned that the river might be an inch or two deeper than the engineers thought. I decided however not to refill her water tanks until we had reached Beaucaire. This would save us half a ton, and half a ton plus the weight of our friends the Hockings, who were returning to England in the morning, might give her a centimetre more clearance, or even two.

The engineer was quite satisfied, for being a sensible man he knew that to be clear of the bottom by four inches was as good as having four feet of water beneath the keel. But he recommended that we should not try the descent unaided. We could if we wished, and he would be powerless to prevent us, but if he was in our place and valued the boat and our lives, he would think a hundred new francs well spent if it were paid for knowledge of the river.

The *Commodore* does not like paying pilots to run a simple and straight course for her, but one glance at the Rhône was enough to confirm the judgment of the engineer that she should try to secure the services of Joseph Pariset, the Rhône pilot whose address — like that of all other French pilots — ended with the picturesque instruction *En cas d'absence, Café de la Marine*. Under ordinary circumstances she would have lurked above the lock until a barge appeared, and locking through in its company she would have trailed it down river at a respectable distance. But there had been no barges up or down during the whole of the month, and if she was to descend the Rhône at all it would certainly be a case for pilotage. And if pilotage, then Pariset, for he had a lifetime of experience behind him in handling yachts amid the very considerable obstacles of the Rhône.

Intending to make myself a cup of tea before trailing off again in search of the pilot, I returned aboard. I had only just finished when the ladies of the crew returned, much sooner than I expected, crowing with delight and carrying a roll of twenty metres of duchesse satin, the most exquisite material for the wedding dress. We were still cooing over it in the saloon when there came a thump on the hull, and the broad and almost purple face of an old sea-dog looked in through the saloon window on the outer side. He was leaning out from the wheelhouse of a small cruiser, and in a voice which shook the timbers in our bilge he asked if we wished to descend the Rhône. Not knowing who he might be we called back that it was conceivable that we might wish to do so during the course of the next month or two, but we had not really decided. However, we bade the man step over, and he did so. Taking off his nautical cap with a suitable bow to the ladies he explained that he was none other than Joseph Pariset, *pilote du Rhône*, and at our service. He was leaving the following morning to take down to Beaucaire the thirty-foot *Isle of Eigg* upon which he had drawn alongside. He would bring an accomplice to pilot us and we could go down together.

We quickly decided that we would leave any further exploring of Lyon until another voyage, for however much we would have liked to visit the country around the city it seemed unlikely that Pariset could be back for another run before the level of the water, which was still falling, was so low as to make our trip impossible. We struck a bargain, shook hands on it, raised a glass of Burgundy to show our complete trust in his ability to find the channel, and arranged that he and his fellow pilot would report on the stroke of nine. The lock-keeper at La Mulatière would be asked to open up at a quarter past nine to let us pass.

With another bow Monsieur Pariset squeezed through our hatch, jumped to the *Isle of Eigg* with a thump that sent ripples washing across the stream, and took her away down river. All our intentions of a pleasant evening at the opera or sitting at a pavement café were quickly abandoned for the less romantic job of going over the engine from petrol pump to plug points and from water filter to the adjustment of the reverse gear. I am not one to find the highest aesthetic experience in a box of spanners and an oily rag, but I have always thought it useful to be as sure as is humanly possible that the engine is in the same sort of order that one would expect to find under the bonnet of the royal Rolls. The Rhône was less formidable in some respects than rivers we had run in Sweden, but it flowed at an impressive pace. I just wished to be sure that there would be no hiccups during the descent of a stream where to be unmanœuvreable might be something more than mildly annoying. Not that I had any reason to expect engine failure, but the motor was a second-hand one at the best of times, and those times were four and a half years earlier. Since then it had taken the *Commodore*

to Alsace and Swabia, through Bavaria and down the Rhine, over
to the Weser and back to Holland, then right down the map of
France to the quays of the Saône. This engine — the *Commodore*'s
fourth — was now beginning its fifth volume, so to speak, and as it
had not even suffered the indignity of decarbonizing it was doing
well. Yet it only performed so splendidly because it was given good
food and a clean bed, and this was no time to begin neglecting its
customary care.

Next morning we pushed our guests into a taxi to take them to
the railway station and soon we were under way. A mile down river
and beyond the railway bridge the port area of Rambaud began,
the Rhône barges and Rhône tankers lying several abreast against
the piles of the shipyards or the wharves beside the railway sidings.
Tall cranes leaned out to peer into their holds but remained
motionless, for it was several weeks now since a laden barge had
arrived from Marseille.

These Rhône vessels were different from the familiar Freycinet-
law barges of the French canals. A certain Monsieur Freycinet
once had the initiative to introduce legislation which standardized
the dimensions of all future canal works to avoid the situation
which still exists between the Midi canals and those of the north,
that the locks of one group of waterways are either too short or too
narrow for craft from the other. He set the standard at 38·5 metres
length and 5·05 metres beam, and left the smaller barges (tradi-
tionally known by the contemptible name of *mignards*) to look after
themselves. Such humble Freycinet *pêniches* also lay in groups
along the quays of the Port Rambaud, but as they had arrived by
the Saône there was considerable activity of loading and unloading.

The proper Rhône-runners may be twice the length of a *pêniche*,
but not of double the beam. They have to contend with a stream
which in places can run at nine knots, and this swiftness of the
river is mirrored in the shape and styling of the hull. A fat and
bluff-bowed body like those of their slow-moving, chugging, canal-
travelling relatives would be useless on the Rhône, and the craft
have altogether more cutting lines. A stem like a butcher's cleaver,
a high-built and strong bow-fairing, competent to deflect the
considerable waves which may be thrown up by the fierce wind of

the *mistral*, these and a body slim and lithe give the Rhône ship an appearance which somehow suggests a clipper on the old China run and has the effect of making the ship, however new and gleaming she may be, seem to be built to old plans from the eighteen-nineties. But the vessels are far from being old stagers. Some of them can make fifteen knots, and lay back between thirty and fifty round trips in a year. A canal boat may carry four tons of cargo per horse-power, but on the Rhône a horse per ton is more likely.

One more bridge, and ahead of us lay the long low line of the weir of La Mulatière, with the final lock of the Saône tucked against the hill on the right bank. From the bullnose below it a shoal extended downstream for some way, the stones being washed out by the Rhône and piled up by the sister Saône. It looked a desolate scene and not very encouraging, the only interesting feature of the confluence being the great contrast between the lowland green of the Saône water and the sterile steely grey of the alpine silt suspended in the Rhône. We slowed the *Commodore*, drew in above the lock, and waited.

Although we had arrived only three minutes before the hour at which we had arranged to be let through, we soon discovered that our eagerness to be ready had been somewhat overdone. The previous evening might just as well have been spent in the opera and the engine overhaul moved forward to the morning, for we were now obliged to spend nearly four hours in delays such as always seem to arise where ports and ships and pilots are concerned. Monsieur Pariset had trouble with his cycle. The *agent* who was to tank up the *Isle of Eigg* with diesel had trouble with his lorry. The lock-keeper had trouble with a paddle, and then needed to restore his strength with lunch and some *vin ordinaire*. Only ourselves and the solitary traveller on the *Isle of Eigg* seemed to live a life free from these little tricks of the devil, and for the whole morning we sat on the lock side and chatted whilst the owners of the various pieces of defective machinery worked to put them in order.

Our companion was a quiet, elderly man, who was taking the *Isle of Eigg* all the way from England to the Balearics to oblige a friend, who owned it. This voyage was a considerable feat, for the skipper was not only alone but had either a wooden leg or one which did not work, and it was a real effort for him to walk fifty yards or to reach the quayside from within his craft. It was this inability to walk which made boating so attractive to him, he explained, and yet the effort of crossing France and passing through more than two hundred locks must have been exacting. Now and again he had hired a local man in some canalside village to come with him for the next day or two, but he had found these individuals not always reliable. The pilot he had booked for the Saône had deserted the ship at Mâcon without announcing his intention until he had packed his bag. Major Eigg (as we called him among ourselves) had already given him his pay, so he added to it such a piece of his mind that the pilot fled without even pausing to take his cycle. The major had limped out to an ironmonger and had bought a padlock and chain, with which he had shackled the cycle to his anchor. It was a presentable and rather dashing cycle with dropped handles. In Lyon the skipper had unlocked it and presented it to some deserving individual on the quay.

We asked him how he managed alone in the canal locks, which one was expected to work for oneself. People were very helpful, he said. If he steered into the lock and just sat there, either the keeper or a drover or a bargee would soon start to work the paddles and gates. His main difficulty was managing the bow and stern lines at the same time.

The skipper of the *Isle of Eigg* then confessed that he had a particular worry. The owner out in Ibiza had guessed it would take three weeks to bring the boat from Britain, and already she had been more than twice that time on the way. Hundreds of miles still lay between her and the most southerly canal exit at La Nouvelle, and then he would have to run her down the Spanish coast and out to the Balearics. It was now nearly November, and with winter gales in the offing it was by no means certain that he would make Ibiza much before Christmas. He himself had all the time in the world, but he was worried about the baby food.

It transpired that the wife of the owner, out in the Balearics, had recently had a baby — recently, that is, at the time of the *Isle of Eigg*'s departure from Shoreham. The parents had sent their friend an urgent message to the effect that there was no good baby food to be had in the Spanish dominions, or at least in the Balearics, and they would appreciate his bringing some. So he had done as he was bidden.

'By the way,' he added casually, 'do you know anything about baby foods?'

We said yes and no. That is, we explained that we had no comparative analyses, but we had a rough idea of the composition one might expect a baby food to have. Certainly infants thrived on the stuff.

He was not worried about the analysis. What distressed him was the dreadful thought that the powder would go bad on him before he reached Ibiza.

We hastened to reassure him. If the milk powder was in a sealed tin it should keep well enough. A much more likely danger, we hinted, was that the child would be at the roast beef stage before he hove in view. Children did not live all their lives on milk, we pointed out.

'No,' he said. 'That's worrying me too.' He looked at the lock-gates and at the grey Rhône rippling in from the left. 'You see I really don't know all that much about babies, but it seems this is just the stuff for one. I'm glad you think it will not have gone sour or anything, all these weeks on the way across France.' He tapped the *Isle of Eigg* on her quarter. 'She's a good old tub, too. Been no trouble at all — though of course I keep her in good trim. And I expect the baby food will help her on the Med.'

We asked him why he thought the baby food would help the sea voyage, and he replied that it would steady her. Curious, we glanced through a porthole near the bow and saw that the entire forward cabin was stacked with row upon row of cartons. Each was marked in blue with the legend: *Creamycow blended milk. Infants only. 6 only 2 lb. tins.*

Without counting the cartons we could see at once that a whole maternity ward could have been kept going for months on the supply he was carrying.

We asked him whether his friends had specified any particular quantity, but he said No, they had just wanted him to bring some.

'I loaded forty cases,' he added. 'Do you think that will be enough?'

We hinted that Major Eigg could rest assured that a fifth of a ton of dried milk would be adequate to meet the needs of even an exceptionally robust and thirsty infant. We had admittedly known those who had consumed less. On the whole we thought he had erred on the liberal side, and as it seemed certain that the babe — unless dead from lack of Creamycow — would almost certainly be weaned before he got there it might be prudent to think what could be done with the load. He might try and persuade his friends in Ibiza to have quintuplets with as much dispatch as possible, or he could start vending the tins on the quayside wherever he stopped. We were still discussing this difficult problem when Monsieur Pariset arrived, broad and boisterous, accompanied by a much younger and paler man named Aubry. This individual, who appeared to have a decided defect of one eye, looked so thoroughly unlike a pilot that I asked to see his papers. I had no wish to pay some unskilled fellow merely to follow in Pariset's wake — a thing I could easily do without assistance. Aubry produced his papers, and sure enough he had been a fully qualified Rhône pilot for some years.

When at last we were ready to leave the Saône, the *Isle of Eigg* moved out first into the water at the tail of the lock with Pariset at the wheel, Major Eigg sitting on a stool nearby, and the load of Creamycow snugly fitted athwart the ship. I let them have a start of nearly a hundred yards and then followed. The Rhône swung in from over our left shoulders and immediately ahead the water rippled down a bank of gravel, dropping more than a foot as it did so.

I have always found it a frightening moment when first a pilot takes over the wheel. The boat lurches and probes and yaws and swings, and however content the pilot may be I find I have to shut my eyes and count to a hundred — by which time he has either got control of the vessel or it is time for me to intervene. I had my eye on the point at which Pariset dropped over the edge of the Saône delta into the grey stream of the Rhône which swung so swiftly past its edge, when suddenly Aubry signed that he wanted to take the wheel. He pointed to another part of the bank edge and made straight for it. I was greatly relieved to find that we had a pilot who could actually steer a straight line, but the fact that he was aiming straight for a place where the water seemed hardly to trickle alarmed me. I could not believe there was water enough to float a soap dish.

'Ah well,' I thought. 'Better be stranded here than lower down. They can always wash us off by opening up the weir.'

Aubry looked straight ahead and shook his finger deprecatingly. '*Pas beaucoup d'eau. Non, non.*' He clicked with his tongue and put the engine to dead slow. The *Commodore* ran to the edge of the bank and slid down it as gracefully as a young princess sliding down the banisters. Very much to my surprise there was water enough for her to do so without striking. Our opinion of Aubry went up and I asked him why he had taken that particular course when Pariset had chosen another.

'*Monsieur Pariset, il fait comme il veut,*' he replied. As for himself, he would do what he thought best. And he relapsed into a silence which lasted almost until nightfall.

Soon we were sweeping at a great pace past the basins of the Port Édouard Herriot. No vessels were on the move, and no doubt this was the reason why the watchman on the dredger just below the bend was inattentive. His job was to watch for traffic and immediately to lower the steel cable which stretched tight as a fiddle-string from the dredger on the left bank to a bollard on the opposite shore, but confident that no ships could pass down the river he had retired to the hut aboard the work boat, where perhaps he was engaged in so exciting a game of cards with his fellows that nobody at first noticed the two small vessels approaching. Pariset hooted, but the sound was probably lost in the screeching of the bucket-chain.

Pariset jumped to the deck and waved his arms, shouting all the while. At last a bell rang urgently on the dredger, for the man working the chute had now seen or heard the *Isle of Eigg*. In a flash the men came tumbling out of the cabin to throw the ratchet off the cable winch, but already the boat was bearing down quickly upon the hawser. Pariset knew that there was no time to turn his ship, even if the *Isle of Eigg* could have stemmed the current, so he quickly made the wise decision to take the cable where it dipped into the water. Following astern we saw the little ship rear up as though she had run on a reef, then straighten and kick up her heels so that for a moment her propeller whirred in the air. She had cleared the wire like a horse taking a fence, and by very good fortune the cable had somehow failed to entangle itself with her propeller or rudder bracket. Astern of her the cable surfaced for a moment clear of the water, then dropped slack with a clacking sound whilst from the dredger came the rattle of the winch being run back. The *Commodore*, who had been steeling herself for an elegant leap, had a free passage accompanied only by Monsieur Pariset's angry denunciation of the watchman, which carried fiercely across the water.

When that evening he told us that he was phoning an immediate protest to the chief engineer at Lyon we agreed that this was only reasonable. All men might be fallible, but to leave a dredger cable unwatched was extremely dangerous, and it was fortunate indeed that the *Isle of Eigg* had not been entangled or overset, else the Rhône might have been converted into a flood of reconstituted full-cream, pasteurised, reinforced and vitaminized milk, guaranteed suitable even for the most delicate child.

c

II

*Downstream to Andance — empire-bank and realm-bank
— Richelieu's last voyage — the King's Rock — rapids at
Valence — ships of the river — lock of St Pierre — the men
of Mornas*

On leaving the Saône, we also left the glories of Lyon astern and
let the Rhône carry us as swiftly as it might through drab
factory suburbs and under clouds of smoke and fumes into the
clearer air of the valley beyond. Yet the ghost of the Saône was
with us still as its water flowed against the right bank, obstinately
remaining unmixed for at least a mile, its slower-moving green
gradually turning to grey and accelerating at the edge where the
Rhône rubbed along beside it, urging it to hurry and join the race to
the Mediterranean. In fact the slower and bulkier river reduces the
speed when the mixing is complete, and it is for this reason that the
Rhône is navigable below La Mulatière and not above that point.

Soon the busy industry of Lyon lay far behind us and our
course lay down a country river-bed. There were no houses by the
stream — for in flood time they would have been swept away —
and always the view was of long wooded aits, or of flood banks
backed by thickets of brushwood and topped with willows and
poplars and an occasional distance board. Backwaters and dead
alleys abounded, for the impetuous river had often changed its
course, and sometimes the main stream appeared almost to be
running through a delta. At kilometre 18 a cloud of coal dust and
smoke signalled the sharp bend at Givors, and as a gap in the
blackened and chemical-stained quay flashed past us we could see
through to a port basin. Fortunately we had no wish to stop at
Givors, because at this state of the Rhône the wharves themselves
were inaccessible by water, and in the port entrance there was so
little water that a stickleback could hardly have made its way into

22

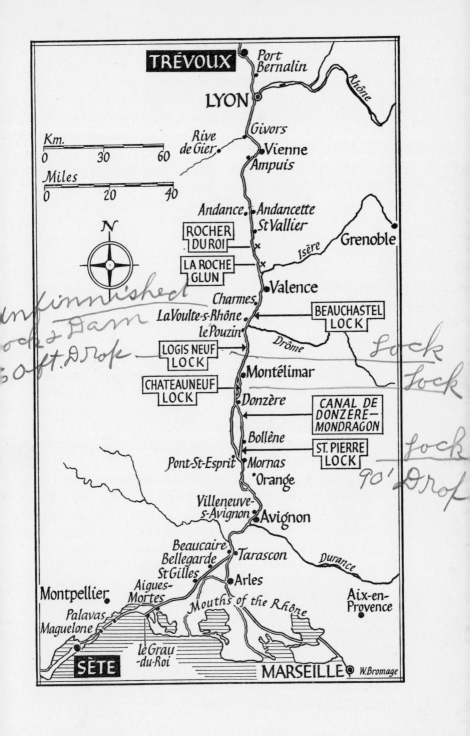

harbour without grounding. Not that it would have tried, for the
scent and colour of the effluent of the little river Gier at Givors
hinted at great chemical enterprises not far distant.

The basin of Givors is all that remains of a grandiose enterprise
which was known in its day as the Canal des Deux Mers — the
same name as that of Riquet's canal for which the *Commodore* was
bound. A concession was granted in the eighteenth century to one
François Zacchari, permitting him to cut a waterway from the
Rhône to Rive de Gier, nine miles up the valley. In fact the canal
was cut for a farther three miles beyond that point, and in the
romantic imagination of its author it was expected one day to reach
the Atlantic — whence the name of the Canal des Deux Mers —
but its life was short, and a century later the tunnel and the forty-
three locks of its twelve-mile stretch were deserted. In 1877 the
last of the small man-hauled barges passed down with its cargo of
coal from the mines of Rive de Gier, and today the products of the
industrial valley are brought overland to Givors for loading, or
taken by rail to their destinations. Zacchari's dream did not come
true, and nothing is left but a particularly dirty basin at the end of
a river which once was beautiful and is now no more than a hideous
chemical sewer. But this is hardly the fault of the engineer; the
Gier valley is industrial, and men of commerce have a habit of
turning even the loveliest rivers into inexpensive sewers to carry
away their scourings.

Aubry spoke little as he steered down the stream. Sometimes we
would have a burst of speed and fly along in relatively deep water,
and then we would reach a rippling and sloping section where he
would take us as slowly as he could, drifting down the bed as
though awaiting a grating sound on the *Commodore*'s bottom.

'*Ici, rochers,*' he would say pointing a few yards to port. That,
together with '*Là, gravier,*' made up almost all his conversation,
but below the long ait of Loire he pointed up for a moment to the
ruins of a tower which, he said, was haunted.

The tower is not hung about with the mere ghosts of the Knights
Templar burned alive there by Philip the Fair, but the spook is
said to be that of the only Roman official whose name is repeated
all round the world in more than a thousand languages every day.

We may never know for certain what became of Pontius Pilate, for whilst Eusebius says he committed suicide there is also the rumour that he was sacked for incompetence and removed to Vienne on the Rhône, to end his days as a minor administrator. However that may be, what is alleged to be his pyramid tomb is to be seen in Vienne, and the tower further upstream is the traditional place of his nocturnal walking.

Vienne itself lies on the outer side of a sharp swinging bend to starboard, and the fleeting sight of its houses crowded down towards the river made us regret that we should have no chance on this voyage of stopping at this attractive city of Roman Gaul. But if the Rhône has one characteristic above others it is that the river declines to wait. It rushes through one place after another, and rarely is there the slightest possibility of drawing in to the bank, or even of anchoring in the stream and rowing ashore. The country-side is whisked past as though on one of those machines used for training drivers, and there is hardly time to establish the identity of a place before it is out of sight astern.

Navigators, it seems, often need the assistance of saints. Below Vienne there is a saintly figure on the façade of a riverside château. The Rhône bargemen would never forget dutifully to cross themselves in his sight before running the fleet passage below Ampuis, but it is said that a tough traveller coming from the Volga was making the grand tour and descending the Rhône by boat, and caring little for the superstitions of ignorant watermen he took aim at the saint with his gun. Being an excellent shot he cracked off the head with a single bullet — and almost immediately his boat struck on a rock and sank. At which the boatmen were delighted rather than surprised.

We had by now run more than twenty miles down from La Mulatière and already we had passed down several ripply patches of water where the Rhône tumbled over a slope of gravel. Aubry was steering us between some eddies when he peered over the side and remarked in his flat, unemotional way, 'Là, rochers.' Sure enough, through the rough surface we caught sight of a few formidable knife edges rushing past the boat at a rate of perhaps ten knots. It was reassuring to feel that the pilot knew what he was

about, and probably it was to convince us of this that he put on a
spurt in the next reach and passed the *Isle of Eigg*. There was now
no question of his following in Pariset's wake. His own position as
an equal was established, and keeping the lead he steered down the
river for mile after mile of a not very interesting course, past tree-
edged meadows and close to high flood banks of silt-sprinkled
masonry, until we had put more than forty miles behind us and we
could see down a long reach to where two little towns faced each
other at either end of a long suspension bridge. To starboard the
single street of Andance lay at the foot of a hill on a shoulder of
which three crosses stood out against the evening sky, recalling the
fate of three beautiful maidens who could no longer endure the
absence of their suitors in the crusade led by Louis the Saint. To
slaughter Saracens was all very well, but the girls grew tired of
waiting in vain, and together they flung themselves into the Rhône.

Across from Andance lay Andancette on the *pèri*. That the banks
of the Rhône should have names of their own in the language of the
pilots and bargemen is one of the most unexpected relics of earlier
times. To the geographer the Rhône, like any other river, has a
right bank and a left bank, but to the boatman the left shore
(facing downstream) is known as the *pèri*, the right as the *réiàume*.

Whenever Aubry closed the *pèri* to follow the channel he was taking a course that would have brought the medieval mariner closer to the shore of the Kingdom of Arles, a vassal state or dependency of the Holy Roman Empire. *Empèire, empèri, pèri* — however the skipper prefers to term that shore the memory is still there, even if the great empire has long since vanished in the dust of history. *Au rèiàume* indicates on the other hand that one is heading for the shore of the Kingdom of France, of which the Rhône was at that time the frontier.

Just above the bridge of Andance a spanking American yacht lay moored to a pontoon where Pariset had left her a month or two earlier. Drawing more than seven feet of water she was likely to stay there for many weeks before he could run her further downstream, and meanwhile she made a handy jetty for ourselves and the *Isle of Eigg*. Turning to stem the stream we drew in for the night and put a regular spider's web of lines ashore to help take the strain of the current.

Pariset was clearly concerned at the low level of the river, which left a broad foreshore of muddy rock exposed at the foot of the Andance embankment. He went up to the village and put through a call to Lyon, and when he came back he carefully marked the level on a stone. There was, he explained, bad news. The upper reaches of the Rhône were so short of water that the barrage below the Lake of Geneva had been completely closed until further notice. He could not remember such a thing having ever happened before, and as far as the *Commodore* and the *Isle of Eigg* were concerned it meant that the last of the Swiss water was already on the way down, even if it was still behind them. The river would fall still further, and we should need to leave at the very first hint of daylight if we were to be sure of making the thirty-eight miles which still remained before we should reach La Voulte, where the damming effect of the first barrage on the lower Rhône would begin to make itself felt.

Next morning there was sufficient light at a quarter past five for us to tumble out of our berths, only to discover that the river was shrouded in a fog so thick that we could not even see the further bank. However, we could see Pariset's mark on the stone, and it now stood ten inches above the water. It was essential to be under way as soon as possible, and yet the Rhône was a river which even Pariset and Aubry could not tackle in a fog. Pariset said he must have half a kilometre of vision, and we had no wish to question his judgment. Although at times the mist parted enough for us to glimpse Andancette across the stream it was considerably too thick for us to start, and after a quick breakfast we settled down to wait with such patience as we could muster.

All down the Rhône the ruins of ageing minor fortresses are perched on the hills and ridges, and but for the mist we should have had several of them in view from where the *Commodore* lay at Andance. Each of them has a history which, if it were known in all its gory detail, would be found to consist of the same familiar ingredients of feudal times — violence, abduction of beautiful women, imprisonments in dark dungeons, sieges to the death, the cries of garrisons put to the sword and knights defenestrated, and the limp bodies of expendable peasants dangling lifeless from the limbs of their own humble fruit trees. The weight of supporting this system fell as usual upon the poor and landless, and upon the shipper whose rich cargo could be held to ransom. Walls, crenelations, heaps of masonry which once were keeps and bastions, the ruins may be less impressive than those of the Rhine for the very reason that they are more ruinous, but they are rarely out of sight of each other. Perched like the birds of prey that once they were, they decorate the cliffs and ridges or the spurs where side valleys join the Rhône, and imperiously overlook the whole of the course to where the broad river flows into the delta of the Camargue.

Looking down from their fortified perches the minor lords must have seen many curious cargoes passing up or down the stream, but none can have been more strange than that carried by a trio of ships which crept up the river to Lyon in the autumn of 1642. Three teams of horses richly decked and decorated heaved and hauled at the tow-ropes, whilst before and behind them rode elegant and aristocratic knights attended by troops of horsemen. Across the river a similar cavalry ambled along the further bank, the horsemen restraining their steeds to match the slow progress of the convoy struggling against the current.

Within the first boat was set a marquee with double walls of red silk and a gorgeous canopy to shield from the midday sun. Inside this tent was a portable bedroom with handles, which eighteen strong men could lift. Upon the splendid brocaded bed reclined a sick and wasted man attended by a personal secretary in the form of a monk. Forbidden by his doctors to undertake even the slightest movement the magnificent invalid, pale and emaciated, lay upon his couch day after day, issuing orders to his secretary, giving instructions in matters of state, or dreaming of literary achievements.

Every evening the convoy halted, and the barges drew in near some suitable mansion. Eighteen strong men of the bodyguard were detailed to take the bedroom ashore and convey it to the house. There may have been those who, because of the exaggerated size of their front gates, were glad to have such an important visitor, but one can well imagine the anxiety with which others would have watched the slow approach of the boats, praying that by sundown they would be past and in a neighbour's territory. For none dared refuse to house the great Cardinal Richelieu, however much they might detest him, and yet his visit was attended with certain inconveniences. The bedroom had to be brought in, and where necessary the town walls and the gateways or fortifications of châteaux would be breached to let it pass.

The third ship contained attendants and a crowd of such hangers-on as would accompany any great statesman of the seventeenth century, but the middle vessel also held a tent, though it was by no means so magnificent an affair as that in the boat ahead. It contained no invalid, but two elegant and aristocratic individuals, the twenty-two year old Marquis of Cinq-Mars and his devoted and faithful friend, de Thou. From the refined and carefree conversation in which they indulged a casual observer might not have guessed that they had been imprudent enough to become involved in political intrigue, and on the wrong side. Their leisurely journey up the Rhône was undertaken at the will of the man in the boat ahead, for they were on their way to Lyon to have their heads cut off. And as they were already aware of this they had every reason to derive the utmost enjoyment from their trip up the valley. A bid for escape would probably have been foiled by the horsemen on the further shore. Besides, it would hardly have been the behaviour expected of gentlemen.

No doubt these men and their captor could be towed up the river even in the morning haze of autumn, but the *Commodore* could not run down until we could see where she was going. Pariset and Aubry sat aboard the *Isle of Eigg*, peering upstream, downstream or straight up in the air, and from time to time looking at the slightly increasing area of wet stone along the shore where the water was now falling at the rate of an inch or more in each hour. The choice was between the risk of mistaking the course in fog, or of running aground by waiting for the mist to clear, or there was the possibility that the *Commodore* would have to remain at Andance with the *Isle of Eigg* and the American yacht until the winter rains came to swell the Saône. It was nearly eight when the visibility rose to about four hundred yards, and even if the fog seemed to have lifted away from the surface rather than to have evaporated, Pariset decided to go. He would risk finding a patch or two of mist further down, he said. But in fact the fog did not thicken, and in half an hour we were past St Vallier.

Three miles short of Tournon the Rhône runs at the foot of a tall cliff on the port side with the main road and railway track from Paris to Nice cramped at its foot. There is dust in the air, and the clatter of cement quarrying, but there is also a remarkable flat-topped rock the size of a small house, standing in midstream. At times of low water this lump is easily visible but in flood time it is submerged and makes a particularly interesting hazard for a ship descending the river. The rock is the Rocher du Roi, the king in question being St Louis.

It once happened that the ownership of this lump of stone was a subject of dispute between the lord of Crozes and another feudal chief who lived across the Rhône. The rock was not a very useful acquisition, but that did not matter. It was no doubt necessary to have some sort of cause for quarrel with neighbours — and besides, the rock might help its owner to hold up and raid the shipping. Armed robbery was the fashion of the times, and neither horseman nor boat could pass down the Rhône without danger of losing his goods and perhaps his life also.

Hearing that King Louis was coming down the Rhône to launch a crusade, the lord of Crozes invited him to a novel and ingenious entertainment in the form of a grand reception and party on top of the rock. The king accepted, and after being plied liberally with the excellent wine from the vineyards of Crozes he must have expanded to the extent of asking whether there was anything he could do in return for such hospitality. The lord of Crozes had the answer ready in the form of a little document bequeathing the sovereignty over the rock to the Crozes domain — a remarkable gift in that Crozes was not in the *réiàume* of Louis at all, but was in empire territory. The paper only needed signing, and Louis obliged with his signature.

Tournon is a considerable town on the river, but as we drifted through its swift and shallow double bend it appeared drab and dirty. No doubt it has its charms, but all we could see of them was the long expanse of embankment walls covered with dried mud, and at their foot a collection of rusting bedsteads and perambulators of the species which always take root in rivers but which in the case of Tournon would rarely have been seen above the surface. Here and there a sewer-pipe did its best to add to the volume of liquid in which the *Commodore* was floating, and from the end of one of them a rat watched her with beady eyes as though hoping she would strike on the bottom.

At La Roche Glun a backwater curving away from the left bank makes a pretty setting for a village half hidden among the trees, and the scene is so gentle that one would not suspect that this place was the seat of such unprincipled and exceptional violence that, as Joinville records, King Louis was obliged to *abbatre* the castle on his way down river to lead his crusade. He had the robber-castle of the Rogiers razed to the ground because it was said that their practice was to *desrober les pèlerins et les marchans*. Highwaymanship with a bit of disrobing was the accepted occupation of anyone of the right class, and one wonders in what way the Rogiers can have exceeded if the good king should have delayed his whole expedition in order to besiege their waterside strongpoint. Or was it perhaps no more than that the splendid wine quaffed on the midstream rock with the Seigneur de Crozes had roused the monarch to come to the defence of the poor and simple?

By now we could notice that the river was effectively banked, the edges of its curves being bounded with massive ramparts. But these works were intended mainly to retain the force of the floods which otherwise might have eroded the railway or the road, and certainly there was no general increase in depth. Aubry, in a rare flash in which he put several words together, expressed a slight fear that the passage of the Valence rapids might prove even more formidable than usual. Much depended upon the contribution of the Isère just upstream of the city, and when we passed the mouth of this great tributary flowing down from Grenoble and the Dauphiné Alps there was little to be seen but a broad and deserted bed of cobbles with the merest trickle losing itself among a few boulders washed down by the floods of spring. Aubry looked even more pained than before.

We had been somewhat unwilling to believe that anything could be more formidable than the miles of shallows and *ici gravier* that we had already survived. Yet Valence with its blank-looking waterfront was soon upon us, and immediately beyond it the river degenerated quite suddenly into a series of waves and breakers set on a slope like that of the defile at Bingen on the Rhine. For perhaps 200 yards the Rhône fell away as though pouring over cobbles — and this, of course, is just what it was doing. The *Commodore*'s stern swayed, her bow see-sawed a little, but she kept ahead. The water jumped, slapping her playfully on her flanks, but the thump and grinding sound for which we had been waiting never came.

'*Ici rochers et gravier partout!*'

Barely overtaking the fleet water we slid down the slope, and when Aubry actually gave a faint smile and began to whistle a tune we knew that we were past the worst. And so we were, for after shooting the torrent of water pouring through the gap of the uncompleted weir of the Barrage de Charmes, another twenty minutes brought us in sight of La Voulte, where row upon row of powerful sleek Rhône ships and tankers were waiting for the day when they could voyage up to Lyon and unload. Probably their skippers already knew something that we did not — that early that morning the navigation below Lyon had been completely closed, and that the two little ships now speeding down the river and flying the Red Ensign would be the last to run the river for weeks to come.

The Barrage de Charmes was being built to close entirely the arm of the river down which we had come, and after its completion the traffic would pass by way of a broad new canal and a lock — the fourth on the lower Rhône to be completed by the *Compagnie Nationale du Rhône*, an undertaking charged with regulating the entire river from Switzerland to the sea in the best interests of navigation, irrigation, and the production of electricity. By the end of the twentieth century much of the work should have been completed, and already nearly fifty miles of the impetuous course had been by-passed or flooded. This section we were now entering. Aubry could at last sit back and allow us to steer as we wished in slow-moving and deep water, to pass the confluence of the Drôme and speed on towards the first lock-cut.

Between the medieval system of towpath haulage *aux bras d'homme* and the modern stream-lined navigation with powerful diesel barges of a thousand horsepower stands an era in which steam tugs were unchallenged kings of the Rhône. The last of them remained in service until 1955, and for nearly a century the splendid craft with their huge paddlewheels threshed their way up the river under a pall of drifting smoke, hauling laden lighters from Arles to Lyon. The voyage involved much sweat and stoking, and there was the more serious difficulty that between Valence and Pont-St-Esprit the gradient of the Rhône was such that even the most powerful paddle-tug could not manage to haul laden craft against the current. For this stretch of river another system had to be used, one which the French describe as *touage* — towage as opposed to tuggage.

The *toueur* of the Rhône was originally a chain-ship like those of the Neckar and Main and Seine, a craft which hauled itself up the river by lifting a chain from the bed, turning it round a capstan, and dropping it again over the stern. But the Rhône was so swift a river that its shoals were always on the move, and the chain would become buried so effectively beneath a few hundred tons of gravel that the chain-ship could not raise it from the bottom, puff and strain as it might. This difficulty was overcome by substituting for the chain a cable which the *toueur* unwound and laid in the river on the downstream voyage and then hauled up again on the upstream trip — this return voyage having of course to be made before the cable was buried by shoaling. Unfortunately this simple solution brought with it a further difficulty, for the cable had to be stout enough to hold the tug and barge in a stiff current, and there were very real limits to the length of such a heavy steel cable which a *toueur* could carry. A twelve-mile reel was as much as could be loaded aboard, and as even this proved enough almost to sink the ship the journey from Pont-St-Esprit to Valence was divided into five sections, each with cable-ships of its own. Barges were transferred from one to the next as though they were batons in a relay race, and even if the system was something of a nuisance nobody could say that it was not ingenious.

The cable ships were introduced after two other curious and unique types of haulage had been tried, neither of which was properly either towage or tuggage within the French conception of such matters. The first was by a type of boat known as a *grappin*, which used the principle that it was better for the towing craft to take a purchase on land, rather than on the water as paddle-wheelers did. But the *grappin* did not take hold of the bank. Instead, it had under its belly a great wheel with knobs on, and this clawed its way along the gravel very much as a tractor might have done.

Perhaps the trouble with the *grappins* was that the river depth was uneven, and sometimes the poor craft would be left floundering, its grappling wheel revolving hopelessly over some hole in the bottom of the river. But whatever the cause, they were replaced by another fantastic brain-child of engineers, the *bateau-écluse* or lock-boat. This ship was built with the particular object of achieving what seemed impossible — to take a barge laden to a depth of six or seven feet through a river where there might be only half as much water as would be needed to float it.

The *bateau-écluse* was nothing more nor less than a floating dock fitted with paddlewheels. The great wheels were set at either side in traditional style, but the engine and boilers and smoke-stack were all perched up at the front. As for the stern, it consisted of a pair of removable lock-gates.

When a barge was to be lock-boated, the ship (but not the barge) was flooded, just as though a lock were being filled. Slowly it would sink far enough for the gates to be opened, and then the laden barge was hauled in and made fast. The gates were closed behind it and the water was pumped out again until the whole affair had risen and now drew no more than three feet of water.

Alas, all these splendid examples of engineering day-dreams have vanished long ago. Their place has been taken by the elegant and powerful Rhône ship, a diesel craft three times the length of a canal barge but little broader in the beam. These vessels, of which we met a couple racing up to unload at La Voulte, can run from Marseille to Lyon and back in a week or less, but they too will disappear when the need for such exceptional power has gone — although this will not happen until the Rhône has been canalized over the whole of its length and its current finally tamed.

The broad canal with its regular banks was a welcome change from Aubry's continual catalogue of rocks and gravel, shallows and rapids and shoals. For mile upon mile it swept ahead in a majestic curve, a waterway twice as broad as Suez and in places so deep that if the *Commodore* had stood on her nose like a stickleback hunting in a stream, her rudders would not have reached up to break the surface. The water lay smooth and clean under the midday sunshine which now at last was breaking through the autumn mists, and the only disturbance was the rhythmic warp of the wake of the *Isle of Eigg* crossing our own to leave a line of little humps down the centre of the cut, with the ribs of wavelets spreading away to smooth out and vanish before reaching the shore. To either side the canal roamed away into bights which served as reservoirs, and there little parties of duck upended themselves to nibble the weed in the shallows along the edge. Behind us the air still lay heavy in the valley. Ahead, a smudge grew slowly at first, then swiftly to resolve into the form of the lithe *Citerna 18*, a powerful tanker racing up to La Voulte as though the devil were after her.

Far beyond her the line of water was cut right across by the turbine house and lock of the first great step at Logis Neuf. Here the *Commodore* was to drop sixty feet to the reach below, and if her engine throbbed with excitement at entering a deeper lock than ever before, she had to try to be patient. The upcoming tanker had left the lock ready and waiting, but there seemed to be some sort of regulation that the pen could only be used for private boats when a barge was present. And this, the engineer added with a shrug, might be a matter of hours; or conceivably we might have to wait until next day.

We had no wish to spend half a day admiring even such splendid engineering works as by the hydro-electric devices of Logis Neuf. Nor had Major Eigg, who was worried about what another day's delay might do to his cargo of dessicated milk. He wanted to move on, and he knew enough of France to suspect that the sound of a cork and the jingle of glasses would make it possible for the foreman to find some reason for working the lock after all. A brief *apéritif* aboard the *Isle* was enough to cause the lockside motors to be set humming to close the gates. Then the level began to fall, and a few minutes later we were steaming out beneath the lower guillotine gate to speed onward past the nougat town of Montélimar and towards the second great lock, the *écluse Château-neuf* — not *du Pape*, but *du Rhône*. This even deeper step is upstream of the Donzère gorge, once the most difficult and dangerous part of the Rhône but now so safe and simple that one can look around and enjoy the splendour of the yellowing cliffs which shut in the great river on either side, channelling it down to Provence.

The final lock on the Rhône is the *écluse St Pierre* on the canal of Donzère-Mondragon. It is the deepest in the world except for the Wilson Dam lock of the Tennessee Valley Authority, and to drop down between its damp walls into the gloom below is to have an awe-inspiring experience of the scale of modern French engineering. Though the descent might seem slow in the eyes of an elevator operator in the Empire State Building, yet the lock of St Pierre holds the world record and needs only seven minutes to fill or empty its ninety-foot depth. Down we dropped, attached to floating bollards which condescended with ourselves and with two empty tankers and Major Eigg's load of baby food. It was now darkening, and the dimness enhanced still more the effect of a descent into some dank and watery hell, until the huge portcullis was raised a little and the sunset light came flooding under its

dripping girders, welcoming us back to the surface of the earth once more.

The lock of St Pierre is *formidable*, but it is made even more so by its immediate neighbour, the hill of Barry which overlooks the barrage. Here, as often in France, one finds the most ancient and the very modern so closely involved that it is at times hard to be certain whether one is living in the fourteenth century or the twentieth, or even the twenty-fourth. The hill of Barry has been continuously inhabited from Neolithic times almost to the present, and its top is riddled with caves carved out of the soft stone. The Gauls living there must have looked down in some alarm upon the Roman columns marching up the valley, but soon they descended from their perch to work the ground of the plain below. Each fresh invasion sent people scurrying back to the rocky citadel, and eventually a real *village troglodytique* was established there, each century bringing new refinements of unnecessary portals and elaborations built on to the mouths of the caverns. At Barry, cave-dwelling persisted right up to the 1890's; and if today the holes in the rock have not long been deserted they yet belong to an age and civilization utterly removed from that of the hydro-electric hum beneath them.

This drone of commutations comes from the great turbine house pouring its electricity into the looping cables which swoop away across the valley. For all its record output of two milliards of kilowatt-hours per annum — an amount of electricity which is doubtless quite as impressive as it sounds — the *Usine Blondel* suggests by its name that the faithful troubador might really have sung his ballads from one hydro-electric installation to another in search of his royal master, and even the discovery that this particular Blondel was a *grand physicien* does not entirely destroy the illusion that the humming which issues from the great towers of the turbine halls is the voice of Richard the Lionhearted, taking up the strain which his favourite minstrel has struck upon his lute.

If the *Usine Blondel* is an invitation to dream of the early middle ages, the village of Mornas recalls some very real events in later centuries. Standing back from where the outfall canal leads the ships out into the Rhône again, there is little to be seen of Mornas but the ruins of a castle crowning a hill on the *pèri* and the creamy little houses of a Rhône village nestling peacefully among the olive trees. This was the domain of a Huguenot family, but in the mid-sixteenth century a Catholic force scaled the castle walls and slew the entire garrison. They then began to make themselves thoroughly at home in the town itself, and as the festival of Corpus Christi was at hand they decided to celebrate it by hanging the fronts of the houses with skins — the skins being those of the former Protestant inhabitants. News of this novel decoration reached the lord of Arles, who promptly sent his fanatically Huguenot lieutenant Montbrun to redress the balance.

The siege of Mornas lasted only three days before the gates were broken in, and the Catholics now found themselves at the mercy of the Protestants. But of this mercy there was little enough trace, for the castle stood on the edge of a 200-foot precipice and it seemed a pity to waste such a splendid opportunity. The defenders were disarmed and driven in gangs up to the top of the wall, where a brief bludgeoning or a few slashes proved enough to send each of them to smash on the rocks at the foot, one more victim of the customs of the times and the implacable hatred engendered by dogma in an age of might and violence.

And even if the actual skinning was unusual, the fate of the people of Mornas was not very different from that of the men of any other place along the valley. Yet for the women the procedure was different. Usually they would merely be raped and then disembowelled — if possible in public.

From Mornas to Avignon the Rhône flows swiftly but without rapids. Hurrying onwards as though it has scented the lure of the Mediterranean it sweeps through thickets to give glimpses of dry hillocks topped with crenelated towers and cypresses standing erect among ruins. Little creamy towns with orange roofs cluster on the slopes as though terrified that the Rhône will flood and wet their feet, although their names of Roquemaure and Montfaucon and Châteauneuf du Pape sound more heroic and recall deeds of knights and lords. And if once a mayor issued an order that no flying saucers should be permitted to land in Châteauneuf, no doubt this was reasonable, for their fiery exhausts might easily have scorched the vines which yield the famous wine of its sunlit slopes.

III

*The Avignon bridge — Beaucaire and the young lovers —
Tarascon — the troubadours — rules of courtship — the
monster of the Rhône — St Martha to the rescue — canals
of the delta — St Gilles — Cougoumasso and prègo-dièu*

The Rhône is a tantalizing stream. Rushing impetuously
towards a city as beautiful and absorbing as Avignon it stays
neither for Pope nor Antipope, nor even to allow the boatman the
opportunity so often taken by the soldiers in *De Bello Gallico* to go
into the city to buy bread. Racing by the long line of the town walls
it gives only the briefest of glimpses of the glories of the palace
within them, and anxious to pour itself into the delta it sweeps
ahead through the course allocated to it by the engineers who
brought it over from Villeneuve. Yet there is one feature of
Avignon which the Rhône cannot avoid, even if it has done its best
to destroy it, and that is the famous institution where

> *Les beaux Messieurs font comme ci,*
> *Les belles Dames font comme ça,*
> *Tout le mond y passe.*

The Pont d'Avignon was one of the most astonishing feats of
engineering of twelfth-century Europe, and such little of the bridge
as still survives gives an impressive idea of what this structure
must once have been like when, in all its length of more than half a
mile, it crossed the river with low arches each of nearly one hundred
feet span. Even now the sheer audacity of the undertaking is
startling enough, but in its own day it must have seemed to the
people of Provence as great an achievement as the Golden Gate
and Sydney Harbour bridges appear in our own century. Nowadays
we assume that engineers bring their works to completion as a
result of proper designing, but almost any sizeable bridge of

medieval Europe seemed to demand supernatural navvying. The splendid Pont Valentré at Cahors on the Lot is only one of many which legend declares to have been successfully erected only because a mysterious mason employed upon it proved to be the Devil himself. Yet somehow the great bridge of Avignon was too sublime to be satanic and the construction was attributed to a direct demand of Christ himself.

The tale of the Avignon bridge is a curious one. Not only is it remarkably complete, but it is recounted in great detail in documents of the period, and testimonies about the hero, Bénézet, were taken from no less than fifteen people. Like the tale of the piper of Hamelin it is remarkably firmly grounded, and it is almost impossible to say where reality ends and legend begins. And as though to discourage anyone who should try to do so, the relevant papers end with the blunt injunction: *Fassan totz ensems a notre Seinghor Dieu et a sant Beneset a cui es honor et gloria.* Let us all bless the Lord God and Saint Bénézet, to whom be the honour and glory.

The year was 1177, and there lived near Viviers, close to the site of the modern lock of Châteauneuf, a woman who sent her twelve-year-old boy to watch her sheep, very much in the way Moses watched over the flocks of his father-in-law. Benoît, Benedict, Bénézet or Beneset as he is variously called, was engaged in this pastoral activity when one day he heard a voice calling him three times from heaven. Samuel-like — for the tale of Eli as well as the boyhood of Moses may have left their mark upon the account — young Ben answered and was astounded to hear the voice announce that the speaker was none other than Jesus Christ himself and that he had an important piece of work for Bénézet to undertake.

'*Ieu vole que tu laisses las fedas que gardas, quar tu mi faras un pont sus lo flumi de Rose.*' So ran the request, as recorded in the language of the day. 'I want you to leave the sheep you are looking after, because you are to make me a bridge over the river Rhône.'

Bénézet quickly protested that he could not leave the sheep, he knew nothing of the Rhône, he had only three farthings to his name, and what with one thing and another he was the last individual to be capable of the work. But the voice insisted that he was to do as he was told, and that an angel would be sent to lead him to the Rhône.

The lad set out, and he had not long been on his way when the angel arrived, disguised as a pilgrim and carrying a staff and scrip. This individual introduced himself as the boy's appointed guide and led him to the bank of the river, the size of which filled Bénézet with such fear that he protested it would be quite impossible to build a bridge over it.

But the angel told him not to worry, and leading him down to a trading ship he told Bénézet to go to Avignon and to show himself to the bishop. So saying, the pilgrim vanished, leaving Bénézet alone at the gang-plank.

The boy then asked the mariners 'for the love of God and the blessed Mary' to give him passage to the town, where he had important business in hand; but the owner of the craft happened to be a Jew, and not at all the kind of man likely to be well disposed to juvenile hitch-hikers. Nor was he impressed by invocations. Maries, he said, were cheap enough. Personally he would prefer threepence to all the love of the blessed Mary, and if the shepherd boy could not pay the money he would have to walk.

Bénézet was not a wealthy lad. To be precise, he had exactly three farthings to his name. But the Jewish shipowner was not inclined to see three good farthings go from his grasp and so he agreed to accept a compromise fare for that amount and allowed the boy to come aboard. At Avignon Bénézet landed, and hurrying into the city he found the bishop preaching a sermon. Obedient to his charge, the lad was tactless enough to interrupt the discourse and announce to prelate and people that he had arrived, sent upon the special order of Christ to build a bridge.

The bishop was not accustomed to having his sermons so rudely interrupted, and he had the lad seized and conducted to the provost of the city with the suggestion that he be flayed alive or have his hands and feet cut off — or perhaps both. Ben was not in the least dismayed, and in front of the magistrate he repeated his tale and explained that he had only come to build the bridge over the

Rhône which was so much needed. But the official was unwilling to take him seriously. How, he asked, could such a simple, common villain, a penniless good-for-nothing, hope to bridge the Rhône where neither God, St Peter, St Paul, nor even the great Charlemagne himself had been able to succeed? And sarcastically he added that he happened to have a handy stone in his residence; if Bénézet could carry it down to the river then he would perhaps believe the lad capable of building a bridge after all.

The stone in question was part of a Roman column, and according to local accounts it measured thirteen feet by seven and needed thirty men to lift it. Bénézet does not seem to have been deterred by its size, and led again before the bishop he explained that the provost was supplying him with a good piece of masonry for the foundations of his bridge, and he would now go and carry it down to the site as the official had ordered. The bishop evidently wished his congregation to share the entertainment, for he led them out to watch.

Taken to where the stone lay, Bénézet braced himself, lifted the stone as though it were a cobble, and carried it to the river bank to set it where the first arch was to be built. Amid the tumult of astonishment the provost flung himself on the ground before Bénézet, and promptly made the first contribution of three hundred sous to the bridge fund — which within the day ran up to a total of five thousand. The authorities and people alike took up the cause of the bridge with enthusiasm, working so energetically under the guidance of the shepherd lad that within only eleven years the bridge of nineteen great arches was complete. As for Bénézet, he was destined never to see the great work brought to completion, for in 1184 he died at the age of only nineteen. A chapel to hold his remains was built above the fourth arch, and it naturally became a place of considerable pilgrimage. Within it Bénézet remained buried for nearly five centuries, until the arch beneath the chapel was so seriously threatened by ice floes that his remains were removed.

The original bridge was brilliantly designed with strong buttresses to protect it from floods and ice, but unfortunately the bridge-building Brothers Pontiff (who were probably responsible for the structure) left the maintenance to the civil authorities, who did little more than replace arches one at a time when they happened to collapse. Much of the repair work was done in wood, and altogether the state of the structure became so poor that as early as 1226 it was too weak for the tramp of the forces of the king of France and several arches collapsed into the Rhône with a loss of life estimated — perhaps with chronicler's licence — at 3,000 men. Again repairs were made, and throughout the centuries the bridge was in use the ravages of wash-out, fire, battle, sapping, ice, storm and flood were continually but not very effectively made good.

The Sade family poured money into repairs, and Pope Clement VI reconstructed the four great arches which still survive to this day, but by 1679 the decay was proceeding faster than the maintenance and the bridge had finally to be abandoned.

The bridge of Bénézet projects from the *pèri* at the foot of the group of fortress towers of the papal palace 150 miles below La Mulatière. As we passed it we knew that only another 17 miles lay ahead of us before we should be leaving the river to enter the canals of the south, and though the stream was still hurrying we now had an easier journey with deeper water, and even some buoys to mark the limits of the channel.

Ashore, the leaves had now fallen to the ground before the blast of the *mistral*, and through the skeleton branches we could occasionally glimpse the distant peaks of Auvergne away to our right, whilst all the while the hills on either shore were becoming more arid, the vineyards stonier and the trees more characteristic of the Mediterranean. Pines and cypresses and the many varieties of sticky evergreen shrubs loaded the air with their scent of the south, and greyish olive trees stretched out from earth-filled crevices to hold out their bare branches as though feeling the warmth of the sun, which even on this morning of late October still had a power more appropriate in Britain to midsummer. We too could sense the nearness of a land with a new sunshine, a climate of its own, and with houses, people, wine, cheese, grass, flowers, and even barges very different from those of the north. For us this country would begin at the Canal de Beaucaire, because though already we might be within its limits we had still to set foot on its land.

A long curve to port led us to where the Rhône ahead was spanned by a new bridge standing by the wreckage of an earlier one, and leading from one little town with a formidable crenelated fortress tower on a low hill to another little town with an even more formidable but equally crenelated fortress tower dipping its feet in the river itself. Glaring at each other across the stream like champions of opposing armies, Beaucaire to starboard and Tarascon to port were obviously confident that if their battlements had already stood for seven centuries they would easily last for a further seven. Indeed the castle of Tarascon is in such perfect order that although the noble duke René has been dead these four hundred years his keep was until the present century the departmental prison, and those who wished to visit the interior could only do so by committing a suitably serious crime. It is now open to law-abiding citizens too — at least in theory, but in practice it is not always easy to be at the gate of any French monument at the time when visitors are admitted.

Tarascon's keep is severe, and it faces directly across the water to its neighbour with such a blank and uncompromising stare that one is not sure whether it regards as a friend or a foe the one solid hilltop tower set among the pines, which is all that is left of the castle of Beaucaire. From the water no more of the town is to be seen at all, for Beaucaire learnt a terrible lesson from the floods of 1840 and its burghers built an immense embankment to keep the river out of the bedroom windows in times of *grande crue*. Behind this bank the houses huddle in such fear that none of them dares to peep over the top to watch the shipping go by.

Below the railway bridge we found a group of Rhône barges lying against some piles, and immediately beyond them the bank curved back to open the way into the Canal de Beaucaire. The *Commodore* ran straight past the entrance, turned, thrust her bow into the current, and with the helm slightly to port she let herself be pushed out of the river into the slack water at the foot of the immense double gates which now stood open but which sometimes had the duty of holding a Rhône flood not just from the town but out of the whole expanse of the Camargue, and the towns and villages along its edge. In still water once more, she seemed to have lost her swinging gait, but she pulled herself together, moved at a respectful speed through the open lock, and turned a bend into such an attractive canal basin as she had not met in France before. Pariset and Aubry packed their bags and stepped ashore, but the fact that they were in no desperate hurry as they bid us *au revoir* reminded us that they had more time to spare than they would have wished. It might be weeks before there would be any other boats to pilot down the river.

Beaucaire and its castle are inseparable from the memory of two young lovers whose tale was sung by troubadours in castle and palace throughout the land. No doubt a minstrel, or perhaps the gentle René of Anjou himself, struck his lyre and sang and recited the lines in his castle set in the stream at Tarascon, recounting once again the story of Aucassin, son of the Count of Beaucaire, and of the captive slave girl Nicolette, a prisoner taken in battle against the Saracens. Who she was, none knew, for she had been taken from home as a child. But she was beautiful in the eyes of Aucassin and on the lips of the story-teller, her hair curling and golden, her eyes blue-grey and full of laughter, her lips of a vermilion richer than ever rose or summer cherry wore, her teeth white as ivory. Her bosom was firm, lifting her dress as though it had been two walnuts, her form so slender that one might clasp her round with one's two hands. So white were her feet, for all their colour, that the daisy blossoms broken by her gentle tread seemed black beside them. Nicolette was as lovely a creature as ever soared from the heart of a troubadour, and it is no wonder that Aucassin should have loved her so deeply that his only joy was in waiting upon her, or thinking of her. This he much preferred to joining in the wars and fighting his father's great enemy the Count of Valence.

But this choice of love rather than war so angered Aucassin's father that he forbade his son ever to see the fair Nicolette again, and to make sure that his wishes should be obeyed he ordered his vassal, the Viscount of Beaucaire, to have the girl shut away in a lonely tower with only a slit for a window. There she was to stay with none but an old woman to watch her, and if Aucassin should try to reach her or to speak to her she was to be burned alive.

When Aucassin learned of the fate of his beloved he retired to his room and wept and wept without ceasing. Meanwhile the ferocious Count of Valence came to lay siege to the place, and Beaucaire was under bombardment with stones flung by every possible engine of war. At the height of the attack Count Garin ran to summon his son and heir to defend the family castle, but all Aucassin could do was to weep. He would never bear arms again, he said, unless his father allowed him to come to his beloved Nicolette and to marry her.

Thus Aucassin wept, and the men of Valence battered at the gates. Never, never should he be allowed to see the girl, his father declared in his fury. But the sound of the onslaught made some sort of compromise seem desirable, and with the enemy thundering terribly at the gates a formula was agreed upon. Aucassin would fight to defend Beaucaire, and if he returned alive from the encounter he would be allowed to see Nicolette once only, and for long enough just to exchange a few words of love and to share a single kiss.

So great was the joy of expectation of that kiss that Aucassin began to daydream even in the thick of the battle, and stripped of his shield and lance he was being led away captive from the battle-field when he most fortunately came to his senses. He still had his sword, and his trusty horse, and little though he cared for Beaucaire and his father's house he would fight, striking down the men of Valence for the love and glory of his adored Nicolette, shut away in her tower. So, setting the spurs to his steed, he ran down so furiously upon the Count of Valence and gave him so lusty a blow with his sword that he stunned him and could lift him up to carry him off as prisoner. The day was won, and Aucassin rode triumphant to claim his prize of the single kiss upon Nicolette's lips.

The Count of Beaucaire quickly let it be known that he had not the slightest intention of keeping his part of the bargain. He were better to be accursed, he stormed, than to allow his son to see the wretched, low-born, worthless Nicolette. And Aucassin, helpless before his blank refusal, freed his prisoner the Count of Valence and let him go in safety. Then he retired to his chamber to give himself up to weeping.

This everlasting crying seems to have worked on the nerves of the Count of Beaucaire, for soon it was Aucassin's turn to be dragged away and thrown into a dungeon. Nicolette came to hear of how he wept and suffered for her still, and one warm night of May as the nightingales sang sadly outside her tower she could bear it no longer. No, she did not throw herself to her death. A more reasonable girl, she waited until the woman set to watch her was asleep, then swiftly knotted together the bedclothes and coverings to make a rope down which she could glide. Being so slim she could squeeze through the narrow window, and so find her freedom.

Fleeing through the moonlit alleys of Beaucaire, Nicolette came at last to the tower under which her true love lay imprisoned. She managed to squeeze her head through a hole, and sure enough she could hear her beloved Aucassin weeping the night away, still sobbing helplessly in his love for her. But already her escape was discovered, and the guards were out looking for her. Warned by the kindly night-watchman she hid behind a pillar, then fled barefoot from the town and out to the forest. And there it was that Aucassin came to her when his father, thinking Nicolette dead, at last released him.

Now the joy of the lovers is complete. Together they reach the coast and sail to a castle on the shore, where they are received with kindness and sympathy. But alas, one day the ships of the terrible Saracens appear, the castle is overrun and many of its defenders slaughtered. Aucassin and Nicolette are seized and carried away to slavery, each on a different ship. The two craft are driven asunder in a swift and dangerous storm such as the Mediterranean can still provide, and Aucassin reaches the coast of Provence. At last — probably still weeping for his beloved — he finds his way to Beaucaire and discovers that he has succeeded to the title.

As for Nicolette, she is taken to Carthage, and there to the great joy of all the people she is identified as their long lost princess. She has no lack of rich suitors, but Nicolette cannot stay. Once more she sets out, and with blackened face and in the guise of a troubadour she makes her way to Beaucaire and there in the castle she sings to the young Count the story of Nicolette and of the Aucassin she has lost and to whom she will ever be faithful. And when the disguise has been discarded and the blackening washed away, Aucassin's tears change to those of unbounded joy. Next day they are married, and they live many, many years in a happiness of such love as only a troubadour can sing.

Of the troubadour nobility, René of Anjou in his castle of Tarascon was perhaps the last. Married in real romantic style at the age of twelve — and to a bride of ten — he lived in that Provence which acquired from the crusaders and by trade with eastern countries an exotic flavour, a tang of love and a zest for life as gay as the scent of the flowers which decked its hills. The troubadours sang and dreamed of beauty, of valiant fights, of chivalry and self-sacrifice, but above all of love. And this ideal of love was such as would send shivers down the spine of any Marriage Guidance Counsellor, for it had nothing to do with marriage. One might well be married, and this was very necessary to preserve the line and raise children, but it had little to do with love. Ermengarde of Narbonne stated explicitly that a husband could only really begin to be the true lover of his wife when she had divorced him and married another. Love was secret, dangerous. It drove men to great deeds of chivalry and daring, it made them strive to win the right to be the lover of another man's wife, and it impelled women to take immense risks — for the double standard had already been invented, and a woman whose chastity and honour were suspect could be ejected, and even murdered by her husband. Clandestine undiscovered love was the ideal, and this meant a mutual trust between lovers as complete as might be the deception of the spouse.

The chivalrous love of the troubadours was played according to definite rules, even if these seem hardly to have fitted the romantic tales of a true love such as that of Aucassin and Nicolette, which involved absolute fidelity leading to lifelong marriage. In fact there was a curious double principle in the romance of the minstrels, as though they suspected that in theory love in marriage was the ultimate happiness but in practice the romantic theft of the spouse of another was preferable. Perhaps this was why cases arose which needed the competent advice of experts in romance. Certain it is that 'Courts of Love' were established, of which those held by René at Tarascon are among the most famous. To them, and to the brilliant and romantic women who formed the bench of judges, lovers brought their problems for adjudication. Their proceedings were as confidential as those of a modern consulting room, and for this reason there is more rumour than certainty about their sessions, but sufficient references can be found in the literature of the troubadour period to suggest at least that the cases they advised upon involved matters of principle in which romantic love was supreme.

Not that the verdict of the women was always in line with that which a modern consultant might give. For instance, a *seigneur* fell in love with a single lady who already had a lover, and although this was in accordance with rule 34 (*Nothing should prevent a lady having two lovers at the same time*) the lady had relied upon the rather contradictory rule 3 (*No person can genuinely love two at the same time*) and had turned him down, but she had generously promised him the right of succession in case of the demise of her original hero. Eventually she married this first lover, and the claimant asked for implementation of his rights on the basis of rule 1 (*The married state is no reason for refusing love*) and the general principle that love and marriage were normally irreconcilable.

The lady refused him, and this was the situation when, in all fairness, he brought the matter before a Court of Love. The experienced women listened to the arguments on either side and then considered their verdict. The decision upheld the claim of the *seigneur* and decreed that the lady who had married should accept him as she had promised. Which no doubt she did — unless she invoked rule 5 (*Favours unwillingly given are tasteless*).

The good René of Anjou at whose castle of Tarascon such proceedings were often said to be held, was a kindly man, well read and generous, a linguist and a mathematician, a poet and painter, a lover of good wine, a ruler simple and philosophical, a peaceable man in an era of violence, and above all a troubadour. His subjects loved him — a thing rare enough in those days — and it was for their amusement and gaiety that he commissioned the construction of the first model of the fearful beast which gives its name to the town and which, had we but known it, might once have destroyed the *Commodore* on her way down to the entrance of the Canal de Beaucaire.

Below the rock upon which is built the castle of René of Anjou there seems once to have been a hole. At least, such a cavity is vouched for by an Englishman, Gervais of Tilbury, writing in about the year 1200. *Sub rupe Tarasconensis*, he said, there was a great hole, and in it lived at the time of St Martha a monster, a dangerous creature of the type of a Leviathan. It was not the only one in the Rhône valley, for there were the dragon of Lyon and the dragon of Arles, and a related but smaller species which lived in the water on the Beaucaire shore. But among all this fauna of the Rhône the Tarascus was the most terrible. It wrecked ships and ate the mariners, and generally held the land in a grip of terror.

A river such as the Rhône is certain to have monsters. At least they can be heard easily enough. Indeed, when lying at Andance we had been aware all night of a great monster sucking at the *Commodore*'s planking, scrabbling at her keel, thumping her underside with swishes of its powerful tail and gurgling with insane and dragonly merriment all the while. Brought up in an unbelieving age we had tried to convince ourselves that this was nothing but the effects of the current, but had we been aboard a medieval vessel our interpretation would have been different. We would readily have identified the sounds as coming from some local type of Loch Ness Monster, and after a suitable draught of local wine either we or one of the pilots would certainly have seen it stealing a case of Major Eigg's baby food for its horrid brood. So, too, at Tarascon the fierce current swirling around the rock may well have produced noises which could only be assumed to emanate from the coarse throat of some strange beast, the terrible Tarasque. And if a ship was sometimes overset, was not this also the work of the same evil creature?

However the story of the Tarasque may have begun, it was soon to be developed and mixed with other legends, Christian and pre-Christian alike, so that the details of the beast's biological origin and final ending were established. And to begin at the beginning, one must appreciate that in a kind of way it was all the fault of the preaching of John the Baptist. When this great forerunner began to preach the coming of the new dispensation there was depression among the creatures who had for generations carried out the vengeance of God, for now there was to be no more vengeance, no fire and brimstone but mere long-suffering and forgiveness. Among those which took a serious view of this new trend in human crime and divine retribution was Leviathan, the fearsome creature described in such intimate detail in the forty-first chapter of the Book of Job. He betook himself quickly to Galatia, and there he discovered a monstress of a different species to himself, an *onaque*. This may have been merely an onager, but some medieval sources describe it as a huge, snake-like creature with one eye, the lens of which was made of a carbuncle.

Occasionally this female dragon would go to bathe in the salty Tatt lake (now Lake Tuz). Before entering the brine she was in the habit of taking out her eye-lens and putting it on the shore — but this was to prove her undoing, for one day the Leviathan stole the lens and then flung himself upon the blind *onaque* in a fit of violent lust.

Evidently the chromosomes of these two creatures were not so dissimilar that embryonic development was impossible. The mating did not prove sterile, and after thirteen months of gestation, a hybrid creature was born, more terrible than either of its parents. The people of Galatia looked at the newborn horror from a suitably safe distance, and they named it the 'Tharrascouros'.

This Tharrascouros grew up, and in his teens he grew restless. Fed up with his home in Lake Tuz, disillusioned about his own ageing parents, he lumbered down to the coast and flung himself into the Mediterranean. So feverish was he that the water promptly began to boil. (This tendency toward epidermal pyrexia was inherited, it seems, from his father Leviathan. According to Job, Leviathan could boil the water as well as any.)

Swimming westward, the creature forged ahead until one

morning his ire was roused by the water actually pushing against him. Unknowing, he had arrived off the Rhône delta, and the current of the great river seemed to challenge him. He turned into the river, beat furiously against the stream of cold and alpine water, so different from the salty fluid of Lake Tuz, and swam vigorously against the current. By the time he had covered ten leagues he was rather enjoying it, and she decided that the land where she found herself might not be such a bad place for a monster to live after all.

The reader will have noticed that the creature changed sex in the course of the ten leagues swim up the river. I have no satisfactory explanation of this, unless there was a streak of oyster in the ancestry, for oysters have the best of both worlds by changing sex every few months. But there is no doubt about it; in Galatia the beast was masculine, but on arrival at Tarascon it was *la* Tarasque, *ung dragon demy beste et demy poisson, plus gros que ung beuf et plus long que ung cheval,* as a medieval writer described her. Naturally she proved a nuisance, killing everything within reach and wrecking the ships on the river. Things would have gone badly for the people of the Rhône valley had they not been unexpectedly liberated from the ravages of the monster, which had already accounted for thousands of victims — though more moderate sources say it was only eight.

During the first persecution of the Christians in the Holy Land a boatload of refugees escaped to Provence. According to some, they were forced into a leaking boat without food, water or sail, and pushed out to await their fate, whilst others suggest they fled by sea of their own free will. The passengers were Mary Magdalene with her brother Lazarus and sister Martha, Mary the mother of James and John, Mary Salome, and two servants. The people of Provence are quite convinced that this is so, and that the boat reached their shores.

St Martha is remembered at Tarascon. The tenth-century church where she is buried stands close to the end of the bridge, and even though it was rebuilt in the twelfth and heavily damaged by British and American bombardment of the bridge in the twentieth, it is very well worth a visit if only because there is

E

really no serious reason to doubt that the lady who lies in a renais-
sance tomb of marble in the ancient crypt is indeed Martha of
Bethany.

The good Gervais of Tilbury — who, being English, would
never lie and could not conceivably be fallible — also mentions
Martha, and the legend of Provence attributes to her power the
saving of Tarascon. She was making her way up the valley of the
Rhône when she came upon a crowd of people weeping and
wailing. On her enquiry the people told her about the Tarasque,
and said that their high priests and magicians had failed to
persuade it to depart, the warriors had blown their trumpets in
vain and clashed their shields to no effect. Armed knights had
courageously sought to fight the beast, and many were those who
had not returned. Meanwhile, the Tarasque continued to sink the
ships and ravage the countryside just as before.

'*Ne pleurez pas*,' said Martha. 'Pray to the only God who can
vanquish dragons.' And with cross in hand she followed the trail of
bones (for the Tarasque was a messy eater) until she came upon the
beast in a wood. It was still engaged in its horrid meal, '*mengeant
ung homme en sa bouche.*'

The beast reared, flapped its wings, cracked its tail, and uttered
such a cry that the whole countryside shook. Martha held up the
cross and the Tarasque at once became so docile that she could
put her girdle round its neck and lead it, meek as a kitten, into the
town. There the people in their fury despatched the beast with
lances and stones.

And that might have been the end of the terrible monster which
lived in the hole under the rock and roamed the forest in search of
prey. But it was to be reborn, made of wood and cloth and with
eight young men inside it to propel its fearsome body through the
streets. That genial ruler René of Anjou first resuscitated the
Tarasque in this way, and from time to time a new one was later
built — as in 1742, when there was some kind of riot during the
annual procession and the poor Tarasque (without the young men)
was thrown down the public well. Naturally the Revolution had to
interfere with it, and the national guard was sent to hew the dragon
to pieces and burn it in the street, so that the happy people of

Tarascon might not have their attention diverted from the more strenuous business of class hatred.

Since then the Tarasque has been once more reincarnated, but for many years she no longer roamed the streets at Whitsun, knocking people down with great flicks of her powerful tail. Instead she lived in a little house near the church of St Martha, and was shown to visitors on request. Now she has returned to activity once more, and on the last Sunday of June she comes out of her lair as large as life, and brings back to Tarascon something of the gaiety that it knew under René, Count of Provence and Duke of Anjou, king of Sicily and Aragon, Hungary and Jerusalem.

At Beaucaire we were leaving the Rhône for the quiet waters of the Canal de Beaucaire, now part of the Canal du Rhône à Sète. Our voyage down the river had not been much less adventurous than it would have been two centuries earlier, to judge by the description given by Tobias Smollett — who decided to go by land transport instead of joining the majority who went aboard the diligence to 'glide down this river with great velocity, passing a great number of towns and villages on each side. In good weather, there is no danger in this method of travelling, 'till you come to the Pont-St-Esprit, where the stream runs through the arches with such rapidity, that the boat is sometimes overset. But those passengers who are under any apprehension are landed above-bridge, and taken in again, after the boat has passed, just in the same manner as at London Bridge. The boats that go up the river are drawn against the stream by oxen, which swim through one of the arches of this bridge, the driver sitting between the horns of the foremost beast.' Our own course had missed this exciting bridge of the Brothers Pontiff, which was bypassed by the Donzère-Mondragon canal, but otherwise the main difference was that the public no longer went by river at all and so missed not only the fun of being 'overset', but the sheer exhilaration of the great stream itself.

There is a general belief that canals are muddy and rivers clear, yet even in time of drought the water of the Rhône is by no means crystal or glassy. The river carries with it the mud and gravel eroded along its hundreds of miles of bed, and just as the Rhine has built the country of the Netherlands out of the pulverized materials of the northern slopes of the Alps, so the Rhône has piled the debris of their southern side into the Mediterranean, and has gradually been driving back the sea. How fast the Rhône delta moves south I do not know, but at least one can see that it has already gone a considerable distance. Once the estuary was right up in the neighbourhood of the modern lock of St Pierre near Pont-St-Esprit, and the accounts of voyages undertaken in the early Middle Ages remind us that places some miles inland were once ports. This does not necessarily mean that they were on the open sea, but at least they could be reached by large ships sailing up one of the branches of the Rhône or making their way through the channels which connected the lagoons of the ever-growing delta. And from earliest times these lagoons were a means of communication for the area between Marseille and Perpignan.

Long before the Canal du Midi was built to connect the Mediterranean and Atlantic, the land west of the Rhône delta was linked to the Rhône itself by a system of waterways through which boats of modest draught could pass from one *étang* to another and even make the voyage from the small ports of the Étang de Thau all the way to Lyon. Some of these channels had been cut for the boats engaged in the salt trade — for the shallow and briny lagoons have always been a source of salt produced by sun-drying. Besides, Beaucaire was for centuries the scene of one of the greatest annual trade fairs in all Europe, and produce could be carried to and from this world market by small craft plying throughout the southern part of what are now the provinces of Hérault and Bouches-du-Rhône. But later, when the Midi barges were able to ply from Bordeaux and Toulouse to Sète, it was obviously of great advantage that they should also be able to reach Beaucaire and the Rhône. The States of Languedoc took the matter in hand and constructed the Canal des Étangs eastwards from Sète, enlarging the medieval channels and linking together the lagoons and salt marshes almost to the ancient and forgotten town of Aigues-Mortes. They also gave to Marshal de Noailles a concession to cut a canal from that point to Beaucaire, draining and reclaiming the land as he did so. After nearly half a century the marshal and his family had not so much as begun the works, so the concession was turned over to the crown. Next, Marshal de Richelieu formed a company and in turn obtained the concession, but once again the project was abandoned. The States then took up the matter themselves and spent nineteen long years in bargaining and negotiation with those landowners whose marshes might be drained and who would thus lose their fishing rights, and those other landowners whose territory might now be cut into by a waterway and who would be obliged to cross by ferry or bridge to reach their land on the other side. These discussions were at last completed in 1777, and the Canal de Beaucaire was begun. It had just reached St Gilles when the States of Languedoc were themselves *supprimés* by the Revolution. Eventually the new régime authorized a company to complete the works, and in 1808 the waterway was at last opened.

This was the canal into which we turned at Beaucaire, and along which we set out westwards towards the marshes of the delta. At first it proved to be a canal of whitish and chalky water, but after leaving the beauties of Beaucaire and its port basin astern we passed along a cutting below a cement factory and reached the open country. Then the waterway decided to shake off its drabness and prove itself worthy of the Midi, running parallel to the grand chain of the Cévennes which stood clear and purple-topped but mysterious to starboard. One lock — the only one before the Canal du Midi — and we were in clean water, gliding along between the reeds towards the sunset. Over the banks lay a patchwork of fields, rich red and decked with vines in the glory of their autumn leaf, or in places black as the Cambridgeshire fens. Sometimes the earth was bare, at others there would be the shining emerald of winter wheat or the stalks of maize lying where the cutter had ripped them.

Near Bellegarde the canal turned a little towards the hills, then away again to converge more closely with the Petit Rhône and run into the delightful little town of St Gilles. Between the two bridges a long stone quay flanked the canal on either side, and the cobbles, earth and even the roadway were all stained a rich and almost archiepiscopal purple which stemmed from the activity of the vintners. The vintage was over, but barrels, winepresses, great

tuns, wooden shovels, boards and slatted wains lay scattered along the canal side, all stained in the same hue of grape-skin. Behind them stood the row of houses of the coopers and vine-growers, with vaulted cellars opening above the ground level through stone arches which seemed to invite the daring hero of some medieval legend to enter fearlessly and face for the sake of his lady whatever horror of dragon or imprisonment, wicked knight or knavery might be concealed therein.

St Gilles is one of the prettiest canal towns imaginable, yet its nautical history goes back far beyond the Canal de Beaucaire to the days when it was a seaport in which might lie the trading ships of half a dozen seafaring countries. These ships have long since vanished, and so has the sea which brought them, and even the canal traffic has so far declined that we ourselves never met a barge from one end of the waterway to the other. At vintage time the wine-tanker vessels may lie along the quays, but on the whole St Gilles is a place of quiet, a little town in which the houses are simple rather than notable and lie tumbled pleasantly about the slope without the least regard to convenience or planning, and with an air that there is really no hurry. At the same time they are sparkling as can be, their doors and windows painted in the bright hues of the Mediterranean, the sills gay with flowers that seem almost to shout the brilliance of their tints, flaunting them in the certainty that no such gaiety could be displayed in the damper and colder climes of the north. It is a town of alleys and queer corners, and of cats watching intently for something which never seems to arrive.

If we first became aware of the full beauty of the Midi when wandering through the town of St Gilles, it was there too that we had a further introduction to the wild life of the Mediterranean. At Tarascon we had stared at a locust on the lintel of the door of St Martha's church, and as it returned our gaze with its compound eyes of shimmering green we wondered whether John the Baptist ate such creatures from choice, or necessity, or for self discipline, or just to add body to the wild honey. Now at St Gilles we were to meet other creatures unexpected, and our first surprise was when a new type of visitor jumped up to the catwalk, and eyed us un-blinking with a cool, imperturbable glance, and with just a trace of superiority in the gulping movements beneath the chin like those of a City of London sheriff who has eaten too much of the fifth course at a banquet but knows he should not belch in the presence of ladies. The creature who thus came to inspect us was a frog little more than an inch long and as brilliantly green as the grass of Ireland. Round his whole body there spread like a continuation of an enormous grin a neat plimsoll line of white. Altogether he was the most pleasant creature, and we soon noticed that he was not alone. The short grass at the canal edge was full of his relations, so ingeniously mixed up with the shoots the wine had not stained that we had to step carefully to avoid treading on them.

The same little frogs we found perched on gravel ledges of a shingle bank up beyond the town, where the fields stretched away to the rising land of the Cévennes. The ground below the bank was hot and baked, and we noticed patches of a tangled plant of bluish green colour with seed heads not unlike the buds of a garden poppy.

I bent down to pick one, and just as I was about to grasp it there was a whoosh, a trail of droplets in the air and on my arm, and the pod had vanished. Propelled by a pressure jet of liquid it had flown past me to land several yards away.

There were plenty of pods, so the next one was approached carefully and lifted very gently with the tip of my finger. The moment the least strain was put upon the point of attachment to the stalk the seal was broken, a fracture spread instantly across the stem, and the fluid held under pressure in the pod issued as a rocket jet powerful enough to send the whole container hurtling away into the scrub. Amused at our delight and astonishment at what was to him a familiar weed, an old man in bright blue overalls and a broad straw sun-hat came over from his vegetable patch to speak to us. The plant was the *Cougoumasso* he said, the *Concombre sauvage*. We later discovered that it also had the name of *Momordique*, or *Pistolet de Dames*, all of which names were better than the *Ecbalium elaterium* Rich of the botanists.

We were still amusing ourselves with firing the Ladies' Pistols when I happened to look down at my own trousers and saw, perched in an attitude of meditation just below my knee, a creature five inches in length and bright green. She was soon joined by two others of slightly smaller size, and I was glad to notice that courtship did not seem to be their intention, for I had no wish that my trousers should be the scene of murder. Perhaps the old man read my thoughts, if not quite correctly, for he hastened to tell me that I need not be alarmed. The animals were harmless. This of course I knew, for although I had never seen one before there was no mistaking from the pious postures struck by the creatures what they were. *Veguère ièu un prègo-dièu*, as Frédéric Mistral said in one of his poems. In other words, I saw a specimen of *Mantis religiosa* L.

The *prie-dieu*, as the French call it, is not so sanctimonious by nature as it would appear to be, but its apparent attitude of being lost in prayer has endowed it in the mind of the people with special talents. It is known to help children who have lost their way. As one writer reported long ago, *puero interroganti de via altero pede extento rectam monstrat atque rare vel nunquam fallit*. Even if he was so certain that the insect was rarely or never in error in pointing out the way with its foot, he did not explain how a lad should set about addressing a question to the creature, and whether the mantis only understood Latin, or Provençal, or what. Perhaps the *prie-dieu* is equipped with E.S.P. on a child's wavelength and just knows the query before the lost youngster has time to formulate a phrase-book enquiry.

The attitude of continual prayer on the part of the female is even more hypocritical than that of the Pharisee going down to the temple, for it covers a trait of character which is decidedly unpleasant — at least as far as the male is concerned. Indeed the love life of the mantis is altogether rather Freudish. The male may only approach his mate from the starboard side, but whether he can do so or not is another matter, for the preliminaries are much like the game of Grandmother's Steps I used to play as a child. He finds the female and watches her, but he can only draw nearer in quick and almost imperceptible darts whenever she is not looking. She for her part behaves in much the same manner as many females of *H. sapiens*. 'The slightest movement made by the male,' as a biologist puts it, 'and the female will immediately snap his head off.' Unfortunately she really does so, with good sharp jaws and not just with a vigorous tongue.

So if he is seen making a move, the male is killed. But if he creeps up to her stealthily and successfully, ending with a final leap which pinions her wings, his fate is not so much better. *Le drame nuptial* takes place, and the moment she has been mated the female turns upon her husband, slices off his head, and settles down to eat him. Frequently she does not bother to wait until he has finished, and a headless torso will be mating with her at one end whilst she lunches off it at the other — for Natural Selection or whatever it is that produces these unnatural tendencies has implanted in the male such a strong pattern of mating behaviour that he can carry on with the job even when half devoured.

Biologists have long been intrigued by this macabre business, wondering what the use or object of it can be. One reasonable suggestion is that the female is about to lay a considerable number of eggs, and to build these she needs an extra source of suitable protein such as her husband can conveniently provide. Another idea is that such brains as the male mantis may have in his poor little head serve only to restrict and lessen the full flow of the mating reflex, and the female is equipped to cope with the situation by chopping off his head and so ensuring a really thorough mating.

Be that as it may, the female is insatiable. She may accept, slay and devour several males within a week. It was the thought that this callous polyandry might account for the portliness of the largest and fattest specimen on my trousers which made me lift her off gently but firmly and replace her among the *Pistolet de Dames* in case she wished to deposit one lot of eggs while waiting for another suitor to arrive for dinner.

IV

St Gilles and the deer — taming the Count — the bull's afternoon — by night to Aigues-Mortes — a medieval fortress — the crusades of King Louis — Le Grau du Roi — the reluctant fisherman — Canal des Étangs — wine of Frontignan

Right in the centre of the little town of St Gilles is a small market place, one end of it formed by the steps and façade of a church which looks for all the world as though it has just been struck by an air raid. It is not just that the portals are chipped and scarred, but that the nave itself runs off into a profusion of broken pillars and tumbled masonry, cracked monuments, blocks of stone and heaps of crumbled rubble. It was a Sunday morning when we saw it, and seated among the debris were an old woman eating olives, a vendor of balloons blowing up his wares, three lizards enjoying the sunshine, and a little girl in her Communion dress. Except for the lizards they reminded me of the people one saw sitting on ruins in Cologne after the bombardment, with nothing left to do in the world but sit, or do whatever one might have done before the city was destroyed.

The abbey of St Gilles has had this appearance for centuries, ever since the zealous if over-vigorous reformers of the Church attacked the monks and threw them down the well, burning the abbey over them. But the magnificent front still remains, and is said by some to be as fine as anything in France. Certainly it must have been a thing of glory before the Revolution interfered with it and made many of the mute statues pay with their heads as though they were real fellow-citizens. Even now it is a thing of great beauty with its classical columns and flutings, and groups of medieval people viewing with very natural alarm the fearsome beasts which seem to want to drag them down and eat them.

Below the church is a deep, dark, but most impressive crypt, laid out in such a way that pilgrims would pass through it in an orderly fashion. For the abbey of St Gilles was a place to which thousands would come as they passed on their way to St James's at Compostella or prepared to take ship at St Gilles quay on their way to the Holy Land. They would file past the tomb of St Gilles himself, the same whose cathedral of St Giles in Edinburgh takes him half way to being a national saint of Scotland. Not that St Gilles himself had any connection with that country, for he began his life in Greece and ended it in the abbey which bears his name. Between these two events he lived the life of a hermit, and he has a permanent place in the legends of Provence.

Aegidius, Gilles or Giles, set out on his wanderings in the sixth century, and leaving his native Greece he eventually reached the forests near the mouth of the Rhône. It was there that he was to become one of the many European saints associated with deer. He did not hunt a stag as Hubert did, nor was he saved from an untimely and involuntary marriage, as was Notburga of the Neckar. But he has this in common with the rest, that his deer was an albino. It is said that he lived alone with it in the forest, and that in return for the hospitality of his rough shelter the doe nourished him with her milk. News of the white doe — which by reason of its albino genes could hardly escape being seen — eventually reached the King of Provence, who at once decided that he must hunt it down. A party was got together consisting of seven score dogs and an even greater number of huntsmen, and as this immense force accompanied the king through the forest a white flash among the trees showed that they were on the right trail.

Fleeing before the hunt the doe led the chase further and further into the forest, and as she drew near to where Gilles lived beneath the trees the din of the pursuit roused him from his prayers. He hurried out to see that his faithful friend and provider should come to no harm, and saw the doe cornered, cowering in terror behind a tree. At this moment one of the royal huntsmen drew his bow and shot, but Gilles stretched out his leg and the arrow lodged in his knee. He pulled it out, the tale says, and prayed that the wound might never heal, so that he should always be reminded of the sufferings of Christ.

This curious incident so surprised the king that he asked his attending bishop to enquire of Gilles who he was, and how and where he lived. The hermit told his tale and the king immediately offered to subsidize him, and to give him a position where he could live in comfort and honour. Gilles preferred to return to his lair with only the doe as company, but now that his secret was out he was continually sought out by the poor and needy. At last he accepted the repeated offer of the king to build him an abbey, and the institution was erected on the spot where he had been pierced by the hunter's arrow. Gilles still slept on the ground rather than in a bed, but he accepted the role of abbot. So good and saintly was he that the great Charlemagne is said to have been willing to confess only to Gilles, and in Chartres a window shows him doing so; but as Gilles lived in the sixth century and Charlemagne in the ninth the tale is not altogether convincing.

The legends of Gilles do not stop even with Charlemagne. When his abbey was to be founded he naturally betook himself to Rome to have the Pope approve the scheme, and it is said that the Pope not only gave his sanction but a pair of fine carved wooden doors as well. Gilles had somehow to take them back to Provence, so he threw the doors into the Tiber — presumably when the Pope was not watching — and sure enough, he had only just reached home when they were washed ashore on the bank of the Petit Rhône close to the abbey.

The forest has long since disappeared, and the low hill of St Gilles now lies at the very edge of the open marshland of the Camargue. And if only the church and crypt are left of an abbey which grew to a position of some importance, they both recall events which unleashed one of the most tragic and fearful terrors ever to descend upon Europe, as the result of which many thousands throughout the southern provinces were burned alive without a word of complaint and an entire civilization was so effectively rooted out that we can only pick up its traces in the few works of art which it has left. Our voyage westward from St Gilles was to take us for hundreds of miles through the lands where that civilization had flowered until, in the thirteenth century, the death of Pierre de Castelnau was the signal for its annihilation.

Pierre was Legate to the Languedoc, and his particular charge was to contain or put down the heresy which was growing so alarmingly in the domains of the Count of Toulouse. Count Raymond VI openly gave shelter and encouragement to those who did not agree with all the dogma and practice of the Church of Rome which, within his realm, had reached an almost unbelievable state of corruption. Pierre set about inciting the lords of Provence to rebel against Raymond, and as this course was not successful he publicly excommunicated him and outlawed his territories, pronouncing in advance a blessing on any who should strike the Count dead. Whether from real terror of the fate of his soul, or — which is more probable — to make an appearance of subservience and so avoid the worst results of the interdict for his people, the Count came to heel and travelled to St Gilles to make formal submission to the authority of Rome. The scene in the abbey was one of victory for the Legate, and certainly it was his day of triumph. But it was also his last, for as he left the town to cross the Petit Rhône, one of the Count's officers ran him through with a sword. That was in 1207, and it roused Innocent III to give the signal for the forces of Europe to be launched against another Christian country in a war of extermination.

The final destruction of the last strongholds of the Albigensians was not to be achieved for nearly forty years, but only two years after the murder of the Legate the crowds were gathered again to see Count Raymond VI humiliated at St Gilles. He was forced to submit in public to the supreme religious authority of the Pope. More than a score of bishops had been summoned to see Raymond submit to whatever the new Legate demanded of him.

There was little that the Legate did not require. A collection of relics (which the heretics despised) was set outside the door, and grovelling before them the Count had to swear obedience to the officials of the Pope. Stripped to the waist he was then led into the church with a rope round his neck as though he were a cow — or perhaps a bull castrated and prepared for public sport like those of the Camargue. At each step the clergy beat him on his bare back, and still stripped and bleeding he was forced to pass through the crypt where not only St Gilles but the Count's own former mortal

enemy Pierre de Castelnau lay buried. Even this was only a
beginning, for the outward humiliations were no more than the
formal seal set upon eight conditions which he had accepted, each
of which involved either submission to the clergy in his domains or
some restriction of freedom for his subjects — for example that all
Jews were to be dismissed from holding office in his territories.
Probably the Count thought that by appearing to accept these
indignities he would hold off the storm which threatened his
people, but he was mistaken. He was a tolerant man, and there was
no place for tolerance in the world of Innocent III. When,
thirteen years later, Count Raymond lay dying, he was refused the
Last Sacrament — a thing that may or may not have been so
terrible to his mind but which showed unambiguously the extent
to which the Church of Rome thought his submission genuine. And
not content with that they refused him burial, and for years his
coffin remained above the ground until finally his remains were
eaten by rats. Yet even this was as nothing to the fate which was
dealt out to those throughout his domains who dared to accept
teachings which had not the stamp of papal approval, and on our
voyage through the Midi we were to pass through one locality after
another where they had been slaughtered without mercy and their
houses razed to the ground.

We had already reached Aigues-Mortes before hearing that
there was to be a *course* at St Gilles two days later, and though
nothing could have induced us to enter a Spanish arena — even as
spectators — we heard enough about the event planned for St
Gilles to turn about and run back along the canal, to draw in for a
second time at the wine-stained quay with its amiable frogs of
jade. From the marshes and the farms people were pouring over
the bridges, excited by the prospect that one of their own young
men was perhaps to make some honest francs in matching his skill
and speed with that of *lou biou*, the bull.

Whatever the delights of the tales told of Tarascon and its
Tarasque, it may not be unreasonable to see in the name a hint of
taurus and of the tauromachy which in one form or another extends
along the Mediterranean from the altars of Mithras to the strange
sports in ancient Crete and to the blood-lust of bullfighting which,

by its sheer cruelty, still delights the crowds in Spain. And if the ancient cult of the bull has left only a name in Tarascon and a carved Roman bull head at Narbonne, across the southern provinces of France there is found a form of bull worship which has not become debased as it has in Spain, and may even be nearer the original.

The people of the south, and particularly of the little towns on the edge of the Camargue, would be lost without *lou biou*. Whether the dark and handsome creatures are the survivors of *Bos primigenius* or came from Persia with the Mithraic cult, there are still some four thousand head of these cattle among the herds of the Camargue marshes. Black and primitive in appearance, they are under the care of their guardians until the day comes when they are old enough to enter the arena — an event which may be preceded by an *abrivado*, when a group of bulls will be driven through the streets to the huge delight of those in the first floor windows, the fear-tinged excitement of those at ground level, and the trepidation of the owners of china shops. For the bulls can cause considerable upturn, even if in fact they are really bullocks and have been castrated.

A bull is allowed to run to the age of three before castration, and by then he has established both the form and the habits of an unoperated creature. To castrate a healthy three-year bull is not so simple, and as the creature has a tendency to resent what is happening the guardians often provide a number of straw-stuffed human effigies upon which the beast can vent his fury as soon as the ligature has been completed. From that time onward he may live a long and successful life as an entertainer, for the *course* is not dangerous to the animal and the onlookers would be greatly saddened if any harm were to befall him. They come to know the creatures as old friends and they are by no means certain that the bulls may not enjoy the *cocarde* themselves. Besides, the people of the Midi are themselves gay and gentle. Blood lust and cruelty do not easily go with their sunlit and happy natures.

The town of St Gilles has a permanent arena, whereas other places may content themselves with erecting barricades or making an impenetrable circle of haywains and barrows to serve as bull-pen and grandstand combined. We followed the people strolling into the town from the marshes, and took our seats in the upstairs stand of a small stadium. Below us was a ground about the size of the centre court at Wimbledon, but elliptical, and this was surrounded by a solid barrier just low enough for standing spectators to rest their arms and chins upon it. Outside this palissade was a second fence formed of steel posts set about eighteen inches apart, which supported the tiers of the upper seating but also served a special purpose of which we were as yet unaware. In the ring of alley between these two fences were planted a few plane trees which bushed out pleasantly above the upstairs seats and shaded them from the Midi sun.

When the mayor and judges had taken their places a group of young men jumped into the ring and marched briefly round the arena behind the flag of St Gilles. They bowed to the judges, the banner was passed out of the ring, and the group spread itself about the oval. Apart from the fact that there were fifteen of them they looked very much like a cricket team, for they were dressed in white trousers and shirts, and wore running shoes. The latter, as we soon realized, were a most essential part of the equipment.

F

At the end away from the judges a door was opened and *lou biou* came cantering into the ring. His name, the announcer told us, was *Le Copain* — The Pal. He looked friendly enough, and he evidently knew what was expected of him, for after surveying the audience like a conductor about to lead in a symphony he took up his position in the centre, put down his head, snorted furiously, and pawed the ground with such practised skill that he managed to scoop a few clods of earth into the crowd. Then he looked up, and waited for the first of the men to come within reasonable range. Making a pass at him, the bull spun round to see who might be coming up from the rear.

'The representative of the Universal Sewing-Machine Company offers one thousand francs for the *cocarde*,' boomed the announcer. 'M. Giraudet the stationer another hundred. *Merci*. And the Angling Club two hundred and fifty. The proprietor of the Hotel La Camargue, five hundred francs. The Administration of the Arena makes it up to two thousand francs. Two thousand francs for the *cocarde*, gentlemen. Two thousand . . . two thousand five hundred — thank you sir — with the gift of the cinema management.'

Two thousand five hundred francs — the French always preferred on such occasions to deal in the obsolete currency, the sums sounding much larger. Twenty-five new francs, or about thirty-seven shillings and sixpence was the sum now staked, and it was not one for which every young man would be prepared to be chased around the arena by even such an amiable creature as The Pal. But the admiring glances of their girl friends, and the sheer fun of pitting their cunning against the horns of a steer from the Camargue were enough to make the *razeteurs* take the matter seriously — and if at the end of the afternoon one had also won a few thousand francs, so much the better.

A *razeteur* had no protection other than his experience of what the bull was likely to do, and his own swiftness of foot. For weapon he had nothing but a small hooked comb called a *razet*, held in one hand. The bull had a small tassel tied to the base of each horn, and a thread connecting the two horns carried a third tassel on the forehead. These objects were so small that at first we did not see them, but they were the standard cockades which give their name to the *cocarde*. To win the money put up by the audience a player had merely to grab a tassel, starting with the one in the centre, which was the easiest.

It is a curious fact that a bull does not like any but a few privileged friends to mess about with his horns. He is not at all amenable to standing still while somebody detaches a thread from his forehead, so the object of the *razeteur* is to have himself chased at such close quarters that he can look over his shoulder, reach behind him, and use his little comb to nick the thread and sweep up the diminutive tassel which dangles so invitingly between the strong horns which are moving swiftly along the track within a few inches of the seat of his pants. The area is not so large that he can be chased for more than twenty or thirty yards, but at the end of the run he has to be able to clear the wooden fence in a single bound, to land among the spectators crowding behind it. The *cocarde* is a sport which certainly encourages speed, and hurdle-clearing too.

'Three thousand francs . . . .' The reward was rising, and one or two of the young men made purposeful runs across the bull but came nowhere near collecting the tassel. Others among the *razeteurs* were more experienced, and knew that there were particular angles from which one could converge with the path of the creature and so stand a greater chance of success. The Pal snorted and tossed his head, and charged at any who came near, but the first tassel was soon snicked away from him and held triumphantly in the air by the man who had taken it.

With one cockade away and forty-five shillings chalked up to the victor, public spirited citizens pledged their offers for the next. And these side tassels carried a better price, for they were much more difficult to collect. Tied very tightly round the base of either horn they could only be detached by pushing the teeth of the comb inside the loop of thread to break it, and there might be thirty passes at the bull and many exciting runs along the arena without the cotton being snicked. Besides, The Pal was not going to hand over his cockades too easily. He could shake his head, and he also had an endearing way of throwing up his horns at the very moment a fleeing attacker was hurdling the fence, giving him such a neat extra push that in one or two cases the young man would arrive in the upper rows of seats, or in a plane tree.

The Pal was guarded by a strict time limit. The *razeteurs* might run themselves to exhaustion, but not the bull. That would not be fair, so after fifteen minutes of chasing the team he was withdrawn along with such of his trophies as had not been won. The crowd applauded his success, and he acknowledged the cheers with a slight inclination of his head.

'And now, ladies and gentlemen, we bring you Désiré.' A charmingly improbable name for a bull, we thought. One could imagine him munching the lush grass of the Camargue and looking appreciatively at the flamingos and avocets and egrets, but hardly indulging in such rough sports as chasing the young men of St Gilles. But Désiré was an old hand and a popular figure. The crowd loved him, and when he appeared smiling in the doorway they roared with delight.

Désiré had plenty of tricks. It seemed he could add up in French currency, for he showed little interest until the five thousand franc mark had been reached — by courtesy of the local paper, a photographer's shop, the greengrocer, the association for the development of distractions in the Province of Gard, the garage down by the canal, the mayor, and two schoolgirls. Thoroughly appreciative of their generosity he decided to give the *razeteurs* a run for their money, and having pursued one of them furiously down the length of the arena he decided that what a white-clad sportsman could do a bull could do also. The *razeteur* cleared the palisade in a single hurdling leap, and immediately behind him Désiré hurdled the fence too.

It is remarkable how quickly a densely packed throng can melt away when a quarter of a ton of charging bull is dropped into it. Even before Désiré was over the fence the faces vanished for a few feet on either side, and then the movement swept swiftly along to the right. Désiré had passed out of sight but we could tell exactly where he was by the swift withdrawal of the onlookers as they shot over the alley to dart between the steel bars of the outer fence and slipped back again the moment he had passed. Twice the gap in the row of heads swept round the arena as Désiré put the crowd through its paces, and then he was diverted back into court to rejoin the men..Thoroughly pleased with himself, and revelling in the appreciation of the crowd, he ran to the centre of the ring, threw up a cloud of dust, bellowed, and spun round just in time to dodge the *razet* of one of the men who had thought to catch him unawares. And so he went on, showing every sign of ferocious determination and fiery aggression until at the stroke of a bell he stopped in his tracks, walked gently towards the pen, licked the hand of an old acquaintance leaning on the fence, turned his head for a final bow, and made a dignified exit.

Eight bulls were run that afternoon, and between them the *razeteurs* combed off about fifty pounds in prize money. At just over three pounds a head it was, we thought, money well earned.

From St Gilles to Aigues-Mortes by canal is a run of sixteen miles, and over the left bank the marshland of the Camargue stretches away into the hazy distance towards the Mediterranean. The land is low and marshy on the northern bank too, but always the hills of the Cévennes are there to set a limit to the distance. Close to the canal the maize grows thick and luscious and there are plantations of bamboo. More surprising, a line of farm labourers

paddling through a waterlogged field, their blue trousers rolled up and straw hats to protect from the sun, are dibbling the rice plants which deck some of the wet areas in so intensely vivid a green. For the Camargue is a countryside unlike any other, a mixture of Wicken Fen, and Burma, and of sunny Mediterranean wine slopes, a land not only of egrets and bulls, rice harvest and mosquitoes, but of the fine white wild horses which may have survived across millennia as descendants of those hunted by early man in the southern parts of France or herded to death at Solutré. Now and again a rustling in the undergrowth would tell us that one of these beautiful creatures had been disturbed at his peaceful afternoon graze and was breaking through to the edge of the waterway to examine more closely the people aboard a boat which dared to pass through a domain which by immemorial right belonged to *lou chivau* as much as it did to the bulls.

There are eels, too, to judge by the nets which can be stretched across the canal and wound up by wooden windlasses placed on either bank, and before ever the canal was cut across the swamps they no doubt formed a welcome Friday feast for the monks of the abbey of Psalmody, of which nothing but a few ruins now remain, scattered and forgotten upon a little rise amid the low-lying countryside close on the starboard side. Its monks are now forgotten too, but they made a brief entrance into history in the thirteenth century when St Louis needed a port for his crusading ventures in the Mediterranean. The French crown had no possessions along that coast, so the monks of Psalmody sold him a parcel of marsh and beach upon which to build the town of Aigues-Mortes. Psalmody was an island then, an islet in the fly-blown and feverish swamp, but how the abbey came to be there is not known. The Saracens raided it more than once, and when finally its monks were disbanded to other houses there remained nothing but the ruined walls, and the beautiful name which still conjures up the sound of plainsong ringing from the choir to float away across the watery flats.

The hot sun beating upon the arena during our afternoon at the *cocarde* made it difficult for us to realize that October was nearly over, but already the days had shortened in so far that after supper at St Gilles we would have to choose either to spend another night there or voyage ahead in the dark. We had no doubts about the voyage, for we had already run the course once in either direction, and as there was no traffic we were not apprehensive. Besides there was considerable starlight, and even if we were to run down a reed bed we should come to no harm.

We had not realized that the fishermen would work their nets at night, but they proved friendly and co-operative. A shout, or matches struck and thrown in the air, would warn us that we were about to pass an eeling point, and we in turn would drop our speed to dead slow and glide over the meshes without the propeller turning. A few cheerful remarks exchanged with men we could not even see, and we would be under way again, following the faint line of stars reflected in the water ahead.

Half a mile short of Aigues-Mortes the *Commodore* seemed very definitely to slacken her speed, and the sound of rowboats knocking together somewhere behind her and on the port bank confirmed our fears that a fisherman had found the proximity of the town tavern too attractive for him to sit out the night at his station, and secure in the belief that no boat could reach him he had left his net stretched across the canal. His belief was a reasonable one, for the railway swing-bridge just beyond Aigues-Mortes quay would not be opened after five o'clock, and any ship coming from the opposite direction would have had to pass the Nourriguier lock ten miles beyond St Gilles, before it closed for the evening. The possibility that a ship might start from St Gilles in the darkness had probably not occurred to him, but that was precisely what the *Commodore* had done, and the reason why she was now straining at the windlasses with a net round her stem and a collection of fishing-craft clattering astern of her.

Aboard the *Commodore* we have always had our own emergency drill. Within seconds of any such entanglement all lights aboard the ship have been extinguished and the motor turned off. We have no wish to disturb the peace of mind of others, and experience has proved that a fisherman has the full enjoyment of his glass of wine somewhat spoiled if he happens to suspect that a 23-ton ship is wrapped up in his nets. And lest untoward noises should also cause anxiety the crew know that they must speak only in whispers, and take off their shoes. We now took all these simple precautions, and as soon as the engine was stopped the *Commodore* began to accelerate stern first in the direction from which she had come, as though shot from a catapult — for a good strong net, stretched to its limits by the momentum of a heavy vessel, proves more elastic than one might imagine.

We waited, hushed, until the tension of the nets had slacked and the *Commodore* was backing down upon the reeds. Then, feeling very gingerly below the stem, we discovered the rope along the edge of the net to be almost awash, and carefully inserting the tip of our bargepole into the netting along its edge we pressed it down and down until it was held more than four feet below the surface. One of us walked step by step along the ship, holding down the net, whilst another poled the *Commodore* ahead. At last the rope was clear of the rudders and we could let it go. Whether or not any eels may have escaped I do not know, but at least we had not torn the net or entangled our propeller. For good measure we poled a little further, then switched on our lights, started the engine, and made for the blank and windowless barrier which shut off the horizon ahead.

This shape was the line of the immense walls of the medieval city of Aigues-Mortes. The only light to be seen came indirectly and as the faintest glow through the low-vaulted gateway of the Porte de la Gardette, just as it must have done centuries earlier when perhaps some boatman was poling his cargo of salt along the shallow Canal du Bourgidou. At the foot of the walls the canal made an abrupt turn, but we drew in against the quay and looked up to where the iron cage-work of the medieval lighthouse was dimly visible as a lattice before the stars, pointing upwards from the turret at the edge of the thick-walled Tour de Constance, built by Saint Louis to defend his port but later used as a prison for those who dared to hold beliefs contrary to the established ordering.

In that heavy tower was incarcerated at the age of eight the girl Marie Durand, and probably it was she who carved the inscription *Au Ciel — Résistez* in the stone of the dark place of confinement she shared with others whom she sustained and comforted in their imprisonment. One day the governor of the Languedoc inspected the tower and had the cell opened. Out of the goodness of his heart, or from remorse, he released the maid and some of her companions. Marie Durand was then no longer a girl. She was a woman of forty-five.

When a film producer decides to rehash one of the great love stories of the medieval minstrels, and to produce a spectacular with plenty of blood, bastions, *trébuchets*, boiling oil, wall-breaching and abduction of beautiful women, he sends his camera team to Carcassonne, for even the most lavish expenditure on carpentry and make-believe could not provide a scene so authentic and so devoid of any modern additions as that extraordinary walled city of the southern marches. Carcassonne is a favourite with others too, and coach tours visit it all the year round. Besides, the famous citadel almost forces itself upon the attention of travellers, being in full view of the railway from coast to coast and lying beside the main road from Toulouse to Marseille and on one of the main approaches to the Pyrénées. Every traveller has heard of Carcassonne and if he has seen it he will not have been disappointed.

Carcassonne's life is Aigues-Mortes's death. Less ambitious, and with only a single circuit of walls, Aigues-Mortes is buried away in the salt marshes on a minor country road which runs to nowhere in particular and which few vehicles seem to have discovered. It does not crown a hill, and the towers of its gateways have no little Sunday hats as do those of the more famous fortress. And because the two cities are in the same part of France, and on the same Michelin map, Aigues-Mortes leaves the glamour and the souvenir shops and the *son-et-lumière* to its big sister and sleeps undisturbed in the quiet which descended upon it after the death of St Louis in 1270. It has had its moments in later centuries but they have been brief. Aigues-Mortes — Dead Waters — has not changed much in the last seven hundred years, and as though Pasteur had never been born a slight flow of ordure still oozes down the central gutterway of each of its gateways to soak into the ground or add to the general stagnation of the bleak marsh which reaches up to the walls on two sides of the town.

It is from the marsh road, or from the canal branch which runs

to Le Grau du Roi that one can best see the town, one of its longer
sides rising from the reeds in such medieval might that nothing
whatsoever is visible but a third of a mile of formidable grey wall
broken only by five posterns. No building inside the place is so tall
that it can hope even to poke a chimney above the line of the
ramparts, and none has dared to venture outside the walls. To
experience Aigues-Mortes in the red sunset of an afternoon of
early winter is to see a medieval fortress precisely as it was when,
inside those walls, the king and queen, the knights and squires and
men-at-arms were preparing to leave for the Holy Land — or so
we could persuade ourselves from our position in the canal,
conveniently overlooking the fact that only the Tour de Constance
was complete when the Seventh Crusade took its leave and sailed
away for Egypt.

Aigues-Mortes was custom-built as a port of embarkation.
Although no longer on the edge of the sea it is still connected with
the Mediterranean at the nearby fishing port of Le Grau du Roi —
the *roi* being Louis IX and a *grau* the particular name given to a
channel by which the lagoons and marshes of this southern coast
connect with the sea.

When Louis assembled at Aigues-Mortes his force of sixty
thousand men, the walls had only just been begun, but planning for
a protracted war with the Saracens he devised a fortified town
which could serve as a permanent point of assembly and supply, and
the building was finished by his son. And while a fleet of Genoese
vessels was being assembled in the *grau*, royal quartermasters were
preparing supplies in places as far away as Cyprus. No previous
crusade had been more carefully conceived, or more magnificent.
French, English and Venetian nobles had their camps, and the
special envoy of the Pope had come to bestow on each knight a
particular blessing as the warriors filed and clanked through the
chapel which is still there, very much as it was at the time but
mellowed by age. The year was 1248, and some of those who received
the benediction bore titles newly received and taken from the heretic
lords of Languedoc whose people they had so recently slaughtered.

Even now one can almost see them embarking, each knight with
a chest to serve him as travelling trunk, as a bed, and as a coffin if

he should be fortunate enough to die at sea instead of cleft to the waist by a Saracen sword on the sands of Egypt. The king, serious, his thoughts fixed only on wresting the Holy Land from the hand of the Infidel, his fair hair streaming from below his helmet, standing with the queen and her ladies aboard the royal galley to receive a final blessing; the soldiers, bareheaded, raising the great strain of the *Veni Creator*, and then the sails unfurled, and the heavy vessels slowly lumbering out to sea — the *Reine*, the *Montjoie*, the *Damoiselle* and their thirty-five companion ships. The banners floated in the salty air and after some hours the fleet was hull down on the horizon.

Months later, Louis leapt ashore at Damietta and would have attacked the Musulman host single-handed. Then came the costly victory of Mansourah, and after it the capture of Louis himself. He was ransomed in gold to return to France with such few of his soldiers as survived.

In 1270 Louis was again at Aigues-Mortes, to launch the Eighth Crusade. This time there was less enthusiasm, and the knights were in no hurry to leave. But their king led them on, and as they crossed the sea towards the African shore an epidemic of cholera broke out. Upon landing, Louis himself assisted with burying the dead 'not holding his nose as did the others', but he was already too old and too sick to see the campaign through. Below the walls of Carthage he died, and the role of Aigues-Mortes in history was over.

As though knowing that it can sleep in the security of a good conscience and a work well done, Aigues-Mortes does not set out to attract people. It is there, and they can take it or leave it. We had difficulty in finding a meal in the place, and by ten o'clock at night the streets were deserted except for a pair of cats which faced each other with arched backs by the statue of Louis the Saint, howling as though for the blood of a Musulman. It knows that its day is done, and that such few canal boats as still turn the bend of the Tour de Constance are unlikely to stop at its quay, and that the old tug lying against the reeds by the Tour des Bourgignons will probably continue to lie there until the brine of the *grau* has eaten through its plates and sunk it.

But however retiring the town may be it has the rarity of a complete walk round the walls, and from the tops of its gateways one can peer down on whatever is happening below — which is likely to be a hen scratching in the refuse, a cat surreptitiously salvaging a fish-head from a dustbin, or perhaps an old woman dozing before her doorway with the knitting lying on her lap. The view extends over the shallow-pitched roofs and past the open-hung bells of the chapel to the walls at the far side, and looking outwards one may see the Cévennes, blue as ever in the afternoon, and the narrowing azure ribbon of canal leading towards St Gilles. Across the waterlogged shallows and away beyond the lagoon several tall pyramids point up to the sky, pure white and apparently of marble. They are smaller than those of Egypt but large enough to be seen for several miles, and in fact they are made of salt. For salt is the only product which can be culled from this desolate landscape.

We were looking out towards the sea when a bell rang in the town behind us, and the school children came out to play. They streamed out of the postern beneath us like the children of Hamelin behind a piper. In the space outside the walls some of them kicked a ball, others sat on stones just as did a group of three old men a little further along. For a brief few minutes they enjoyed the freedom of the outside world, and when the bell rang once more they hurried back so obediently that we almost expected to hear a gate-keeper drop the portcullis behind them.

There is nothing to detain the visitor at Aigues-Mortes — nothing, that is, but the sheer delight of walking round the machicolations of a town which has decided that the Middle Ages were good enough, or bad enough, and that the world can go on to invent rockets and power stations if it wishes but Aigues-Mortes is not prepared even to widen a gate for the traffic. To live there might be dull, but to pause at its quay for a day or two on the way to the Canal du Midi is nothing short of enchanting.

We could not visit this stronghold of the salt marshes without also running round the edge of the walls to follow the *grau* down which Louis had sailed on his two crusades. It is a Fenland type of channel, but at its end lies the pretty fishing port of Le Grau du Roi, its two halves spread along either bank of the waterway and joined by a swing-bridge. Beyond the bridge there are shrimp saloons and shell-fish saloons, oyster saloons and in fact saloons for every sort of invertebrate one might fancy extracting from the sea, and at the extreme end a line of hotels tries to find its feet on the sandbank which flanks the salt marsh on its seaward side. It is a little resort, unsophisticated and without any ambition of attracting droves of foreigners, and if the town itself is of no great beauty the waterway is lined with dozens of small fishing-boats, sunbaked and salty, their faded paint of sun-bleached blue and blank white or russet brown bringing gaiety to the pinkish tints of the houses. They seem ready and waiting to sail out bravely past the lighthouse to net such poor fish as the Mediterranean can offer, but though the craft are prepared the fishermen are not, for it is more pleasant to sit just one hour longer in a heavy wine-vapoured stupor enlivened occasionally by an argument.

We found it difficult to decide whether the sailors at Le Grau du Roi were malevolent, drunk, or just plain stupid. No less than three of them in turn signed to us to bring the *Commodore* alongside the sloping shore at points where there was not enough water to float a duck, and we liked to think they did so from ineptitude rather than the hopes of wrecking us. But when in the evening we turned the *Commodore* to point her back again towards Aigues-Mortes we encountered an individual whose wine seemed to have gone to his head. With the help of his son he had just laid a net right across the waterway, and rocking in his rowboat he declared in a rather abrupt fashion that we could not pass. The navigation, he said, was closed.

Technically, navigation ended at five o'clock at this season of the year, and though any ordinary man would have dropped the net to allow us to pass it did not matter to us whether we slept at Le Grau or at Aigues-Mortes, so we informed him that we did not mind in the least. He then declared that as the next day was Sunday the navigation would be closed all day too, so we could not proceed until the Monday. However, we happened to know enough of the rules to tell him that navigation began at seven o'clock on Sunday, and that the *Commodore* would then proceed.

The fisherman said he did not rise early on Sundays. He might arrive by midday, but he could not say for certain. To this we replied that if he chanced to come he should allow himself plenty of time to collect the fragments of his nets. The *Commodore*, we added, had enough *chevaux* to convert his netting into so much waste twine. As for the stout ropes, they were easily severed too — and just to emphasise the point we showed him an axe which we kept aboard for splitting logs.

The man seemed indignant at these suggestions, for much of what he said was lost in sheer choler. However, he conveyed that he would see us in hell before he got up at seven to take in the nets. We said maybe he was right, but at the stroke of seven the *Commodore* would move up the *grau*, and any obstructions would be dealt with effectively. This only brought more invective, so we wished him goodnight and plenty of fish, and went below.

Next morning we took in our lines, and at three minutes to seven we started the engine, pushed out into midstream and gave one long blast. A moment later we saw the fisherman tumbling out of his doorway some hundreds of yards down towards the town, still struggling into his shirt. His son was already ahead of him, and came streaking up the bank with an assurance that his father was approaching with every knot he could muster. Just to encourage him we put the *Commodore* slowly ahead. Meanwhile, the lad leapt into the rowboat and ferried himself across to the further shore to start releasing the windlasses.

The clock struck seven just as the fisherman came up. 'You are late,' we said. 'The navigation must not be obstructed. . . .'

In his anxiety he slipped on the bank and nearly fell into the *grau*. But the wine of the previous evening had ebbed away, and no doubt the early morning trot had done his liver no harm. Slightly ashamed of himself he dropped the net, and gave a wry smile. Then he began to laugh, and so did we. As we moved cautiously over the net he gave us a cheerful wave and wished us a pleasant voyage. No doubt we should have replied with the traditional greeting used of old by the sailors of such ports as le Grau du Roi —

'*Diu que-b goarde de la coude de la balène e dou can de la serène.*' God save you from the tail of the whale and the siren's song. Both of which, in their different ways, could be the undoing of any fisherman, and even of the *Commodore*.

From Aigues-Mortes the canal to Sète follows the line of the old Canal de la Radelle, then cuts along the side of the broad salt lake of the Étang de Mauguio. It is a wind-swept course when the mistral is blowing, and we found the waves large enough to break upon the canal embankment and throw up showers of exceedingly salty water which stung the face and encrusted the *Commodore*'s windows and upper works with salt.

The waterway runs along the edge of no less than six of these meres, which stretch all the way to Frontignan and are separated from the sea only by the sandbar which carries a road to connect up the minor resorts west of le Grau du Roi. The Mediterranean is virtually tideless, but an onshore or offshore wind will make a surprising difference in the sea level, and as all the *étangs* are connected with the sea the result is to cause a strong current inwards or outwards. The *graus* cross the canal at its surface level, and the result can be exciting for the steersman when he comes to a point where a stream running at several knots enters the canal at one side and leaves it immediately opposite. Just to encourage the bargee these watery crossroads are beset with notices about *Danger de Mort*, and the administration of the Department of Bridges and Highways not being responsible for loss of life or limb or cargo. Sometimes it is impossible for craft to cross the gap, and a real flood sweeping through the channel may interrupt the navigation for days on end.

On this occasion there was no great *risque ou péril* for ourselves, even if a barge might have been swept into the wrong watercourse, and after four hours of edging along beside these beautiful lakes with their little fishing ports and their cypress-sheltered farmsteads set on islands and outcrops, we saw ahead of us the chimneys of the refinery town of Frontignan. Here at last the quays were lined with barges, tankers shorter than the craft of the north and able to pass through the Canal du Midi, but spick and span with sun-awnings and blinds, and gay gardens of cacti in their windows.

Frontignan has a cat-cracker, but it is also the home of a particularly excellent wine with a flavour all of its own. Rabelais and Louis

XIV both extolled the delights of Muscat de Frontignan, and so did Voltaire in a letter to a friend whom he implored to save his life by sending him a quart of it. And a very good wine it is, rich pinkish brown, sweet and aromatic, pressed from the grapes which grow along the canal bank and beneath the equally aromatic clouds floating downwind of the Mobil refinery.

It is said that Hercules himself — in whose legends the coast abounds on account of its shipping contacts with the Greeks — arrived at Frontignan at vintage time. He was so taken with the wine that after drinking as much as would not upset his performance of labours he filled his wine-skin in order to take the muscat up to Olympus to delight the chief of the gods. And Zeus, when at last he tasted the wine brought to him by the victorious hero and traveller, declared that he was through with ambrosia. From that day onward the official food and drink of all recognised deities would be the sweet muscat of Frontignan.

It seems that what was good enough for the people on Olympus was O.K. for leading diplomatic circles in the United States. Thomas Jefferson had tasted the wine when plenipotentiary in France, and recalling its excellence he wrote to order one hundred and twenty bottles for President Washington, and five dozen for himself. Which at least shows that there was good taste in the White House, and that ambassadors in those days knew what was desirable.

V

*Sète, port of pipe-lines — ships for jousting — the Étang de
Thau — Bouzigues and Mèze — Marseillan — the Commodore arrives at the Canal du Midi — Riquet of Bonrepos
— the Canal Royal — day-dreams unadopted*

A glance at the map would suggest that nothing could be less
interesting than the twenty miles of canal leading along the
edge of the Gulf of Lions towards Sète. Yet the shallow meres with
their silted and forgotten ports are beautiful in their wildness. They
are the haunt of duck and scoter, of flamingo, and of men who sit
in little green boats armed with a gun or a rod, a net or a trident, for
whatever kind of game comes closest. Between these wide and
reedy waters and the sea there is only the low and narrow bar of
sand which has been dropped by the current and flung up by the
waves to seal them off, and this tenuous line of dry land is utterly
deserted except for a cluster of fishermen's huts and perhaps a
small hotel or a caravan-site clinging to the shelf where a *grau* breaks
through to the sea. Though romantic the scene is one of extraordinary solitude, and the loneliness is made suddenly more acute
when one realizes that a simple cracked and buttressed building
clustered about by pines on a knoll to the seaward side of the canal
is all that remains of the cathedral of Maguelone, a see which has
been extinct for centuries.

At Frontignan we had reached the last of the meres, and with
the refinery behind us and the muscat vineyards to starboard we
could already see vaguely in the distance the port of Sète. Two
miles ahead we turned into the Canal de la Peyrade, and diving
under the railway we were soon approaching the maritime basins
where some of the cranes stretched their necks high as though
looking for a new arrival, perhaps another cargo vessel from
Madagascar, or Tunisia, or Morocco, and others drooped their

jibs in languid inactivity as if they had drunk too much of the pinkish wine or eaten too much of one of Sète's gastronomical specialities — a term which embraces fish so small and bony that any fisherman of the Scottish coast would not even use them for bait.

Before leaving Holland on our voyage to Southern France it had occurred to me that we might leave the *Commodore* at Sète through the winter, and so I had written to the harbourmaster to enquire in a general kind of way what sort of harbour he mastered. His reply stated Sète to be the most considerable French Mediterranean port after Marseille. It had great activity of refineries, it seemed, and tanker vessels arrived continually. The port area was equipped with one pipe-line for hydrocarbons and seventeen for wine. The *Commodore* would be welcome to stay there if she wished.

This answer obviously left much unsaid, but it was enough to intrigue us. Now that we had passed the huge refinery of Frontignan — fed, we presumed, by the single hydrocarbon line — it remained to discover the other facilities, and we began to picture to ourselves a town so swilling in the fluid leaking from the joints of the remaining seventeen pipe-lines that the very air would be intoxicating. And so perhaps it would have been but for the fact that the mistral was sweeping through the streets with such tremendous force that to stand erect was difficult, and to bring the boat in to a corner berth no easy matter either. But we persevered, and encouraged by the calls and advice of the Sètois we drew in right in the centre of the town, three weeks and two hours after leaving the Place de la Concorde in Paris.

Sète was as intriguing a place as one could wish to find. It did not arise as most towns do, but was planted deliberately and by edict, and almost all at once. For years the lack of a proper port on the Languedoc coast had been a matter of concern to the government, and the conception of the Canal du Midi provided Colbert with the incentive to build a harbour town. Pierre-Paul Riquet — of whom we shall hear more in the course of this voyage — was charged by him with designing and constructing Sète (or Cette, as it then was spelled) as a terminus for his canal and as a point where Mediterranean cargoes would be transhipped to barges.

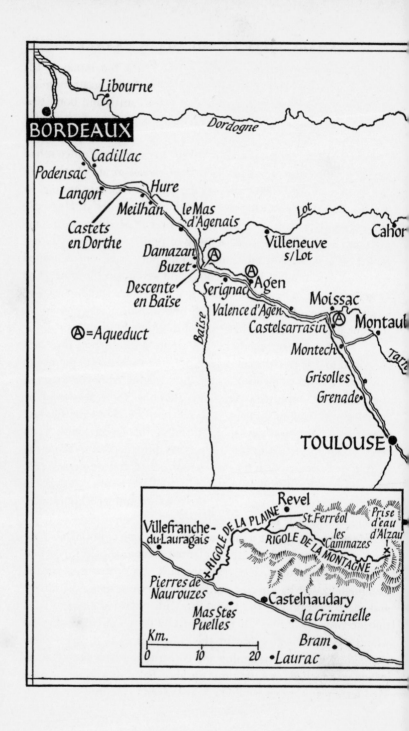

Libourne

BORDEAUX

Dordogne

Cadillac

Podensac

Langon

Hure

Meilhan

le Mas
d'Agenais

Castets
en Dorthe

Lot

Cahor

Villeneuve
s/Lot

Damazan

Buzet

Ⓐ

Descente
en Baïse

Serignac

Ⓐ Agen

Valence d'Agen

Moissac

Ⓐ = Aqueduct

Baïse

Castelsarrasin

Ⓐ Montaul

Montech

Tarn

Grisolles

Grenade

TOULOUSE

Revel

Villefranche-
du·Lauragais

RIGOLE DE LA PLAINE

St.Ferréol

les
Cammazes

Prise
d'eau
d'Alzau

RIGOLE DE LA MONTAGNE

✕

Pierres de
Naurouzes

Castelnaudary

la Criminelle

Mas Stes
Puelles

Km.

0   10   20

Bram

Laurac

Km
0   80

Miles
0   50

Km
0   5   10

Bouzigues   Frontignan
Mèze
Etang de Thau
Sète

Hérault

Marseillan
Bagnas
Prades
les Onglous

Agde

Mediterranean

SOUTERRAIN
DE MALPAS

•Revel
illefranche

Fresquel   la Redorte   Capestang   Béziers
Homps   Poilhes
Bram•   Trèbes   Aude   Agde

SÈTE

Fanjeaux

Carcassonne
Salleles   Narbonne
Gailhousty   Gruissan
Limoux   la Nouvelle
•Lavelanet
Montségur

W Bromage

Devoid of anything earlier than 1666, when the first stone was laid, Sète lies at the foot of the Mont St Clair, which rises about 600 feet from the sea and was once an island. The chain of sandbank which runs along the Gulf abuts against this lump at either side, and Riquet rightly selected the lee quarter of the hill for his port. The sandbank was cut through to connect with the Bassin de Thau, the deep salty sea behind the dunes, and Sète itself was laid out and built somewhat in the style of a Dutch water town. Louis XIV gave it immediate tax concessions, and it was quickly settled by a polyglot collection of merchants from Mediterranean lands, whose descendants mixed with the folk of the Languedoc to produce the people who live there today, the Sètois. Small, dark and full of fun, the men of Sète are renowned for their story-telling, but so strange is their language that one cannot easily identify it as French and the stories are like to fall upon uncomprehending ears.

In designing the port to serve the Canal du Midi Riquet did his work well, and the town canal has on either side one of the most casually beautiful and matter-of-fact waterfronts imaginable. The houses are not built to conform, but as they nearly all come from the same period they have a harmony about them which is rare. Ironwork balconies carry a hint of Spain, the swingbridges a savour of Holland, and the wide expanse of waterway a tinge of Venice. The broad wharves are stacked with tuns and barrels of every size and shape, the flags of many nations stream in the dusty wind from the flagstaffs of the waterside consulates, and along the quays rumble tanker lorries and trailers, just such vehicles as in Britain would be painted in the colours of Shell-BP or Esso, but which in Sète bear such names as Dubonnet, Noilly Prat, or Cinzano. Others are the tankers or bowsers of various wine-transporting companies, and they leave in their passing an odour like that of a public house in the morning, before the windows are opened.

Along the quays are ranged small vessels of many kinds — the large *cargos* being two blocks away in the more modern Nouveau Bassin, or the Bassin du Midi. At the seaward end, not far inshore of Riquet's original jetties, a collection of drifters is packed along the stone wall as though the fishermen of Sète are determined to cram the largest number of craft into the closest possible space. Their low bulwarks hint that the storms here are not quite like those of the British coasts but the vessels are good solid craft well suited to their job, and their brilliant reds and greens and yellows make startling splashes of colour to be reflected up from the clean and brilliantly clear water of the port towards the azure above. Further in towards the town centre is a smaller group of curious wooden craft with high sterns and scrolled quarters, their machinery rusty and their paintwork done in pale blue and pink and lemon yellow. There is something faintly piratical about these ships, and if their appearance is oddly exotic this is because, as the peeling paint on their transoms reveals, they come from Sfax in Tunisia. Whether or not they are derelict is hard to say, but in their day they must have landed a good supply of tunny, and perhaps engaged in a little healthy smuggling too.

Small one-man craft continually chug up and down Riquet's canal on their way through Sète to the passage leading out under the railway bridge to the fishing grounds of the Lake of Thau, and from the lake itself come wallowing into the town the open barges laden with the wines of Marseillan, and wine-tanker boats of Canal du Midi dimensions bringing the exports of Béziers or the Corbières to be bottled, or blended, or just consumed.

Down near the railway bridge itself another type of boat is lying, a craft shaped like a ship's lifeboat and with seats for ten oarsmen. White, and rimmed elegantly in scarlet, this boat has a counterpart in blue and white, and the most extraordinary feature of their decoration is that the sides are painted with baroque curtains gathered into folds and tied with tasselled cords of gold. At the stern a long raised ramp projects far above the water to end in a tiny platform. Several times in the year these battleships will engage with each other in a duel upon the waters of the town canal, the relays of jousters of the two teams ready to be poised on their perches for the attack. Each craft has its musicians, and the two vessels are rowed furiously towards each other with oars straining, drum and oboe playing, and the people of Sète shouting deliriously from the wharves and balconies and windows. A moment of sudden silence, and the boats glide swiftly past each other with a powerful

momentum which is transferred to the shields of the combatants as
each parries the lance of his opponent.

The jousts are as old as Sète, and so is the music played in either
boat, like a relic of the days when a drum or gong beat out the
rhythm for slaves at the oars of galley. Perhaps the contests
originated in sheer ecstasy over Riquet's canal, or maybe those who
migrated to the new port brought with them memories of Lepanto,
or of other stirring clashes at sea. However that may be, Sète still
buzzes with excitement when *La Lance Sportive* (blue) rows up to
challenge once again *Le Pavois d'Or* (red), and without this
traditional fight on the water the place would never be quite the
same, for all the unselfconscious beauty of its waterways.

As this was to be the end of the *Commodore*'s autumn run we let
the mistral blow us along the quay towards the offices of a *courtier
maritime*. We expected a grave and serious individual who would
bow, flourish his hat and perhaps even kiss our hands, but the
courtier proved to be a man whose busy office shipped olive oil
from Tunis, signed on Moroccans as deck-hands, sent cables to
Lloyds, extracted refugees from Algeria, and arranged salvage
claims. In spite of all this urgent business the courtier himself was
anxious to help us in any way he could, and he said he would
contact Messrs. Scotto and Repetto. Although he assured us that
they were shipbuilders of the very highest repute we could not
entirely divest ourselves of a belief that they must be a circus act.
This effect of their name was actually enhanced when we heard a
knocking on the hull and saw on the staging a thick-set man so
short that he seemed only just able to peep over the catwalk. He

proved to be Scotto, and after we had helped him aboard we conversed long and earnestly with him about such matters as we wished to be put in hand during the winter. We got on splendidly with M. Scotto, except that we could not understand much that he said. He spoke the weird tongue of the Sètois, and when at last he took up his hat to go he asked us to do something for him.

'*Vou m'envoya una carta di Chrissmassa, de Angellaterra?*'

We promised not to forget. A Christmas card would indeed be sent to him, we said, and we pictured to ourselves the joy of Scotto showing Repetto his picture, and Repetto sharing with Scotto his stocking. Then, after we had lifted him down to the quayside and bade him good-bye we took the *Commodore* through the streets and under the bridges of the docks, to leave her floating in Riquet's town canal, made fast alongside the quay outside the police station, close to where the major was in process of laying up the *Isle of Eigg* for a few days so that his cargo would be under the watchful eye of the law while he journeyed down to Spain by train to inspect the harbours along the route ahead. Having packed our bags we knocked on the door, asked the man with the machine-gun to convey our respectful salutations to the inspector, and on being admitted to the presence we announced that in twenty minutes time we should be taking the night sleeper to Paris and *Angellaterra*. In five months we should be back. Meanwhile, the *Commodore* would be moored outside the front door, and we should expect to find her afloat in the following spring. If she sank, perhaps an *agent* could tell the courtier, who would no doubt know what to do. So saying, we placed a packet of nineteen cheap cigars on the table, and withdrew. (There had been twenty, but I had tried one, which was enough.)

Next spring the *Isle of Eigg* had gone, and no doubt Ibiza was being overtaken by the population explosion. But the *Commodore* was indeed still afloat, and if Scotto and Repetto had not done the work they intended this was either the result of linguistic difficulties or of *la grève*. This time the strike was over government action in Algeria — the previous one having been called over government inaction in the same domain — and however little it had to do with shipbuilding it had emptied the yard of workers as effectively as a saint's day, or the anniversary of the capture of the Bastille, or the plague. But within a day we had the boat shipshape, spruced up and ready to tackle the journey across France from coast to coast through one of the most enterprising canals ever constructed.

Though Sète was built as the port for the Canal du Midi, the canal itself ends eleven miles away, at the far end of the Bassin or Étang de Thau, a sheet of water which can be rough when lashed by the *mistral, mistràu, maéstral* or *magistràu*, that masterly or magisterial wind which controls the climate of the littoral. '*Lou mistràu, lou parlomèn e la Durènco soun lei trés flèus de la Proubengo*' — the mistral, parliament and the Durance (a temperamental river, violent in flood) are perhaps still the three scourges of Provence. But *lou marin es couquin*, a knave, because his apparent gentleness deceives, and the *marin*, blowing off the sea could be as much of a danger as could the *mistral* in the days before barges had motors. Sailing-barges were sometimes held up for days before they could run down the lake in safety, but the bank-hauled boats had an even worse time of it. Naturally, this inland sea had no towpath, and before the advent of steam-tugs the laden craft were hauled along the windy water by row-boats. As a travellers' guide to the canal once so pleasantly put it 'A number of serious accidents indicate the temerity of owners who exposed themselves to a battle with winds and waves in time of storm.'

Having a reasonably reliable engine we did not need great temerity to enter the Lake of Thau. Besides, it was evening. The wind had fallen away and the wonderful warm stillness of a Mediterranean evening lay over Sète. We moved past the freighters from Piraeus and Cairo and Tananarive, turned the corner by the handsome old training ship which lies beside the railway station, and just squeezed beneath the last of the dock bridges without having to bring the *pontier* from his evening wine. Then we headed out between the marine biological laboratory and the old canal breakwater of Riquet to aim north-west past the headland of St Joseph towards Bouzigues, a few miles distant on the opposite shore.

Bouzigues is not the canal entrance, but just one of those pretty little ports on the northern shore, where the vineyards run down to the oyster beds and the hills dip down to the salt. Each of these towns or villages is clustered on a knoll of its own, and even if they are less spectacular than the Mont St Clair it does not need much imagination to guess that once they were sunbaked and smiling isles set along the Mediterranean coast before the sandbanks were deposited to shut them away inland. This isolation has pushed them away from the limelight and their beauties have remained undiscovered by guide books. Nobody ever goes to Bouzigues, and it rests happily on the edge of the lake as it has done for centuries.

Fortunately it was not quite dark when we approached the port, for the lighthouse shown on the chart we had bought that same morning was fictional and what appeared to be a jetty proved to be a mass of piles from which tiles could be hung to provide suitable homes for oysters. But the harbour with its bright little boats was one of the prettiest we had ever seen, and the old men of the town came to give us a great welcome. There being no quay other than an elongated heap of rocks they helped us arrange a mesh of lines so that the *Commodore* could rest like a spider in the middle of a web, and then they settled down to talk. Most of our conversation was in smiles and nods, for the good people of Bouzigues spoke as little of the President's French as of the King's English. We were definitely and decidedly in the Languedoc.

In the Middle Ages the language of the area which includes modern France was not standard, and the officers of the French crown distinguished three parts according to how the people spoke the word for 'Yes'. In the north and centre one said *oïl* — the forerunner of *oui*. In what is now the Italian littoral the form was *si*. Finally there were the wide domains roughly co-extensive with the territory of the Counts of Toulouse, and here the language was quite distinct. Instead of *oïl* the people said *oc*. And for their benefit the royal proclamations had to be promulgated in *Occitan*, the *langue d'oc*.

This is not to say that the old salts of Bouzigues use the affirmative *oc*. But the Occitan tongue has no more been wiped out than has Welsh in the mountains of Wales, and it still persists sufficiently for poets to write in it, for it is so expressive a language that Dante seriously considered writing the *Inferno* in Occitan. People may understand French, just as the Irish and the Welsh will know the meaning of English, but it does not follow that they will speak it. The fishermen of Bouzigues talked to us at length, but I do not think we picked up much of what they said, except that the dry year might produce *boun bî* — good wine. They also hoped it would be a good season for oysters. Bouzigues has its wealth in the oysters sitting on the offshore slates or waiting to be scratched up with the long rakes which littered the harbour's edge where we had drawn in, for these oysters are the best in France, and are sure of selection for banquets in honour of all the most important people. In spite of this the town does not advertise itself but just sits there on the edge of the lake, its menfolk young and old gathering for the evening in the only wine-house and leaving the narrow and crooked streets to the cats. Never have I seen so many cats. Large and small they seemed to be on every window-sill or roof pitch, beside each doorway, or lapping waste water from every gutter, into which spouted kitchen sink water through holes knocked in the walls of the houses. Cats are not usually great water drinkers — and no more are the French as a nation — but perhaps the dishwater at Bouzigues has a pleasant oysterish taste which appeals to them as much as a bowl of milk.

There is little to Bouzigues except that it is a most pleasant place to spend the night, provided one has a boat and is not hoping to find hotels. It was not until we had left their harbour that we discovered the Bouzigauds to be known to their neighbours along the lake shore by the name of *lous crans* (the crabs), perhaps in reference to the shellfish which thrive in the water as happily as do the exotic sea anemones in the town canal of Sète, to judge by the hundreds of elegant violet or peach-pink specimens which clothed the *Commodore* from water-line to keel. But there may be more to the name than a hint of fishing, for the people of the village have a reputation for being somewhat cloddish. When in 1710 an English force landed at Sète in that mysterious way the English had of suddenly materializing from nowhere, a single musket shot was enough to make the population of Bouzigues take to its heels — or so the people of Frontignan relate, adding that their own courage made the *Anglais* re-embark very quickly. Perhaps there is malicious misrepresentation in what is said about the fate of their parish priest, but those of nearby towns relate that when the good father fell into the water he was drowned, because his parishioners were so conscientious that not one of them would presume to lay their hands upon a man of God.

One of the voices uplifted in derision of the people of Bouzigues proclaims that they are imbeciles, brutes as black as Moors and walking barefoot.

Brutaou de Bouzigaou
Négrès como de Maudous.

The lines are not sung by the people but actually by the bull of Mèze, the great *Bœuf* which is certainly of great antiquity as a local celebrity. Like his relation the Tarasque he appears on special occasions, and his motive power is provided by eight men inside his hide of cloth. He is led meekly enough by a drover armed with a goad, but he can roar as gently as any sucking-dove, for he is equipped with a pitched or resined cord attached to a sort of drum made from a barrel over the end of which is stretched the skin of a donkey. When the cord is pulled through the hand, a most fearful and ominous bellowing is produced — enough to send any poor native of Bouzigues running for his life. That Mèze, another little port on the Étang de Thau, should have this unusual creature woven into its life is not so very strange, for what is the Étang de Thau if not the Étang *du Taur*?

The voyage to Mèze was one we could undertake while the coffee was percolating for breakfast, and with the early sun shining aslant on the yellow cream walls and orange roofs of Bouzigues we backed out from among its fleet of diminutive oyster boats of azure and red, green and black and lemon yellow, and cut out past the mile or more of oyster-piling. To port, the Mont St Clair stood in the sunshine above the mist which lay over Sète and the long line of banks, and astern the smoke rose as ever from the distant refinery of Frontignan. Within half an hour we were turning in between the harbour moles of Mèze.

Although a larger port, and one at which barges may call, Mèze is as lost to the world as Bouzigues. Once its wooden barrels made

from the chestnut of the Cévennes provided a trade which reached as far as Portugal, the West Indies and America, but now it is a market town where one may scoop from roadside barrels delicious walnuts in pickle, or black olives, figs, and *marrons*, not to mention the grapes and peaches and apricots laid out in baskets beside the pinioned ducks and chickens and the great bowls of *pâté* and the rounds of cheese. There are stranger dishes, too, for the French have a way of eating anything and everything which moves in the sea, and even such unlikely creatures as tunicates were there for the eating, raw. And though most repulsive in appearance, these degenerate descendants of our earliest semi-backboned ancestors proved extremely good to gnaw. Perhaps one could not describe the creatures better than by saying that their colour was a blackish green, the consistency like that of perished rubber, they had a slight grittiness about them, they squirted one in the eye when they were squeezed and had a taste half-way between sea water and saturated tincture of iodine. I admit that this outline of qualities would not go far towards selling the creatures in a restaurant, but none the less we found them delicious.

The last port along the shore is Marseillan, from where wine barges continually run down the lake to Sète, hugging closely the northern or southern shore according to whether the *mistral* or the *marin* is the wind for the day. It is the least interesting of the three, even if the most frequented by ships, but it has a place in romantic legend as the home of that lovely and innocent girl Scribotte, who was seized upon the shore by Moorish pirates and sold as a slave to a caliph. Her young swain, Mas of Marseillan, nearly died of grief, but pulling himself together he determined to rescue her. Having suitably disguised himself he enlisted with the Moors and worked his way up the army of the Saracens until through sheer ability he attained the rank of general. Now he had the opportunity to come more closely into the company of the Caliph, and having spied out the land he entered the harem, swiftly snatched up his beloved and fled. Many were the fights and hair-breadth escapes which still lay in their path, but at last they reached their home port of Marseillan, where they married and lived happily ever after.

From Marseillan it is less than a mile to the lighthouse of Les Onglous, the mark without which it would be difficult to pick out the mouth of the canal which leaves the Bassin de Thau at its foot. For more than a mile the cut runs straight across marshes which are half land and half lake, and the first experience a boatman has of the famous Canal du Midi is not a particularly attractive one. Were it not for the salt drying in the pans, the mountains away to starboard and the scattered faded farmsteads with cypresses planted to break the force of the prevailing wind the scene might be on the lower Somme. But soon the canal swings sharply right to avoid the conical Pic St Loup, wavers along the edge of some salt pans and runs between a pair of dry meadows to turn a sharp bend to port, straight into the *écluse Bagnas*, the first of the long climb towards the watershed more than a hundred miles distant. It is the same stone pen which has served for nearly three centuries, not

rectangular but built as an ellipse — a shape which may be waste-
ful of water but which is an excellent one for withstanding the push
of the surrounding land. And having managed to jump, catch hold
of the edge of the wall and haul ourselves up to the lockside — for
there are no ladders on the Canal du Midi — we can leave the pen
to fill and turn to what Monsieur Michelin would call *un peu
d'histoire* about the waterway itself.

In 1604 the contract was granted for the first watershed canal in
the world, the Canal de Briare which was to link the Loire with the
Seine. Later in that same year a christening was held in the
cathedral of Béziers, and it is said that the godmother prophesied
that the child would be the means of securing a great highway of
communication across the Languedoc. The lady was the Marquise
Riquetti, the child Pierre-Paul Riquet, a relative whose Italian
origins already lay some way behind him, so that his parents now
used the name in its French form.

If the godmother breathed a word — and it would be difficult to
prophesy in complete silence — nobody paid much attention. The
young Riquet was anything but a success during his years of
learning, and he left college with no attainments beyond reading,
writing and arithmetic. As the professions were therefore closed to
him his father put him into the Inland Revenue, where no particular ability was required. There he worked, a reasonably honest
man with no very obvious future except that of enriching himself
at the expense of others.

Tax-collecting involved travel across the hills and valleys of the
Languedoc, where tracks might crack and crumble in the heat or
be washed away by torrents. No doubt Monsieur Riquet soon had
more than enough personal experience of the bad state of the roads,
and he may also have known that soon after the conquest of Gaul
the Romans had wondered whether the two coasts might not be
linked by a canal, so that ships might be spared the three thousand
mile voyage round the Spanish peninsula. They did not attempt to
construct one, but at least they joined the city of Narbo Martius (or
Narbonne) to the sea by means of a fourteen-mile canal called the
Robine.

In 1515 the monarch Francis I had returned from his Duchy of

Milan, bringing with him to his castle of Amboise the decorator Leonardo da Vinci, who was also a notable engineer of canals. Together they planned cross-country routes in the centre and in the south, and a survey was actually made for a Canal des Deux Mers which would join the Aude at Carcassonne to the Garonne near Toulouse. But before anything could be undertaken the king's attention and money were fully occupied in wars and rumours of wars, and the next step forward was taken by Henry IV, who charged his eminence the Cardinal Archbishop of Narbonne to report in general rather than in a detailed mathematical way upon a course for such a canal. The good bishop selected roughly the same route as the surveyor of Francis I, and he reported to his royal patron that any canal would have to cross the pass of the Castel-naudary plain. He correctly identified the lowest point of the divide as the Pierres de Naurouze, a jumble of rocks some 30 miles east of Toulouse, but this point was more than 620 feet above sea level, and it had the unfortunate characteristic that it was com-paratively dry. As no streams of any size could be found within several leagues in any direction, it would obviously be impossible to provide the canal with water.

So things remained until the day when Pierre-Paul Riquet the tax collector, Baron of Bonrepos, was reposing in thought upon that same spot, the Stones of Naurouze. He was fifty-five and undis-tinguished, and any prophecy of his godmother still lay utterly unfulfilled. He had made a heap of money and bought some farms, he was a baron, and in the eyes of the world a respectable and successful man. Yet his dream was that the canal which the kings of France had planned might actually be built, and this was the strange fancy which brought him to haunt the locality of the rough pile of rocks which stood like some monument placed by inexpert giants to mark the pass of Naurouze.

It happened one day that Riquet, lost in thought, strayed a short way from the rocks and noticed a little spring, the Fontaine de la Grave. Watching the trickle of water he observed that at one point it divided into two streams. By an odd coincidence the one trickle ran eastward, the other west, and in a flash of genius Riquet saw the solution to the problem of a canal across the Languedoc. The

H

water of the spring divided, and eventually reached the two seas. If he could somehow convey to that point an infinitely greater source of water, enough to float ships, then this supply could be split in the same way and the land spanned by a navigable waterway from coast to coast. The real question was how such a great and continual flow of water could be achieved.

Riquet's next step was to betake himself to the Montagne Noire, an upland area fifteen miles to the north-east of Naurouze, where hills up to 3,000 feet were covered in deep forests. The rainfall there was much higher than in the arid lands through which much of the canal would have to pass. After tramping through the forest and riding over the hills the Baron of Bonrepos was convinced that there was water enough and to spare, provided the streams could be diverted and an artificial course cut to take the flow all the way to Naurouze. Satisfied that it could be done, he shared his idea with a lad named Pierre, son of the well-borer and smith at Revel. Pierre became enthusiastic, and it was partly through his practical energy that the canal was eventually to be completed, but for the moment he and the Baron contented themselves with building a miniature canal in the park of Bonrepos to study some of the practical problems.

At this stage Riquet was advised by his friend the Bishop of Toulouse to take into his private service a young engineer named François Andreossy, who had seen canals in Italy and had some practical knowledge. The only person thoroughly opposed to the project was the Baroness, who was convinced that this mad scheme of canal building would sooner or later swallow up the whole of the family fortune and estates. Besides, she could not abide that young man Andreossy. In both these opinions she was right. Like all the great canal men Riquet was to die impoverished. Andreossy was to introduce many ingenious ideas, but he turned against his employer and attempted to persuade the king to recognize him as the genius behind the scheme. Even as late as the beginning of the nineteenth century, his namesake and relative, who was general of artillery in the army of the new republic, returned to the attack upon Riquet, who had by then been dead for more than one hundred years.

With the explorations complete, Riquet very wisely wrote to

First Minister Colbert, outlining in some detail his conviction that
the Canal des Deux Mers was a practical proposition. That energetic
and imaginative man seized upon it as a truly great enterprise, and
he realized that by its sheer scale and audacity it would appeal to
le Roi Soleil. This it certainly did, and Louis XIV ordered commissioners to examine the scheme. Riquet himself took them to the
Black Mountain, explained just how and where he proposed to
convey the water, and as they still seemed reluctant to believe
that such a thing could really be done he offered to have a trial
feeder dug at his own entire expense, all the way to the Stones of
Naurouze. This offer was accepted, and in five months Riquet and
the faithful Pierre had achieved the construction of a pilot channel
for his proposed Rigole de la Plaine, to bring water from the River
Sor. The commissioners were summoned, the sluice was opened,
and the officials could see for themselves a copious flow of water
arriving at the vital point.

Louis XIV appointed Riquet contractor, and in 1666 the work
was begun. Fifteen years later the first ships passed down the
canal — the Canal Royal as it was now called — and when Voltaire
came to write of the era of the *Roi Soleil* he had no hesitation in
declaring that '*le monument le plus glorieux par son utilité, par sa
grandeur, et par ses difficultés, fut ce canal de Languedoc qui joint les
deux mers.*' In fact it was the greatest feat of civil engineering
between Roman times and the nineteenth century.

The edict of Louis XIV proudly pointed out that not even the
most ambitious and able princes or nations had been able to think
actually of putting this great work in hand, and stressed that the
waterway — a great work of peace — was to be constructed in a
manner well worthy of the royal interest, and capable of perpetu-
ating for centuries to come the grandeur, the abundance and the
happiness of the reign of its royal patron. And this it most certainly
does. It is impossible to pass over the aqueducts, sail through the
first canal tunnel in all the world, mount the locks and see the
means devised for supplying water to the canal without being
impressed — even if it is Riquet and Colbert rather than Louis XIV
who are remembered.

The letters patent also placed the charges of maintenance of the

canal upon Riquet and his descendants in perpetuity, and in return
they were to levy the navigation charges. Thus the crown obtained
the credit without the risk. Twelve hundred men and five hundred
women were soon on the job, most of them at the personal charge
of the Baron himself, but Louis XIV was at least represented on the
obverse of medals struck and buried in the foundations of the dam
of St Ferréol — of which more will be told in a later chapter.
Around his head were the modest words:

Undarum terraeque potens atque arbiter orbis,

whilst on the reverse was a representation of Toulouse with a canal
joining the river, and the legend *Tolosa utriusque maris emporium.*

The crown and the States of Languedoc eventually subscribed
considerable sums, but the Canal Royal, or Canal des Deux Mers,
or Canal du Languedoc, or Canal du Midi, as it is now called,
proved more expensive than had been foreseen. Although it was
completed in the very short period of fifteen years the project had
actually cost sixteen million pounds of gold, of which Riquet had
personally provided almost one third, thereby so impoverishing his
estate that more than half a century was to pass before his descendants could work off the debt and see a slight profit on the
management.

In May 1681 the Royal Commissioners came to view the completed canal before it was filled. Then the water was admitted from
the feeders at Naurouze, and within a few days the level was high
enough for them to go aboard ship at Toulouse for a ceremonial
voyage, their ship being followed by 23 laden barges bound for the
fair at Beaucaire. Music, flags, acclamations of the crowds and
blessings of the clergy accompanied them all the way, and poets
vied with each other in the eulogy of commemorative odes and
sonnets. Verses survive in Latin and Italian, in French, and of
course in the Occitan tongue. Never had there been such delight,
such unrestrained pride in an achievement of which the country
and its people could justly be proud.

Yet there was a sad note, too. *Ta perto Riquet, nous coumblèt de
tristesso,* one of the poets wrote. Only seven months earlier
Pierre-Paul Riquet, Baron of Bonrepos, had died in poverty, his

farms and estates mortgaged to the hilt to finance the canal. It was
Pierre, the wellman's son from Revel, who had doggedly seen the
work through the last few months of difficulty to its completion,
and who accompanied the Royal Commissioners on their voyage
through to the new port of Sète which his friend and master had
designed.

Riquet's canal flourished, and as the years went by his descendants were able to see with satisfaction an increasing traffic in
passengers and in goods. Fly-boats set out daily from either end,
and in the nineteenth century steam tugs helped to make the
passage of the Bassin de Thau safer and more rapid. Then in 1850
the main railway from Sète to Bordeaux was opened, and the canal
was threatened with decline, or even extinction. As usual in such
circumstances, canal enthusiasts were very ready to come to the
rescue with wild schemes for bigger and better waterways which
would make the railways appear vastly inferior. Among these men
was one Louis Verstraet, who was convinced that the canal
should be greatly enlarged. After he had doggedly argued his
scheme through seventy-eight committees and more than a score of
chambers of commerce without having it either accepted or
rejected, he put an end to the discussions by blowing out his brains.

Then there was the worthy Monsieur Manier, who in 1875 hit
upon the excellent idea of enlarging the canal to a depth of 33 feet
to take the largest vessels then afloat. He also proposed to dispense
with the locks by digging the waterway down to sea level — an
excavation which would have involved a cutting 657 feet in depth
at the Stones of Naurouze. As a result there would be a ship canal
without impediment, he stressed, melons costing threepence at
Narbonne could be carried direct to the London markets, and the
English fort of Gibraltar would be bypassed. Besides, not a single
snowflake falling on the northern slope of the Pyrenees would be
wasted. The Garonne could be diverted at Toulouse to precipitate
itself through a series of water wheels into the canal 420 feet below,
and if much the same were done with all the other rivers the 'Grand
Canal du Midi will be lined by factories as far as the eye can reach,
whose machinery will be moved by a power costing nothing.'

Manier was a barrister, not an engineer. But in the 1920s his scheme was revived, except that the sea-level ship canal was now to be even larger to accommodate the increased size of vessels and bring it up to the dimensions of Suez. There is no record of the *Ponts et Chaussées* having taken up such an ambitious idea with enthusiasm, or even without it, and one wonders what they may have thought of the still more original ideas which were to follow. Among these was the notion of a *nautostrade*, a sort of nautical *autobahn* similar to some of the fantasies of early American canals but even more extraordinary. Vast docks, fifty feet in depth, would rise gracefully from the sea terminals, holding within them the floating liners which would then be whisked across the country on rails at a speed of up to sixty miles per hour.

This system, combining *mal de mer* and train sickness in one mad rush across the Languedoc, would have proved one of the winning wonders of eccentricity of the modern world. So would its rival — the notion of a *subterranean* ship canal from coast to coast. Certainly the human mind is inventive; but it is always easier to day-dream than to bring the dreams down to practical execution. Weird ideas are common enough, but the Riquets and the von Platens, the Brunels and the Telfords, men who actually see their brain children through to achievement, are rare.

We can leave the world of fantasy and return to Riquet's own waterway, for the lock chamber of Bagnas is now full and it is time to wind open the gates, jump aboard, push out from the wall into the centre of the lock, and continue our journey. Soon we are gliding through an avenue of trees and after a mile or two a right-angled bend leads to the lock of Prades, which is open right through and is only there to be used when the Hérault is in flood. For the River Hérault lies immediately beyond it, a broad stream with high banks set with poplars. It is reminiscent of the Seine in its upper reaches except that the water here is almost chestnut brown with the rich vineyard earth washed down from the foothills of the Cévennes — a fact which accounts for the absence of fishermen along its shore.

The river is not now in flood. On the contrary, its water is low, but there is still enough to run at a gentle pace towards the weir and the town mill, half a mile ahead. Before the weir we must obviously leave the river course, so we can confidently aim for the small cut which disappears among the bushes on the right bank. Soon we are passing a number of old canal hulks which seem to have given up the idea of voyaging and have metamorphosed into floating homes for their families. Ahead is the *écluse ronde*, the circular lock of Agde.

VI

*Agde — netting the river — the canal at Béziers — the
Cathars and the crusade — the great massacre — Fon-
séranes locks — the long pound — tunnel of Malpas —
Poilhes and Capestang — the* Commodore *in Roman waters*

The round lock of Agde is an example of the ingenuity of the
designer of the Canal du Midi. Whether it was devised by
Andreossy, or young Pierre, or the Royal Commissioners, or by the
Baron of Bonrepos himself, the lock was a brilliant solution to a
particular problem. The old mill weir which spans the Hérault in
Agde itself causes a step in the level, and the Canal du Midi needed
access to both parts of the river — the upper section for navigation,
and the lower reach so that barges could visit the port of Agde
itself and ships could sail out to the sea beyond. So the round lock
was devised with a gate at each end and another in the side, each at
a different level. The roundness is merely to give space for a ship
to pass straight across or out at the side, according to the skipper's
intentions.

The lock stands by a group of magnificent plane trees at the end
of the curving cut from the upper Hérault, and the deserted towpath along the quiet and reedy side canal leads to a splendid view
of Agde itself. Nothing of the town is seen until at the very last
moment, when all of a sudden it is there, straight across the river,
its broad stone quay and cramped little houses making one of the
prettiest waterfronts in all France. Once Agde used to be on the
sea, but that was long ago. The port is now inland, with more than
two miles of channel leading down to the salt water. Sitting beside
the summer Hérault Agde looks safe enough, but the great iron
rings in the walls of the houses across the quay show how high the
river may be expected to rise, and no doubt there is sometimes a
chance of catching fish in one's own kitchen. Fishing craft, heavy

and sunbleached, still lie along either side of the stream, and the humble life of the fishermen and sailors in their waterside houses is emphasized by the enormous black mass of the cathedral of St Étienne, built eight centuries ago of lava from the nearby hill and so tough and unweathered that it looks as though consecrated only a month ago and made of some new and resistant breeze block.

It is abundantly clear that the Bishop of Agde, back in the days when infidels were on the prowl by sea, was going to brook no nonsense. This was the Church Militant, even if others might think it the Church Decadent. The cathedral would stay there, standing fast with all the impregnable rigidity of a dogma. That is why the black building resembles a fort more than a church. There is not so much as an arrow slit or embrasure to let a chink of light penetrate its astonishing blank façade. Instead there are machicolations, battlements, and all manner of handy places from which to pour boiling oil or shoot down attackers with arrows. The tower is a fortified keep with turrets commanding a view of the walls. There is even a means of hauling up supplies from ground level. Naturally, the nave is as dark as a dungeon, and nothing could be more eloquent of the state of affairs in twelfth century Agde if the church had thus to be protected, not just from possible sea-borne Saracens but from the humble Agathois themselves — *lous bochs* (the madmen) as they are known to their neighbours, on the grounds that they are supposed to spend much of their time in pleasure.

Agde is one of the oldest towns in France, and when the cathedral was built in the twelfth century the port was already two-thirds of the way along the line of its history leading to today. Like Marseille, it was founded by adventurous seamen from a city state of Greece. Richelieu furnished it with an immense mole, for he intended to make Agde the premier port of the Mediterranean. Whilst he was still alive the States of the Languedoc could only dare accept the idea and foot the bill, but as soon as he died they stopped the works. Then came the plans for the Canal du Midi. Had the port been completed it would certainly have been the terminus of the line, but the royal commissioners chose to build a new harbour at Sète instead. Agde was only allowed the short branch canal as a sort of consolation prize.

We had arrived at Agde in the evening, and on the following day I set out early on the usual morning errand of buying fresh rolls from the baker. Agde lay bathed in a soft and misty light, and below the road bridge a man in a green fishing punt was about to make his morning haul. He had spanned the Hérault with a net, the down-stream side of which was raised to just above the water level, and the upstream edge was now being wound up by an accomplice who strained at a wooden windlass whilst the fisherman sat in his boat inside the trap, helping to drive the shoals of prey to one end. It was a simple way of fishing, and I wanted to see what the fisherman would find as a result of his labours. I waited on the grass under the spotty plane trees, wondering what strange monsters of the river would soon be brought into view.

The line was tightened little by little, but the net was still not fully raised when another individual came to stand nearby and watch. I wished him a good morning and he replied only with a somewhat sheepish grin.

'What do you think he will have caught in his net?' I asked, not in the least discouraged. 'Big fish? Small fish? Or perhaps nothing?'

My neighbour looked at me in something like alarm, and with-drew a step. He shook his head decidedly. '*Anguilles!*' he said. '*Anguilles!*'

That there should be eels in the Hérault did not astonish me, but I found the man's behaviour rather disconcerting. However I decided to carry on the conversation as though I had not noticed anything strange in his demeanour.

'I like eels,' I confided. 'There's nothing so good as a fine eel, properly cooked. Fried, or better still smoked. Don't you agree? If he brings up a good one I'll see if I can buy it for breakfast.'

The man looked wildly around as though seeking a way of escape from some dangerous lunatic. Again he gave a faint smile, pointed his thumb towards his own chest, and repeated his assertion.

'*Anguilles, anguilles,*' he exclaimed.

The fisherman was nearing the moment when he could pounce. He took up a fold of net and shook it, sending any eels he might have trapped down into the small portion still under water. Care-

fully he gathered up another fold of the net until he could raise the final dip of mesh clear of the river. Flipping and tossing within it were five silvery fish the size of moderately adult sticklebacks.

'Not much of a haul of eels,' I said to my neighbour. 'And I wouldn't think there's a living to be made out of a handful of sardines, would you?'

The man shrank back, and raised his arm as though to ward off an attack.

'Look here,' he said in English. 'I'm sorry, but it's no use your jabbering away at me. I can't understand French. You see, I'm an *anguille*.'

'Are you sure?' I replied, somewhat surprised. 'You don't think ...'.

'Good heavens! Don't tell me you're English too,' he broke in. A great wave of relief spread over him. 'I thought you were one of these French chaps — that's why I kept on saying I was English myself, as I couldn't understand. See what I mean?'

Beyond Agde the Canal du Midi begins to lift very slowly above

the marshes and after three locks and sixteen miles it seems about
to plunge into the River Orb when it thinks better of it and cuts
round close to the river to start climbing up the side of the valley
towards the city of Béziers, hidden behind the trees. Had we been
making the voyage before 1857 we should have run out into the
river itself and turned to the right up its course, for that was the
way that Riquet devised this part of the journey. He happened to
be a native of Béziers, and perhaps General Andreossy was right
when he alleged that it was for this reason alone that the Baron
wished to take the canal to that place. He wanted to ensure that the
advantages of increased trade would be conferred upon his own
city.

There is no doubt that to take Béziers into the course raised the
worst of many difficulties which the canal had to encounter, for the
city was perched on one side of a deep valley with the canal
approaching from the other. The Baron of Bonrepos decided to
lead the waterway on a contour to the very edge of the valley and
then drop down a flight of eight locks to the Orb, pass down the
river itself for half a mile or more, and then strike out through the
left bank towards Agde. To do this he had to find some means of
leaving the valley of the Aude and taking his waterway over the
ridge to the Orb basin. The whole success of the canal depended
upon his original vision that water could be made to flow from
Naurouze all the way to the sea, and naturally this meant that the
canal had to fall all the way. There could be no question of
suddenly climbing again, as this would make it impossible to supply
the hump with water.

So it seemed impossible to take the waterway out of the one
river valley and into another. Although the ridge between them was
not very high, even a single lock rising the wrong way was something which could not be contemplated. But Riquet was not to be
beaten, and he decided to pierce the ridge with a tunnel, the first
canal tunnel in the world. With it he brought the Canal Royal to
the valley edge, straight across from his native town.

Béziers tout entié countemplo soun idolo dessus soun pèdestal, and
not content with having him on a pedestal the Bitterois have
named the one splendid double avenue in the centre of the more

modern part of the city the *Allées Paul Riquet*. Nevertheless, to take his canal down into the course of the Orb and out again below the town was one of the few mistakes in an otherwise brilliant design. The rest of the way from the summit the route had deliberately been kept out of the bottoms of river valleys, so that navigation would not be interrupted, but here this wise principle was thrown over, with unfortunate results.

The rivers of the Languedoc are temperamental streams, draining large and often mountainous areas of very erratic rainfall. The Orb does not have to cope with thawing snows from the Pyrénées, but the hills along its upper reaches are more than three thousand feet high, and they can deliver great quantities of water. Riquet found the Orb at Béziers to be a river which for much of the year was so shallow that it could not float a laden barge, whereas at other times violent floods could raise new shoals and race past the city with a current too formidable for boats of any kind. To combat the first difficulty he raised the water level by a weir, but this made the river deposit more of its mud. Several groins and moles were added to deflect the current and scour the channel, and in this way the dry-season troubles were overcome. But nothing could prevent the serious interruptions caused by floods, and in 1779 shipping was held up for seventeen days on end. The many craft delayed included — according to General Andreossy — a convoy laden with some seven thousand tons of grain destined for Provence, and the hold-up caused something like a famine throughout that area.

Riquet could have thrown an aqueduct over the river, but this would have been an undertaking even greater than other river crossings he had dealt with in that way. Perhaps he considered it and decided against it, or it may be that he was confident that the floods and shallows of the Orb could be tamed. Nevertheless, the passage of the Orb proved so unsatisfactory that the aqueduct had eventually to be built, and in 1857 a new piece of canal was cut from half way down the great flight of locks opposite the city, and the waterway was made to fly over the river. This also cut out the old port down by the river, so a canal basin was dug on the city side of the valley.

The *Commodore* was soon climbing the double lock into this

Port Neuf, and here for the first time she came upon the broad and beautiful craft of the Canal du Midi, the wine tankers with their gay splashes of red or azure or emerald on curving bow and elegant stern. *Perrucho* and *Bram*, *Couret* and *Epargne*, *Montauban* and *Roussaud*, *Bicon* and *Larose*, the wine carriers lay all along the quay beside the bleached warehouses of the vintners co-operative and the blenders, the snake-coiled pipes across the wharf pulsating with the suction of the pumps which drew the wines from their cargo-tanks to the huge containers in the sheds. Beyond the wharf a second pair of locks led out to the aqueduct, and as we sailed across the broad river-bed below us Béziers suddenly burst into full view in all its astonishing beauty. Two road bridges, an old and a new, crossed the stream at a lower level than ourselves towards roads that disappeared between jumbles of brown limestone houses which looked as though they had been spilled down the slope and somehow had stuck fast. Up at the summit the city spread away behind the fortified bishop's palace and castellated cathedral of St Nazaire. This view from by the aqueduct is the finest along the whole length of the Canal du Midi, and it is impossible to look across to that splendid and beautiful city without a pang of realization that there, on the feast of St Mary Magdalene in the year 1209, a terrible event occurred which was to put off the Reformation for more than 300 years and seal the destruction of the highest and finest civilization which Europe then knew.

The very day after the murder of Pierre de Castelnau as he left St Gilles, the signal was given for a war against the heretics, a crusade against those who did not accept the authority of the Church of Rome, and in particular upon the Count of Toulouse and his young nephew Raymond-Roger Trencavel, Viscount of Béziers and Carcassonne, in whose territories the heretics were firmly established and tolerated. These heretics were of two distinct kinds; there were the Waldensians — followers of Pierre Waldo of Lyon, a wealthy merchant who had the scriptures translated from the Latin and who then renounced his wealth and position to live in charity with the poor. Shocked by the abuses and pretension of the Roman Church, Waldo and his friends attempted to live like the Apostles in poverty, preaching the gospel as they wandered from place to place. They recognized no ecclesiastical authority but God, and they not only threw over the Pope and a corrupt priest-hood but much of Catholic doctrine and dogma, too. They could not accept the ideas of purgatory, or of transubstantiation, and they ruled out praying to saints. Indeed the Waldensians were the first breath of the Reformation, and a serious menace to the authority, power and revenues of the Church of Rome — which they un-compromisingly identified with the Great Whore of Babylon.

The same identification was made by the Cathars (or Albigen-sians, after the Languedoc district where they flourished). The Waldensians were more to be found in the Alps, but there were certainly a number in Béziers even if the vast majority of those who opposed the Church of Rome were the Cathars, the 'pure ones'. Some of the beliefs of the Cathars have been lost for ever, because the crusade against them endeavoured to destroy every trace of their Church, but certainly they emphasized the wisdom of Christ rather than sufferings, and they abhorred reverence for the Cross. If one's son was slain, they logically demanded, would one revere his memory for what he was, or would one worship whatever weapon or accident had killed him?

There was more to the Albigensian heresy than just a revolt against the abuses of the Catholic clergy, great though they were. The movement came from the Bogomils (or beloved of God) who flourished in Bulgaria in the tenth century and spread across to the Languedoc a theology which contained various elements from the East. The chief 'heretical' point was the Cathar insistence that the world was under a sort of dual control, everything physical being the work of Satan, alias Jehovah. The good God sent Christ as a Mediator, but because it was unthinkable that he could have had a genuine or Satanic body Christ was not 'really real'. From this it followed that he could not genuinely have suffered or died, but the Devil cleverly founded the Roman Church to make believers think that he had done so.

The notion that everything physical was created by the evil deity led the Cathars to abhor anything associated with repro-duction. Eggs and meat were banned, and so was milk. The Cathars themselves had a horror of sexual relations as aiding the Devil in his creative activity. How far these notions were understood and accepted by the *credentes*, the rank and file of adherents, is another matter. Probably much of the doctrine was above their heads, and certainly the great majority of them were married.

There was a single sacrament, a laying-on of hands which conferred the Holy Spirit. This was only given to a person after he had spent a year or two in study and preparation, and when he had received it he thereupon became a *perfectus*, a *bonhomme*. From that moment he gave away all his goods, he ate no food of animal origin, he lived ascetically, gave his life to prayer and preaching and service, and dressed in a black robe. Whether a man or a woman he swore never to retract for fear of death by fire or any other means, and amid all the barbarity of their persecution there is only one single recorded case of an initiate recanting.

The *perfecti* or ministers of the Cathars thus lived in a state of poverty and purity and dedication which stood in complete contrast to the affluence of many of the Roman clergy. Inevitably they were respected, and their logical and liberal preaching based on the Gospel of St John mixed with the romantic ideas of the troubadours to make the Languedoc an area of such freedom that Jews held official posts and professorships, Arabs taught in medical schools, women were largely emancipated, and capital punishment was regarded as barbarous. It was against this splendid flowering of justice and equality and faith that Pope Innocent III, a sincere and fanatically enthusiastic defender of the faith, announced a crusade. He wrote to all bishops, archbishops, counts and barons and knights of France and the North summoning them to root out the heretics.

For a while nothing happened — nothing, that is, but preparations for launching a murderous assault in the name of the Christian Church. Great forces of knights from France and Germany and Brabant gathered at Lyon for the crusade, their numbers swelled by many thousands of mercenaries — outlaws and brigands and cut-throats who were prepared to fight anybody — and by a horde of pilgrims who hoped to be in at the death and earn the wholesale indulgence granted by Innocent III to any who might strike down a heretic in the lands where the Cathars had taken root. In the same month that Count Raymond made his second and humiliating journey to St Gilles, there to be flayed by the Legates, an armada of lighters began to float down from Lyon. Within a short space of time the largest army Europe had ever seen was camped at the walls of Béziers, its leaders determined to teach these damned barons of the Languedoc a lesson.

Every member of the vast beleaguering force had a reason for enthusiasm. The nobles could have the credit of doing their forty-day crusade service without the dangerous voyage to the holy land and the menace of Saracen hordes. The Cathars, abhorring bloodshed, were complete pacifists and — at least in the early stages of the war — would be cleft asunder rather than raise a hand in self-defence. They were hardly a dangerous enemy, and there was freedom to seize their goods and lands for oneself 'in the name of Christ'. The mercenaries were after the loot by which alone they lived. The pilgrims, thousands of them led by a kind of wild mass hysteria, had the chance accorded to them by the Pope of winning salvation and forgiveness by the mere act of murdering a heretic.

Yet in spite of such attractions the siege of Béziers promised to be a long one. Though hurriedly fortified, the city was well placed and ably defended.

The crusading forces issued an ultimatum. Béziers could hand over some two hundred known heretics and their families, and the rest of the population would go free. Otherwise the city would be attacked.

This choice was put to the townspeople by their Catholic bishop, and though the burghers must certainly have been predominantly Catholic they respected the saintliness of the Cathars and burned with indignation at the suggestion that they should hand over their fellow citizens. They would rather be drowned, they said, than submit to such terms.

The details of what happened at Béziers have never been fully known, but it seems that the defenders made a rash sally and the attackers managed to wrest from them the control of one of the gates. Almost at once the fortified city itself was open to the full fury of the mercenaries, and of the frenzied pilgrims pursuing at

I

their heels in the hope of achieving salvation through slaughter. Behind them came the knights in armour, furious that the mercenaries and mob were smashing and wrecking so much of value that might have become their own.

It was not the heretics who were thus cut down, but the whole population, much of it loyal and Catholic. The difficulty of distinguishing heretics, other than the Cathar ministers in their black robes, had already occurred to some of the nobles, and according to the testimony of a German monk who took part in the assault they posed the question to Arnald-Amalric, the leader of the troops and Abbot of Cîteaux.

'Kill the lot,' he replied. 'God will recognize his own.'

And so it was to be. House after house was broken open, every man, woman and child was clubbed to death or cut down and trampled upon. As the insane fury spread down the streets the citizens fled in panic to the sanctuary of the great cathedral and the other churches of the town. Priests and monks tolled the bells to summon them, and beyond the clanging and pealing the din of destruction and the screams of the victims filled the air.

But the crusaders had no intentions of respecting sanctuary. The prize was too rich for them to be robbed of it so simply, and battering in the doors of the churches they slaughtered the people where they prayed and the priests at the altar. Seven thousand were said by a contemporary report to have been murdered in the church of the Madeleine alone, and the Abbot of Cîteaux was able to write to Innocent III to report on his success. 'Some twenty thousand citizens were killed by the sword, without regard to age or sex,' he announced.

The wholesale destruction in the city infuriated the French knights. They cared little for the citizens, but they could not abide seeing the rough mercenaries plundering the wealth of so fine a city. So, among the score of thousand corpses, they turned on the unarmoured mercenaries and stripped them of their ill-gotten gains. Furious, these men were steeled to destroy everything in sight, and rather than let the riches of Béziers fall into the hands of the lords and barons they fired the houses. Quickly the city was swept by the flames, and the cathedral itself cracked, trembled, and crashed to the ground to bury the dead and dying under a heap of rubble and hot masonry.

For three days the crusaders rested from their exertions, taking their ease in the meadows beside the Orb in the good conscience of a worthy deed well done. Then they moved on, and ahead of them travelled the news of their ruthlessness with such effect that the people of the country fled from their path and many of them took to the forests, or the mountain fastnesses of the Pyrénées.

Today, the Béziers which arose from the ashes of the massacre is a centre of the wine trade. It seems that the city was also once a place with its own specialities of the table, but the Englishman approaching Béziers is not likely to be greatly enticed by discovering that the town was particularly famous for blancmange. One of the most celebrated of French gourmets described the dish as frequently insupportable when made by the chefs of Paris but a treat when made by many a simple cook of Béziers, and he went on to say that indigestion was the only serious disease to be found in the place. This he declared in a work dedicated to a certain Monsieur Aigrefeuille, who later attained to such heights of indigestion when devouring a fifteen-pound salmon single-handed that he collapsed on the last plateful and was carried out dead. This, however, took place in Paris. It would be a noble gourmet indeed who could die by stuffing himself with blancmange.

With the crossing of the Orb the Canal du Midi leaves the less interesting country behind it and becomes as enchanting a waterway as any in Europe. On either bank the cypresses soar high in an elegant unbroken screen, and the canal curves majestically towards the locks of Fonséranes, the nightingales on either hand vying with each other in their welcome to the boatman. Exotic butterflies flit across the water, and that delightfully named bird *Upupa epops* pops and poops from tree to tree, always keeping level with the boat and flashing its elegant orange and black feathered head-dress like an Indian brave at a pow-wow. The hoopoe is a beautiful creature and its downward-curving bill gives it an air of somewhat haughty disdain. Thomas Bewick noted that its crest was only erected when the hoopoe was surprised or irritated, so perhaps these pretty birds were as surprised to see us as we were to see them. Certainly they rarely paused to stare at the *Commodore* without flashing their crests, and it was hard to credit them with being — as Buffon put it — a bird of the pie kind.

We had had plenty of time to visit the city, for the lock-keeper at the entrance to the aqueduct explained that the *Commodore* would have to heave to for four hours, because there was a one-way-traffic system in the locks ahead. This was because the *écluse de Fonséranes* is in fact a staircase lock, in which no passing is possible. It is also one of the splendidly ambitious feats of engineering which Riquet conceived, and which had no parallel elsewhere for a century or more to come.

The Fonséranes locks form a magnificent ladder of water which rises seventy feet from the Orb to the *long bief* of the Canal du Midi, in the existence of which the ingenuity of Riquet can be seen. Such a flight of locks set end to end can use an enormous quantity of water, particularly when a boat is going up and needs a new lockful at each step instead of travelling only on a single basinful as does a *bateau avalant*. To draw off so much water from the pound above would drop the level seriously, and also cause a strong current, unless the pound itself were large enough to form a considerable reservoir. In fact the pound is the longest on any French canal, and runs for 35 miles all the way to the lock of Argens. Such an immense body of water is unaffected by the lock operations at the Béziers end, as a whole flight of water would not make half an inch of difference to the level, or cause any noticeable flow.

But the *long bief* has always had one disadvantage of another kind. Just because there is so little current it is an excellent place for weeds to grow, and the engineers soon found that it had to be provided with a weed cutter of its own. All kinds of devices were tried, and eventually a barge was installed which had in front of the stem an arrangement of double-edged scythes fixed to a post. A couple of labourers see-sawed with a pair of handles, and by means of a wooden gear wheel this caused the scythe blades to rotate and slice away at the weeds. The machine wrought a certain degree of havoc among the water plants, but General Andreossy stated in his history of the canal that it was not as effective as was desirable. The trouble still exists, but is no longer so serious, because the modern motor-barges keep down the weeds rather better by the slicing action of their own propellers. Not that weed cutting has been stopped. On the contrary, it was very actively in progress when the *Commodore* made her voyage towards Toulouse, with results which we were later to discover.

The long and level pound beyond the flight of locks wanders hither and thither like a lost soul, forbidden to leave its contour. Sometimes its gentle and erratic course is spun through pastures, or it may pass along a twisting avenue of cypresses or mulberries, or plane trees so huge that those of the London streets would appear like seedlings beside them. Now and again the canal bends round the edge of a hill as though anxious to give the boatman a conducted tour of the landscape, and one can look over its bank toward a wide expanse of arid semi-desert, dry and stony and cracked with the heat, a waste of limestone blocks eroded by wind and interspersed with prickly pear and other cactus-like plants which flourish on the poor ground. Bright yellow brooms smother the banks, helianthemums and orange-centred cystus bushes lay their flowers wide open to the brilliant heat of a sun so intense that the *Commodore*'s catwalk would steam off a bucket of water flung over it and be dry again and too hot to walk upon within less than a minute. To stop outside the shadow patches of the tall trees would have been to blister the paint. But that is why the trees are there at all. The good Baron of Bonrepos overlooked nothing and was well aware of the desirability of shade. Many of the gigantic planes which stretch along the banks are of his planting.

Six miles beyond the Fonséranes locks we twisted through a beautiful wood beside the manor farm of Colombiers and turned a bend to see ahead of us a ridge rising to a crown of rough stone and tall cypresses, and scattered shrubs set in crevices of the rock. With the binoculars we could make out a few regular geometrical patches and even the top of a pillar, for this was the Iberian town of Enserune, dating from the fourth and fifth centuries B.C. Almost at once the canal gave another swerve to the left, and ahead of us was the mouth of the high vault of the Percée de Malpas, the tunnel which Riquet had cut through the barrier of the Enserune ridge.

Today there are three tunnels under the hill. The Bordeaux–
Sète railway takes the same opportunity to change valleys, and the
track actually passes through the hill far beneath the canal,
entering on the starboard hand and emerging to port, so that the
boatman may unknown to himself be passing diagonally over an
express at the same moment that a car on the winding road to the
Oppidum of Enserune is somewhere above him. But beneath all
these is an even older tunnel, dug by Roman engineers to drain the
Étang de Montmardy into a similar swamp beyond the ridge.

It may well have been the existence of this subterranean
aqueduct which gave Riquet the idea of tunnelling instead of
making a very deep cutting in the soft rock, but in so doing he was
trying something never before attempted. When his force of
labourers arrived at the Enserune ridge they found the rock to be
an extremely soft tufa stone which, though easy to excavate, was
not very firm. The engineers hesitated, refusing to cut a passage
lest the roof should fall in. Word that the works had run into
difficulty reached Colbert, who appointed M. d'Aguesseau, governor of the Languedoc, to investigate the matter with a commission.
The governor immediately ordered the works to be suspended
until the commissioners could arive, view the obstacle, and make
their report to the chief minister on the bad passage or *mal pas*. At
the news of trouble Riquet's critics and enemies were delighted,
and they brought every possible intrigue to bear with Colbert to
have the canal stopped altogether. The First Minister was content
to await the report of the commission, but the reaction of the Baron
de Bonrepos was typical. Having brought his canal thus far he was
not to be beaten, and summoning his workmen he harangued them.

Did they know, he asked, what the people of Toulouse were
saying? No? The folk of Toulouse were laughing at their cowardice,
and saying that these men could not drill through the mountain if
they tried! The works, they taunted, would have to be stopped.
Did anyone want that to happen?

The labourers were roused and swore that nothing could stop
them. They would show the world what could be done, and the
Tolosans could eat their hats.

They had exactly six days, Riquet told them. In six days the commissioners would be coming, intent on closing the works. In six days they must be through the 520-foot thick ridge and out the other side, or else . . . .

Six days later, Governor d'Aguesseau and his colleagues of the commission arrived. The Baron bowed a welcome and offered to conduct them on a tour of the works. By the light of torches he led them through the tunnel, carefully evading their questions about the purpose of the great vault in which they found themselves. At length they reached the further end, and the governor somewhat impatiently asked to be taken to the *mal pas*, the difficult passage which was holding up progress.

'You have just passed through it,' replied Riquet. And as the object of the investigation was no longer there the officials could report that the work was progressing without hindrance, whilst Riquet's men dug and dug on their way towards the Orb.

The tunnel of Malpas was thirty feet in height and it had been cut without difficulty and without accident. But Riquet wisely accepted that the rock was too soft for permanent safety and decided to line the vault throughout. A wooden ceiling was erected inside, but water percolating through the stone and falls of earth from the excavation shafts brought about its decay, and after only ten years it had to be replaced. A masonry vaulting was built into the tunnel, and the roof has held ever since.

Having bravely plunged through the Malpas the Canal du Midi runs along the foot of the ridge of Enserune, with a splendid view to port across the wide basin of the Capestang marshes, now transformed into orchards and vineyards, fields of maize or groves of peaches, but with dykes and ditches damp enough to provide a haven for the thousands of frogs which cannot even wait for dusk before singing their Occitan love-songs to the wide vault of the sky. Beyond these rich fields the land rises to hide the valley of the Aude, and further distant the foothills raise themselves indistinct to disappear into a purple haze of mystery from which the snow caps of the Pyrénées stand up like plywood mountains in a theatre set. Along the canal edge itself planes, planes, and more planes are ranged to port, but to starboard the vegetation is that of the hot stony slopes, the broom and bay and olive, splashed with the dark

green of the cypresses and here and there the vivid magenta of
bougainvillea or the royal blue of the giant convolvulus. On either
side the land seems inhabited by cicadas engaged in competing for
the honour of the year's loudest zizzer, but the hoopoes pay no
attention. Perhaps they are no better at finding the source of the
sound than we were.

At a bridge the canal swung into a deep cutting and we were
passing through the village of Poilhes. It had nothing unusual
about it, but it seemed a pleasant place to rest for the night and
we drew in to the bank opposite one of the pretty and useful
tile-roofed washing-houses which a benevolent Department of
Bridges and Highways always provides for the benefit of the many
who have little or no plumbing at home. Laundering was over for
the day, but the slab served as a diving point for the girls of the
village and a spotted setter. Hanging a rope-ladder over the side we
joined them, and quickly learned to appreciate the blessing conferred by Riquet in devising such a copious water supply for his
canal that it is as sweet and clean as a river.

Poilhes has no claim whatsoever to fame, but we found it to be a
fair sample of a small town of the Midi. The houses are of a rusty,
dusty brown, their walls trailing with vines but the interiors dark
and shuttered off from the heat outside. A curtain of bamboo — or
more probably of coloured strips of polyvinyl chloride — dangles
and rattles in the doorway, and behind one such barrier is the table
which serves as the village bar. But there are no seats. The cus-
tomers sit outside, tanned and wiry men with the red earth dusted
on their boots, gentle and genial men who talk quietly without
gesticulating, who laugh but do not shout, and who are always
ready with a smile or nod for anyone passing. Their chairs are
ranged on the pavement outside the inn, or in front of their own
houses, and content with a glass of non-Algerian wine they watch
the world go by — the world at Poilhes being a single wine-bowser
in the course of the hour we spent over our evening aperitif.

Our chairs happened also to be the spectators' grandstand for a
refined form of hopscotch played by the junior girls of the village.
Over-twelves passed by with averted eyes, conscious that they had
outgrown such childish sports, but from about sixteen onwards the

young ladies would stop and watch with undisguised interest, it being accepted that the game was one which figured in a childhood too far gone for any such demonstration of newfound superiority to be necessary. They watched the sport, and so did we, for it was happening right in front of us.

The first round was simple enough, a single hopping kick of the stone from one square to the next all the way up one side of the chalked course and down the other. Those who finished this first lap would then do a zig-zag diagonal course, and after that a circuit with the stone kicked into alternate squares. Then a player had to hop the same rounds on one leg, repeating the performance with the stone balanced on one shoulder and then on top of her head.

The unchallenged champion of Poilhes was a studious-looking little girl in a pleated skirt before whose skill the other girls stood more in awestruck wonder than envy. From her deportment and dress she was obviously a cut above her fellows, not just in hop-scotch but in brains, but there was nothing condescending about her manner. She was just a born hopscotcher, that was all, for having run through all the preliminary rounds without failure she went on to tackle a further refinement, which consisted of hop-scotching the whole course a square at a time, or diagonally, or in twos, but blindfolded.

The cobble might not stray out of its proper square, so very gingerly she would hop on one shoe, twisting and turning until she could feel the stone against her instep. To help her with direction she was allowed to have another girl standing in the centre of the right square and calling to her, but she had even to find the hop-scotched stone again without any indication of whether it was just inside the line, or nearly out at the other side. Each correct hop and kick was met with cries of '*Mama, mama!*' Or, if the stone went outside its destined square, with a commiserating groan of '*Papa*'. To the girls of Poilhes, or perhaps to hopscotchers in general, mothers were good and fathers a disappointment.

Next morning we set out again down the long pound, and almost at once we could look across the fields to see the tree-line of our route winding to and fro before arriving at a sunbaked town with an immense church tower proudly dominating the country for miles around. This was Capestang, the name of which suggests a lake or *étang* teeming with carp. If the lake has now been drained away to form rich silty fens the people of the market town are still described as *Lous mango escarpas*, or carp-eaters. But it was not to eat carp that a party of burghers from Narbonne entered the town in 1209, led by an archbishop of whom even the Pope could declare that he knew no other God but money. They had come to Cape-stang to promise the obedience of their city. Rather than suffer the fate of Béziers they would themselves hand over their heretics to the crusaders. With that single episode, which was no fault of the people of Capestang, the town disappears from history to lead a life of wine-dressing and farming and marketing disturbed only from time to time during the ensuing seven and a half centuries by the Black Death, wars religious, wars national or international, and the ravages of *Phylloxera*.

Our arrival at Capestang coincided with market day, and we found that the church tower had learned a way of joining in the commerce and earning its keep. There was no chiming of church bells — and for this we were thankful, for the continental idea of bell-ringing is to toll all the bells at once, regardless of time or harmony, as though driving out the devil. Instead, four loud speakers broadcast pop music over each quarter of the town and a voice would then break in with an announcement.

'*Hallo, hallo!* Monsieur Cruzy the clockmaker of Béziers is in the square, close to the fountain. He has clocks, watches, jewels of great purity but of an unbelievable cheapness. And today alone he offers to the people of Capestang the unrepeatable bargain of watches at a discount. Hurry yourselves and visit Monsieur Cruzy, the clockmaker of Béziers.'

Treacly music would waft down for a minute or two, and then it would be the turn of Madame Gabbarat the specialist in corsetry, or of Monsieur Pujol the hatter from a nearby town. Each had his wares proclaimed to the winds in a wattage which stirred the jackdaws in their ecclesiastical niches, rattled the bars of the church windows and even drowned the scissoring of the cicadas in the trees below the church and the cricket trilling from within the houses.

The country through which Riquet laid his canal was usually dry but it could be subject to heavy rains, and for this reason he was persuaded to keep the course well above the level of adjacent rivers. But the canal itself received the waters of various brooks in addition to the feeders cut from the Black Mountain, and weirs and spillways and sluices were provided in great numbers so that surplus water could be got rid of. Even then, flooding was such a menace that the great military engineer Vauban diverted more than fifty brooks in 1688, providing culverts or siphons for the water to pass under the canal instead of through it. As a result, it was some-times short of water in drought periods, but an exceptionally violent storm could still flood the canal and inundate the fields alongside. In 1766 a tremendous cloudburst raised the water level in the long pound by six or seven feet.

Where the canal lay in a dip this merely caused a flood, but at Capestang the course ran round the contour of a gentle hill. Here the water pouring over the bank and into the town washed away the side of the canal itself, and more than ten thousand labourers worked for two months to plug the breach and restore navigation. This was always one of the dangers of the long pound — if it slid, it slid magnificently.

The long pound was eventually fitted with two siphons like those in a public lavatory, where the tank fills and then discharges completely as soon as it is full. At Capestang and also at Ventenac further up the line, siphons built of stone were inserted in the canal, the bends some eighteen inches above the normal water level. An eighteen-inch flood would start the siphons, and the entire contents of the canal would then be discharged into spill-ways until there was only two feet of water left. At that level air pipes would be exposed, the siphons would be interrupted, and the canal could refill again.

There seemed no end to the wonders devised by Riquet or Vauban, or their successors, but as we moved westward along the waterway we appreciated Riquet's trees most of all. *Soulèu de jun, rouino degun*, says the native of Occitania, and even if the June sun does indeed ruin nobody a little shade may do no harm. We had never been ones to huddle away from the sun, but a stationary boat can become so baked in the midday of the Midi that the joints open, the timbers crack and groan, and even the steering wheel is too hot to touch. One of the great delights of the long pound was that the canal, twisting along its contour, headed in every direction successively from north-east through west to south-east and back again, and the shadows of the great planes would often cut across the water to bring us a sense of coolness.

Twelve miles beyond Capestang we came suddenly upon a junction of waterways. On the port side a channel led away, dead straight and dropping sedately down a series of locks set like the steps of a baronial castle between a magnificent double line of cypresses. Turning into this waterway we worked away at the lock-gates of five steps in succession to enter the canal village of Salleles.

This was the course which Riquet intended to follow when he first drew up his scheme of 1664, but it was much later that the Canal de Jonction was cut. As a junction canal it must be joining something, and in fact it was dug to connect the Canal du Midi with the River Aude at a point where once the small port of Gaillousti stood — a place merely for unloading salt gathered from the marshes. This salt was brought on small boats along a water-way which reached the further shore of the Aude at a point not far away, and which we were now to enter, after swinging into the Aude, running upstream a short way to avoid the shoals hidden below its pinkish surface, and turning to run down the opposite shore.

Another two hours brought us to the lock of Gua, at the outskirts of Narbonne. A laden tanker was creeping round the bend towards us, and it was curious to reflect that three hundred years earlier the craft might have been a shallow lighter with a cargo of salt, hauled from the bank by manpower. Earlier still it would have been a Roman craft, for since crossing the Aude we were in the Canal de la Robine, a waterway dug by the Romans, and in use along much of its course ever since.

Under footbridges and along the centre of an elongated village green we pursued our way into the city until we reached the town lock, set among a jumble of old houses which looked as though they might at any moment collapse into the canal. The *Commodore* waited patiently in the pen while one of us set off down an alley in search of the lock-keeper. At last she was lowered to the town reach, to disappear under the vaulting where the course was spanned from side to side by a bridge which bore a double line of ancient houses, an Old London Bridge in miniature. The bridge was the Pons Vetus, the street between the houses was once the Domitian Way, the highway built in the second century B.C. to serve all the ports and coastal towns from the Rhône delta to Gibraltar.

The Roman road was now carrying motor traffic, and the Roman bridge still held on its broad back the weight of a row of houses. When she emerged from beneath them into the hot evening sun the *Commodore* could swing round to draw in at a quay where, two thousand years before her, a Roman admiral's barge might have pulled in to the wharf where the rich merchants of Narbo Martius were preparing the cargoes of cheese and wine, hemp and flax, for shipment to the Tiber and the city of the Emperors.

VII

Narbonne — the canal game — crossing of the Cesse —
post-boats of the Midi — Homps — Carcassonne of the
troubadours — the betrayal of Raymond-Roger — the
victims of Bram — crime on the canal — the Commodore
comes to Castelnaudary

'Narbonne the glorious-pasted' extended a welcome to the *Commodore*. At least, that was the sobriquet attached to the city in the English edition of the leaflet issued by the municipal bureau of information. In our simplicity we thought this to be a reference to the effect wrought upon the citizens by the wines of the district, but to clear up any doubts we asked for the French version too. And there it was, *Narbonne au glorieux passé.*

Pasted though the place may be, little remains of the Roman city which once had Mark Antony as its distinguished governor. Here and there an odd column has been brought to light, and one of the churches has been converted into a museum where Roman sculptures survive by the hundred. One of them even shows a pleasant representation of a Roman fishing-boat with a lateral rudder in the form of a broad oar. But there is no amphitheatre, no temple or triumphal gate. Narbonne was too often sacked for its glories to have survived.

And yet the appearance of the place is dramatic. It is theatrical, like a set for an opera. Below the Roman bridge a chorus of women wash their laundry on the public steps — at least we presumed this was what they were doing, although the rusty red of the water of the Robine caused us to wonder whether perhaps they were not laundering the clothes but dyeing them. Above the quayside walk, other women sit to sell flowers, or just to gossip, and across the water a dozen more squat under coloured umbrellas along a line of trees which leads to the corner of the town hall square. The square itself has all the appearance of an imaginative backcloth, for one side of it is ranged by the three stolid, squared, and fortified towers of the palace of the Archbishops of Narbonne. Most formidable of all is the great keep nearest the Robine, and for six centuries it has frowned down upon the shipping at the quay. During our visit the concourse of ships consisted only of the *Commodore*, but this gave us all the more opportunity to select her berth to the greatest satisfaction of our senses. The nose demanded a mooring upstream of the discharge of the public conveniences, and the eye was more than satisfied with the view from the hatch, which looked upward and over the river to the four defensive corner turrets from which in earlier times the archiepiscopal bowmen might have drawn a bolt upon us if they had suspected our intentions to be overtly hostile.

Through one of the strong gateways one enters the trap of a battlemented and fortified street, leading to the buildings of the palace itself, with its two rounded guard towers topped with coolie hats. Nobly these strong-points sustain and protect the whole range of buildings from attack at the rear, and even an archbishop must have felt secure. No archbishop now lives in this splendid place but one can imagine his eminence of earlier times seated in the audience chamber with an important personage from the Vatican.

There would have been talk, no doubt, of the fact that even now, four and a half centuries after the burning of the last of the

Albigensian thousands, heresies obstinately reappeared, actively encouraged by the wayward lost sheep of the Protestant fold. There were intrigues and power politics in every see, and only the unexpectedly good vintage was a sign that better things could still happen. That, and the opening of the Canal Royal, so soon after the death of poor Monsieur le Baron de Bonrepos.

'And talking of the canal, Monsieur the Legate, perhaps you will join me in a game. We shall navigate from Toulouse to the new harbour of Sète, over a bottle of Corbières. You agree?'

The Archbishop of Narbonne, His Eminence the Right Reverend Lord Cardinal de Bonzy, rang the bell and a servant set before him the jug of wine and the game. It was a kind of snakes-and-ladders with no hazards. The board showed the feeder channels dug by Riquet, and there was a space for every lock and aqueduct all the way from one end to the other of the waterway.

Each cast the dice in turn, the legate choosing to start from the Mediterranean end.

'A six and a two, my lord. That brings my ship to the famous tunnel of Malpas, I think.'

The Archbishop took up the dice. 'A five and a four. Congratulate me, Monsieur the Legate. In only two turns my ship has reached the basin of Naurouze, the very top level of the canal. You will need to look to your tow-rope or I shall beat you to the half-way mark at the lock of Villepinte.'

The Archbishop's game-board was shown to us in the offices of the *Ponts et Chaussées* at Toulouse, where letters from Colbert and P.-P. Riquet and Louis XIV are filed away on the shelves almost as though they were the last year's traffic returns. It is reproduced on pages 140–1 of this book, and the *Commodore* is greatly indebted to Monsieur Blaquière, archivist of the administration of the Haute–Garonne *département*, who kindly restored the playing surface so that it could be photographed and made available to her friends.

At the back of the palace is the cathedral of St Just, or what little of it exists. Not that it was bombed or burned, but owing to oversight on the part of the architect or an overweaning confidence on the part of the Archbishop in the decay of things secular, the

edifice was unfortunately begun so close to the fortified city walls
that when the choir was completed it already reached to the
ramparts and no further growth was possible. The pillars and
vaulting remain incomplete, all tailored for the moment when the
city should crumble into dust and leave space for the cathedral to
grow a nave as any proper see would wish, but for the last seven
hundred years Narbonne has obstinately refused to crumble and
the poor cathedral has been thwarted. Yet it is well worth the
climb to the roof, just to enjoy the view across the old town with
some of its streets too narrow for modern transport to pass.
Beyond the canal the still older churches of St-Paul-Serge and
Lamourguier stand up boldy amid the sun-bleached roofs, and to
the south the Robine leads out through the salt marshes to the sea,
past the curious medieval village of Gruissan clustered around a
ruined fort on a knoll in the lagoon.

While at Narbonne we needed to tank up with fresh water. In
France this was often a problem, for taps were rare, and usually
we would seek out a quayside toilet and set to work at dead of night
to dismantle the plumbing with our pipe wrenches and connect
one of the joints to a hose. This favourite trick of ours usually
resulted in the lavatories being sprayed from ceiling to floor with
gushing water, but we had formed the opinion that few French
Dames and certainly no *Messieurs* were the worse for the treatment.
I doubt if the *Dames* at Mâcon on the Saône had ever been so clean
as they were by the time we had finished tanking.

The Narbonne toilets proved however to be so ancient and their
pipes so corroded that I dared not touch one with a wrench. But
fair caravans frequented the space by the bandstand and a stand-
pipe was there, right to the bank. It had no proper tap — the key
being no doubt in the keeping of some municipal janitor — so once
again we got to work with the wrenches and produced what looked
like an oil gusher. We let it gush, too, for it was our only defence
against the mosquitoes which swarmed up from the reeds to bite
anyone within range. Then, with tanks full, our legs covered with
bites and the decks with drowned mosquitoes, we reconnected the
plumbing and left as quickly as we could, blowing cigar smoke in all
directions. Through the Roman bridge and back to the Aude, and

up the flight of locks leading to the long pound the *Commodore* plugged ahead in the boiling heat of sheer sunshine, and at each lock we bathed.

Cool and refreshing though it was, the bathing was forced upon us. Many miles ahead of us the maintenance men were proceeding westward along the main line of the canal, scything and slashing the reeds along the banks and leaving those swathes which fell into the water to be wafted along by the current. Much of the debris came down the Canal de Jonction, and at almost every lock there was a rich green haystack of weed and reed laboriously raked out by the keepers — and by ourselves, for often we could not open the gates at all until a ton or two had been dragged out. At the head of each lock there would be a green belt anything up to fifty yards in breadth, and through this the *Commodore* had to force her way. By the time she had reached the further side of it the propeller would be seized tight, and steering was impossible because of the herbage round the rudders. If necessary we poled ourselves clear, then leapt overboard with saw knives held in our teeth like pirates, and got to work under the stern.

It is remarkable how high a tensile strength the leaves of ordinary sedge reeds have. Twined round the propeller shaft they could defeat all the *chevaux* we had aboard, and they were strung too tight to sever with the fingers. But a bread knife is a wonderful weapon for weeds and we soon became extremely skilled at freeing the screw and rudders. We had only bathed six times before we reached the main canal again, turned to the left, and found a suitable bend where we could moor in the shade of Riquet's giant trees and where we might bathe in a more leisurely fashion through the heat of the day.

The point we had chosen was just before the aqueduct over the River Cesse, a splendid three-arched and confident bridge of stone bearing all the marks of the grandeur and determination of the great engineer Sébastien Vauban, who designed it after Riquet's death. France is littered with fortresses built by this master of defence and bastion, and the construction of the 200-foot long aqueduct over the Cesse was one of the rare occasions when he let himself design anything but military works. But Vauban was an enthusiast for the canal, and if today the barges are still passing over his mighty bridge that is something of which a historian of engineering can be proud.

Looking down from the towpath we could see that the river sixty feet below us was for the most part shoaled and shallow, but beneath the aqueduct it was deep and clear. We made our way down for another bathe on the lower deck, and found two boys busily hunting something in the shallows. Each had an ordinary table fork lashed to a stick, and they would move through the river overturning the stones as they went. Suddenly they would jab, and jab again, then set off to splash after whatever it was that had escaped.

We soon discovered what their quarry was, for one of the lads had a piece of wire hooked on to his belt, and from it dangled the corpses of half a dozen eels. They were not large — in fact the creatures were small enough for us to ask with genuine curiosity whether they were to be eaten. Yes, indeed, the boys assured us. The eels made an excellent dish, they said, but in what style they were to be cooked we did not hear. After the boys had left we prospected down the river, turning up the stones as we went. We had no desire to kill the poor creatures, of which there were plenty, but just to try to catch them in a bucket. Yet eels are not so easily trapped. The moment they are exposed they can insinuate themselves into a crevice and vanish completely. We caught none, and contented ourselves instead with pulling wild onions from the canal bank to garnish our salad.

A mile or more beyond the Cesse aqueduct is Le Somail, a place which did not exist before the canal was built and hardly exists now, for it is merely a quay. It was established as a useful loading point for the produce of the area around, and later it came into its own as a passenger depot.

Before the birth of the Sète–Bordeaux railway, which appropriated to itself the passenger traffic between Marseille and the Atlantic coast, the management of the Canal du Midi operated an excellent service of horse-drawn fly-boats which connected at the Sète end of the line with ships to Mediterranean ports, and with the trains to Marseille. At the western end the traveller could change in the canal basin of Toulouse to a fly-boat of the Garonne lateral canal, which in turn had *correspondance* with a river steamer at Agen, on board which the journey to Bordeaux was completed. What with this, and the voyage down the Bassin de Thau, behind the steamer *Colbert* or the *Riquet*, or the *Vauban*, it must have been a splendid journey. The boats were divided into three classes, somewhat after the fashion of the American canal boats, and they were literally packet-boats, for they carried the mail. At the quay of Le Somail they would draw in for a moment to hand over the passengers and mail for Narbonne.

When the post boats were first introduced, thirty-six vessels were needed. The canal authorities decided that time would be saved if the boats did not pass through any of the flights of two or more locks, and of these there were twenty-two. A passenger from Toulouse to Agde would certainly have a speedy journey behind the horse-teams, but during the course of it he would have to change ships more than a score of times, jumping ashore at the top of every lock-flight, stumbling down the towpath with his bags, and boarding the next vessel below the bottom gates. It was healthy exercise and an ingenious mode of travel.

The thirty-six ships with their relays of horse-teams and their postillions brought plenty of life and bustle to the canal, but there was not much profit to be had from the business. Later a smaller number of craft achieved the journey at a slightly lesser speed but more conveniently, passing through the locks like any other boat. The only exception was at Béziers, where the long staircase and the awkward traverse of the Orb were not worth the effort.

Every morning a boat would leave Toulouse, stopping for midday dinner or for an overnight halt at prearranged places which had suitable inns and arriving at the top of the Fonséranes locks about noon on the fourth day. The passengers then drove into Béziers for lunch, and afterwards embarked on another packet on the further side of the Orb, to reach Agde by evening.

Before running to its end at the lock of Argens, the long pound led us close to the village of Ventenac, and the *Commodore* had the privilege of flying over the Répudre on an aqueduct. She had been over many other aqueducts, and that of the Cesse lay only an hour astern, but the crossing of the little River Répudre took her over an arch which in its day was considered an almost incredible feat of engineering. Just as Malpas was the first canal tunnel ever to be bored, so the aqueduct at Ventenac is the oldest in the world designed to carry ships and a stone reminds the boatman that it is not only the first but was an invention due to the genius of P.-P. Riquet himself. From end to end the Canal du Midi is a succession of bold and imaginative inventions, and if many of them have since become commonplace it is an indication of the brilliance of Riquet that with neither training nor ability in mathematics he could see how to pierce a hill, bridge a valley, or provide an unending supply of water, and go ahead and do it. What is more, his ideas actually worked.

By now we were gradually leaving the dry and rocky desert lands behind us, and with every mile the country was becoming richer, the hills more wooded. Occasionally we could look down across the fields or vineyards to the Aude on our left, but the waterway led us through no villages at all until, a few locks beyond the end of the long pound, we climbed upstairs into the town of Homps. It is easier to spell this place than to speak it, for when properly pronounced it sounds like the groan uttered by a cricket fan when his favourite batsman is clean bowled. But Homps is a favourite with the bargemen, for it has a long and broad stone quay against which several can lie whilst night approaches and a glass or two of the famous Corbières wine is taken in the evening sunshine at a table outside the simple inn at the end of the row of quayside houses. With its wine barges lying at the wall and the families taking their dinner under the awnings on deck, Homps is a place of slow-motion activity until the first barge gets under way at six o'clock in the morning in order to be at the next lock by half past.

Three miles short of Carcassonne the canal rose steeply up a trio of locks to leap the River Fresquel and turn sharply away into a course different from that originally dug by the crowd of soldiers and labourers who laid down the waterway under the orders of Riquet. The fact is that the Baron had cut the city out of the itinerary. Considering that Carcassonne is much the largest and most important place between Béziers and Toulouse it may seem odd that Riquet decided to lay his canal near it but just out of reach. In fact he had his own reasons. By the time the canal was well under way the good Baron of Bonrepos was finding himself increasingly short of money, for Colbert was a man of such precision and neatness that he always demanded a full and immediate return of the taxes Riquet collected for the Inland Revenue and often pressed him very hard financially whilst encouraging him over the canal project. In need of funds, Riquet approached the Carcassonne council for subsidies; but as they could see that the canal was progressing and was likely soon to reach their door without their having to spend a copper coin, they prevaricated and then graciously declined. This seems to have been the factor which drove Riquet to re-route the canal on the other side of the hill to the north of the town, along an easier course. And if he chose thus to requite the burghers one can hardly blame him. He even remained deaf to the entreaties of the Bishop of Carcassonne, who was most active in trying to have the line laid through the town.

Hardly had the canal been opened when Carcassonne found itself out on a limb. Bargemasters, merchants, the council and the bishop and dean and chapter all wanted something done about it. After one hundred and four years of discussion the works were begun, an aqueduct was built to carry the canal over the Fresquel, and a deep cutting was excavated to bring the waterway in and out of the town. A good port was also dug. This immense amount of navvying would have been very expensive, but by good fortune there was a plentiful supply of Prussians captured at the battle of Jena. They were set to work on the canal, and the product of their toil was used to fill the city moats and build up the roads and promenades on the outskirts.

The cut dug by these hard-worked men starts at the flight of locks by the Fresquel, and this point — or more correctly the next bridge — is known as Pont Rouge. We had a particular errand at this place, for a master and his wife from the Hall School in Hampstead had left Suburbia to settle in the Fresquel valley and build up a market garden. As the *Commodore* climbed up the stairs we enquired of the lock-keeper where we might find Monsieur and Madame Howe.

To our surprise he had never heard of them. We told him they were English and actually lived there, at Pont Rouge, a place of no more than twenty inhabitants as we could see for ourselves. Monsieur Howe lived within 200 metres of the locks, we had been told. Surely Monsieur Howe and Madame could not be entirely unknown.

The keeper thought for a while and asked us to give a minute description of the man we sought. When we said that the man we were looking for was a schoolteacher recognition dawned on his face.

'*Ah, c'est le Monsieur Auve!*' And we heard that Monsieur Auve was a *grand professeur*, *un homme très très propre*, and verging on the *formidable*. He lived indeed very close to the lock, down past the stone in the hedge which commemorated the forward-looking enterprise of the Carcassonne burghers in having second thoughts and taking the canal over the Fresquel towards the town.

The Howes were delighted to have visitors, including a former boy of the school in my son Hugh, and a governor in myself. Certainly nobody had sought them out by boat before, and as they had never yet been on the canal beside which they had lived for a year or two we invited them up to the locks to accompany us on the voyage into Carcassonne.

Our progress was majestic. In the Howes we might have had the President and his Madame, to judge by the deference shown to us by people passing along the road in their cars or in the local bus. Monsieur le Professeur Auve was known to everybody — as well he might have been, for he seemed to have established a great reputation as a teacher of English in many schools around Carcassonne. This meant working the acres and packing the produce for the wholesalers before school began, but he and his wife were thriving on living an unorthodox and interesting life in such an enchanting place as the valley at Pont Rouge.

As we passed under the Pont Rouge itself we noticed that it was white, and could never have been red. There might, of course, have been an earlier bridge, but that seemed unlikely. The Howes told us that the locals alleged it to have taken its name from the quantities of blood spilled over it — and this not in battle but

merely in car crashes, because the road was a main one and there was a blind right-angle approach at either end. To judge by the squeals of brakes and the squeaks of hot tyres as we passed beneath, this explanation might have been the correct one, we thought.

The Howes were as excited as ourselves with the breathtaking approach to Carcassonne, for the canal gave us a grandstand view across the valley of the Aude to the astonishing medieval fortress set on a hill of its own. Even through the binoculars it seemed quite unreal, a coloured illustration from a children's book about princesses and wicked barons. For the place is intact, thanks very largely to the intelligent restoration of Viollet-le-Duc, who also renovated Narbonne. Even from a distance one can distinguish the two outer rings of walls and within them the final redoubt, the castle of the counts, standing within its own separate moat. Scores of towers peep over each other's shoulders to see who the attacker may be, and the little cathedral stands at attention, its battlements ready to shield the defenders. It needs no effort to believe that in the days before artillery it was impregnable — except by treachery. Provided, that is, that one accepts the place as being real, for there is something so enormously improbable about the existence of this fortified town now, in the twentieth century, that it appears as much of a mirage as does the Disney background of snow peaks against which it is set.

In fact Carcassonne is double, and approaching it along the canal we could look over both cities, distinct enough to be on opposite sides of the River Aude. The canal runs into the 'new' town and from the distance of its course the other city, the fortified cité, looks dreamy enough, with just a trace of the same mystery about it which hangs over Oxford when seen from a quarter where the motor works are invisible, or over Cambridge viewed on a misty June morning from Madingley Hill. And as one toils up the slope to cross the empty space of grass between the two outer circuits of walls one is not greatly surprised to discover that of all places Carcassonne is one of the richest in tales of love and heroism, of murder and hauntings.

There is the story of the troubadour Geoffroy Rudel who fell in love with a lady of Carcassonne whom he had never so much as glimpsed, but whose beauty and grace had reached his ears in a far country. The love-lorn minstrel had no other desire than to come to her, and after terrible journeyings he reached the city and fell at her feet. So great was his love for her that he could not even frame a single word of speech or song to tell her, and gazing up at her he died, of sheer adoration.

And then there was Pierre Vidal, another troubadour, whose love-sickness took a different form. His lady love was named Louve — the she-wolf, a strange name perhaps for such a beautiful creature. To her he wrote his songs of adoration, ballads which dealt with the virtues and graces of the female of *Lupus lupus* L., yet in spite of his utmost and lyrical attentions the fair Louve gave herself to another. In a final demonstration of his eternal devotion to the only lady he ever could love, Vidal became a wolf. Dressing in fresh wolf-skins procured from the hunters he let himself be chased through the woods by the wolf-hounds of the Count of Carcassonne, and when the dogs had caught him and practically torn him to pieces he had the huntsmen carry his mutilated body and lay it at the feet of the one he adored. After such selfless devotion it is disappointing to discover that Louve was not moved to take him. Perhaps she thought he was just a little bit crazy.

That Carcassonne is ancient, one cannot fail to notice. There are Gallo-Roman sections in the walls, and there are towers from the era of the Visigoths, those dark-age characters who flit in and out of history books, broadsword in hand, without ever coming to rest securely in the memory. Without doubt there was a fortress on the hill in the days of Charlemagne, and one of the troubadour tales explains prettily if improbably how the city came by its name. The great monarch invested the citadel, which was in the hands of the Infidel, and when the Saracen king fell into his hands and refused to become a Christian Charlemagne had him strangled. This was a terrible blow to the defenders, but the Saracen Queen Carcas took her husband's place and stirred the men to withstand the onslaught of the emperor.

Five long years the forces of Charlemagne encircled the be-

leaguered city, and five long years the defenders held out against
spear and arrow, famine, and lack of water. Or so it appeared, but
in fact by this time only the Queen was alive. She had made
dummies of straw, and dressing them in the clothes of the dead
defenders she propped them in the embrasures. She herself ran
round the walls from one position to another, hurling darts and
spears in the guise of a soldier, but changing hats between appearances. The soldiers of Charlemagne — simple fellows no doubt —
were thus deceived into believing that the citadel was still held by a
formidable force of Saracens, and had it not been for their belief
that the provisions would run out they would have packed up and
gone home. In fact the brave and beautiful queen had almost come
to the end of the rations, but not of her stratagems. The very last
bucket of grain she gave to a surviving piglet, and when she had
made it gorge itself to the gullet she tipped it over the battlements
so that the poor creature burst asunder before the eyes of the
emperor's troops. Again the poor fellows believed what they saw,
and when it was reported to Charlemagne that the garrison was so
well supplied that good grain could be used for rearing pigs he
ordered the siege to be raised. Soon the army was ready to start
trekking back towards France.

Carcas was no doubt relieved to see them go. And then, all of a
sudden, she felt terribly alone. Everyone in Carcassonne had long
been dead, and the emperor's men were the only people she had.
Running out from the fortress she cried after the troops, blowing a
trumpet or perhaps (as some say) ringing a bell. One of the officers
heard the call and hurried to tell Charlemagne.

'Your majesty,' he said, 'Carcas is calling.' Which being
interpreted is *Carcas sonne.*

With his customary generosity Charlemagne forgave her for
tying down his forces so long and in vain, and as Carcas was
willing to surrender the fortress and be baptized he turned back
and entered the dead city. Then, as a mark of his esteem, and so
that she might for ever be mistress of the city she had held so
bravely, immediately after her christening he presented her with
one of his most chivalrous officers as a new husband, to become the
first Count of Carcassonne.

Thus the troubadours tell their imaginative story of the naming of the city, with minstrel's licence that conveniently ignores the earlier name of Carcaso which the citadel bore long before Charlemagne. But not every tale of the troubadours is so romantic, and it is from them that some of the details have been handed down of a siege more fatal in its effects than that in the story of Carcas. For it was there, outside those splendid and confident walls, that the second hammer blow was dealt to the cause of reformation (or heresy) and thereby to freedom of religion, by the rapacious northern knights under the leadership of the unscrupulous legate Arnald-Amalric.

Only ten days after the slaughter at Béziers the fearful army of the Albigensian crusade was stopped before the intimidating walls of Carcassonne. The fortress was held by a strong garrison, commanded by Raymond-Roger de Trencavel, Viscount of Béziers and Carcassonne, a young man of only twenty-four, strong, handsome, utterly fearless and chivalrous, the ideal not only of the troubadours but of all the people of the Midi and of those who had flocked to Carcassonne to fight or die at his side. Not many weeks had passed since he had been summoned to Montpellier, where the authorities of the Church of Rome ordered him to give up the heretics, the refugees and the Jews who enjoyed freedom in his domains. Alone of all the nobles of Europe he faced them with the challenge that he would offer home and food, shelter and clothing and the defence of his own sword to all who had cause to flee, or were in want. No wonder that the young Raymond-Roger was the object of the hatred of the Legates, nor that his stand caught the imagination of the threatened people of the Languedoc.

But the Viscount was a skilled warrior as well as a hero, and when war was unleashed upon him without warning he swiftly and rightly decided that whether or not Béziers could withstand an attack it was Carcassonne that could hold up the flood tide of the invasion. Had he been at Béziers on the day of the terrible assault things might have turned out differently for that unfortunate city, but there can be no doubt that his decision to lead in person the defence of Carcassonne was the right one. He had only been there a few days when news of the fate of Béziers began to sweep across the land ahead of the invaders, and the country people fled to the stronghold, bringing with them their families but also driving their stock and hauling in great quantities of provisions.

In spite of deep wells bored in the hill, water was a serious problem for the crowd of tens of thousands of refugees which now supplemented the garrison, but of other supplies there seems to have been plenty. It soon became clear to the crusaders that there was no chance of taking the city by assault. Nor could they attempt a protracted siege, for the crusading knights were only bound to serve for forty days. And besides, Raymond-Roger himself led the most destructive sorties, laying about him with his axe to deadly effect. His troops loved him and they would have died for him, yet the prospect of their having to do so must have seemed to the attackers to be somewhat remote. Carcassonne was as secure a stronghold as any heretic could have.

Yet attack the crusaders did, and for two weeks without ceasing the onslaught continued. Raymond-Roger was always to be found where danger threatened, and as assault towers and scaling ladders were laid against the walls he himself would counter-attack and hurl the besiegers down to the ground below. Taking off his helmet he was there for all the people of Carcassonne to see, and many a woman would have died to save such a hero.

At the end of two weeks it was clearer than ever that the fortress was not going to be taken. The invaders had suffered heavy losses, and if many of the townspeople had been crushed or maimed by the stones hurled from catapults, the number of mercenaries and knights whose corpses lay in the moat, or who were dying from the terrible burns of boiling oil must have been immense. The time had come to try other means, and the legate Arnald-Amalric now invoked his moral principle that it was not necessary to keep an oath to the enemy of God. What could be easier than to ask for a parley, guarantee the young viscount safe conduct, and then seize him as a heretic?

And so the knights were persuaded to invite Raymond-Roger de Trencavel to their camp. Certainly the heroic young viscount could not have been duped by the legate himself, and probably some of his fellow nobles were deceived into inviting him in all good faith.

However that may be he was seized, and loaded with chains. Bereft of its valiant leader, the city surrendered.

Raymond-Roger was taken into the fortress and shut away in a dungeon. A few months later he 'died', as imprisoned enemies so frequently do. His wide possessions in the Languedoc were forfeited, and awarded to an eager new owner in the person of Simon de Montfort, the most brutal if sincere leader the occupying forces could have had. The great crusade had won a victory which disposed of the most dynamic leader among its opponents, and set the seal on its future success as a war of extermination.

The canal port of Carcassonne is a place for loading wine, but when the *Commodore* was there the vintage was not yet in sight and dredgers were busy deepening the basin and removing the mud which seemed to have settled in such quantities that there were few points where a barge could draw in. The sunburned dredger-men in shorts and singlets and broad panama hats sweated at the controls of the grabs and buckets, much as the sappers of the crusaders must have toiled at the walls of the *cité*. As our presence was inconvenient we left them to it, and taking our leave of the African lock-keeper we steamed out to the west through the deep cutting made by the city fathers.

For some distance our route wound to and fro among the hills, following the erratic valley of the Fresquel and sometimes meandering for several miles between locks. By evening we had reached the lock of Beteille, thirteen miles from the city, and after another bathe to clear the screw and rudders we moored for the night. Never had we seen the snows of the Pyrénées more clearly, and on this evening the peaks of the tiny mountain state of Andorra stood out pink in the glow of the western sun. Andorra, we realized, was one of the very few countries of Europe which the *Commodore* could never hope to enter in person, a frustration afforded also by San Marino and Liechtenstein, though not by Monaco or Luxembourg. And for that matter, Andorra is as inaccessible by railway too, for there is no such thing within its borders. The country can only be approached by road or on foot, and the pass which leads in by the Port d'Envalira on the French side zig-zags through the narcissi and gentians, primulas and anemones, at a height of 8,000 feet. On horseback or by car the place is approachable, but not even a canoe would be a small enough boat with which to penetrate the icy torrents of the Andorran heights.

As we went on our way towards Toulouse we were following the trail of destruction wrought by Simon de Montfort in his zeal to be the scourge of God, laid upon the enemies of the Church. Béziers, Carcassonne, and now Bram were on our route, and we were up to the lock of Bram shortly after seven in the morning. The little town lay over a rise and out of sight, but the name is famous on account of Simon de Montfort's treatment of it. He had resolved to subdue the Languedoc by terror, and when the peaceful community refused to hand over its heretics he attacked it, and after three days broke down the defences. The garrison consisted of rather more than one hundred men, and Simon ordered that they should have their noses and lips cut off, and their eyes gouged out. Only one man he graciously left with a single eye, so that he might lead his fellows to another town and strike panic into the hearts of its defenders when they saw the kind of man they had to treat with in Simon de Montfort, the new Viscount of Béziers and Carcassonne. That such a sight would fill people with terror is certain, but it was actions such as these more than theological disputations which aroused the hatred of the people of the Languedoc and turned the war into a struggle to the death, without mercy for any.

Beyond Bram some of the locks have intriguing names. There is the *écluse de la Criminelle*, but we were unable to discover just who this wicked woman might be. The good lady who looked after the lock merely expressed the opinion that it might have been a poisoner, or a murderess, but nobody seemed to know. Nor did the engineers at Toulouse when I later asked them, though they had in their files the records of another *criminelle*, but one whose deeds were not immortalized in a lock. In fact there were two women involved in the dreadful offence, and a legal notice dated 1779 declared that Marguerite Journet, of Cordes in the Albigeois, was sentenced to six years' confinement, and that Hypolite Collongues was outlawed. The trial was held before the *juge châtelain du Canal de Jonction des Mers en Languedoc*, and the offence of which the women were found guilty was stealing and receiving washing taken from one of the public washeries on the canal, just such a washing-place as is still in use in many places today.

Both the accused were washerwomen, though Hypolite was also described as a prostitute. Yet she had much the lighter sentence, for the unhappy Marguerite had to suffer still more. Before she was taken away to her six years in prison she was to be delivered to the proper authority, who would place her in the pillory for two hours on each of three days, with a notice on her back and on her front bearing the words *Voleuse de Linge*. Theft on the property of the canal was severely frowned upon.

The *criminelle* of the lock of that name cannot have been either of these unfortunate women, for the lock bore its title from the moment it was constructed. Perhaps one of the women employed on the works pushed another one into a paddle hole, but there is evidently no record. The next lock is that of La Peyruque, but on the Archbishop's canal game it is spelt more nearly in the usual fashion, and one can only assume that when bowing his flowery respects to the Baron of Bonrepos one of the Royal Commissioners dropped his wig into the water.

Next is the *écluse de Guerre*, and we were confidently informed that this had to do with a fight against the Duke of Wellington's forces, but here the keeper was wrong. It had the same name more than a century earlier, and one is free to imagine a fight between navvy gangs as more likely than a long-nursed resentment over some skirmish of Albigensian times. More probably the recollection of a fight involving the English is correct, but the date wrong, for in the Hundred Years War that wicked nation was indeed engaged in burning and sacking, besieging and wrecking all along the valley.

Then comes the lock of St Sernin — Saint Saturninus, the first bishop of Toulouse who was probably martyred under the Decian persecution, but whom legend places still further back in time as a disciple of John the Baptist and a companion of St Peter in Rome. The story tells that when Saturninus was passing the capitol at Toulouse the portents failed and the augurs could get no results.

Furious, the pagan priests seized Sernin and demanded that he should sacrifice with them, and when he refused to do so the idols fell at his feet, shattered in a thousand pieces. For this, Sernin was tied to the tail of a bull which was about to be sacrificed, and dragged round the town by the enraged animal. He is commemorated in the splendid church of St Sernin in Toulouse, but it is pleasant to think that he has a lock also.

We were climbing steadily now, and another six steps in quick succession brought the *Commodore* to the foot of the ladder of St Roch, the young man of Montpellier who, it is said, was born with a red cross marked on the left side of his belly, an undoubted sign that he was destined to be a healer. In fact it was St Roch who first broke through the custom of burning the clothes of a leper and driving the sufferer into the country as an outlaw, sworn to speak to no man down wind, to visit neither church, nor fair nor market. After years spent in tending the lepers in the Languedoc he returned to his native town, and when asked who he might be he answered only that he was a poor pilgrim. Tragically, this led to his being thought a suspicious character, perhaps a spy. He was arrested and imprisoned, and five years later he died in gaol without ever having disclosed his identity.

The ladder is a flight of four locks leading up through a magnificent avenue of stately planes to the port of Castelnaudary. In former times the passengers on the fly-boats had forty minutes or more to wait while their ship ascended or descended the steps, and on Sundays they were all disembarked and a mass was put on for them in the canal-side chapel of St Roch, to fit the timetable of the post-boats.

The locks are now electrified, and in only twenty-eight minutes the *Commodore* had climbed to the top, to enter one of the most beautiful canal basins in the world. Once again the genius of Riquet can be seen, for here he had no long pound to take up the shock of the quantity of water used to bring a boat up the flight.

Instead he made his port basin so immense that it would serve as a suitable reservoir, and in fact it is more than a mile in circumference. One side has quays with trees to shade the waiting barges, and across the water the town of Castelnaudary clusters on a hill and spills down to the edge of a basin which is as large as a lake.

It was in 1681 that twenty-three boats were hauled into the basin in solemn procession. Commissioner d'Aguesseau was aboard, and with him was a whole orchestra of harps and violins to play martial music. As they moved out over the water the convoy was met by another flotilla, that of the Archbishop Bonzy of Narbonne, which had come up the steps of St Roch. With him were several other bishops, and they ranged themselves behind the Archbishop as he solemnly blessed the waters of the Grand Bassin de Castelnaudary.

And it is pleasant to imagine that after the official business had been dealt with, the Archbishop drew alongside the barge of the Royal Commissioner and invited Monsieur d'Aguesseau to step aboard. Afloat on the basin they would play a hand of the Archbishop's new canal game, while the orchestra played a suitable solemn musick.

VIII

*The museum of Cucurrou — Laurac and Guirauda —
Dominic Guzman — a mission of reason — the Montagne
Noire — forty miles of hydraulics — the St Ferréol dam —
the Stones of Naurouze — the fate of the Languedoc*

At Castelnaudary the southern shore of Riquet's giant basin is provided with a long quay, generously shaded by trees. It is so pleasant a place to stay awhile that one has a feeling that the town on its hill across the water must have been built merely to delight the eye of the bargee. But on closer acquaintance the place turns out to be curious rather than beautiful, and in the words of a song of the Languedoc *ni Castelnaudary es pa Carcassonno*. It is certainly not Carcassonne, for that fortress city is unique indeed.

Perhaps the town was a fine one before it was sacked by the wicked English in the fourteenth century, but without the Canal du Midi and the splendid works of Riquet it would today be dull. It suffers much from being on the main lorry route from Bordeaux and Toulouse to Marseille, and almost every other house along the main street seems to have been converted to a heavy haulage garage, tyre depot, spray shop or truck-drivers' rest. The remainder offer to those who can be induced to stop for a moment the culinary specialities of the town. The *cassoulet* is an unappetising reminder of school-day beans and pork, and the others are even worse. I hope the worthy Castelnaudarians will not mind my confessing that after one bite at an *alléluia* and an attempt to gnaw a *gloria* we were obliged to feed both these strangely named delicacies to the swans and hope the birds had stronger digestive systems than ourselves.

We happened to read that a mile or two outside the town we should find the magnificent park and château of the ancient lords of Cucurrou, containing the splendid Museum of Natural History founded by Dr Ancely, so we set off one afternoon to walk out from the town and along the edges of rich fields of corn towards a copse which was pointed out to us as being the Cucurrou domain. Certainly there were traces of what might once have been ornamental pathways curving through the neglected undergrowth, but all we found in the way of a mansion was a small farm, one end of which had little corner turrets. Two men with long-tined forks were throwing up straw from a wain towards the doorway of a loft, where a third was catching it. The catcher was an old peasant, but one of the pitchfork men appeared to be perhaps the bailiff, and nodding towards him we advanced to the doorway beside the cart to ring the bell. Probably it was not connected, but that did not matter. The hay-pitching stopped, and the burly bailiff asked us what we wanted.

Although no place could have looked less like a Museum of Natural History we said that we wished to see the collections. The men looked at each other in surprise and the bailiff asked who had sent us. We tried to explain that we had come on our own initiative but he cut us off with a friendly wave of his hand. If we were friends of Monsieur Mordagne, he said, that was enough.

We had no idea who Monsieur Mordagne might be, but evidently he was a figure whose acquaintance we should be unwise to deny. Not that we had the chance, for the farm-hand on the cart was sent running to the back door of the house to call out that some *amis* had been sent by Monsieur Mordagne so that they might view the birds. He beckoned us to follow him, then left us to await the arrival of a lady of middle age who welcomed us inside without hesitation or enquiry and led the way across the stone-paved hall towards a staircase with a splendid mahogany bannister. In spite of the dust and the peeling plaster we could see that this had once been a place of some style.

Few people ever came to the house, the lady told us, and she did not live upstairs. There was no need to. The house was large enough, and there were no servants these days.

Our companion was, we presumed, perhaps the last of the Cucurrous. Obviously she was what Burke would have classified as Landed Gentry, a mixture of Old Girtonian and County Hunt and farmer. At the same time we could see that things were not what they once had been, for dust lay over the stairs, cobwebs hung in the corners, and altogether the place had the air of slow but relentless decay.

Turning a double corner into an upstairs passage she led us on, and we noticed that blinds or curtains shut out all but the most insistent rays of the bright light outside. Nothing could have been less like a museum, and for a moment I had a sensation that we were to be confronted with something weird and horrible, perhaps with the bones of the ancient lords of Cucurrou mummified where they died, or the corpses of mistresses strangled by jealous spouses, or of wayward daughters walled up alive with their unwanted infants. Or perhaps the bodies were hidden and were those of victims murdered just for the fun of the game, visitors like ourselves. There was a sweet and sickly smell of decay, and though I tried to assure myself that this was nothing worse than a dead rat or two the frequent brushing of cobwebs on the face as we groped our way forward rippling the dust on the walls with our fingers, gave a sinister tone to the adventure.

Our companion drew up outside a door. 'Here is the museum,' she announced. She drew out a bunch of keys and rustled through them. When she had unlocked the room she led us into such complete and unrelieved darkness as one might find in a laboratory darkroom. For a moment I seriously wondered whether this could be as it seemed, or whether some sudden lesion had affected my optic nerves.

'Follow me,' her voice said from somewhere close behind us. And then, 'We are there.'

We had no idea whether we were in a great hall, or a room of moderate size, except that the sound of our guide's voice did not float away into space as it would have done in any very large chamber. It was clear that we were in the museum, however unlike it was to any idea of one we might have.

'Yes,' she continued. 'It was the doctor who made the collection. It was his life's work — just to amuse himself, you know. He must have been a rich man, a great man. But all that is past now. It was very beautiful once, but people do not care for those things nowadays. When the doctor died it just stayed as it was. It has never been touched. From year to year nobody ever sees it.'

'No,' I said sympathetically, though acutely aware that I myself could see absolutely nothing. I moved one foot cautiously forward, for there was still the feeling that in spite of the gentility and chat of our hostess the whole thing was some sort of trap. An innocent phrase tossed into a guide-book, and every now and again some foolish tourist would be lured to the isolated house in the woods, led up the stairs, conducted into a place of total darkness, and then quietly murdered and robbed. Dr Ancely's museum, if it existed at all, was probably a sinister cache of dismembered bodies. Not all the assurances printed in the front of a British passport would be worth much in these circumstances, I reflected.

'Do not move,' the woman's voice went on. 'It is safer so. Wait just a moment until I find the handle.'

After a moment of fumbling there came the clang of a heavy steel bar against wood, but instead of a trapdoor opening beneath our feet to drop us into some sword-filled dungeon shaft the room was flooded with light. Blinking in the brightness we saw that our companion was swinging back the tall and solid double shutters and as the sunlight streamed in we discovered that we were in a room some fifteen feet in length and no more than six in breadth, the wall of which was one long glass-fronted cabinet. Inside it stood a great array of birds large and small, mostly European but with a few exotic species, some of them on perches and others on plinths, a few on lichen-clad branches of trees. Faded labels identified them, and beneath many of them a little pyramid of mouldering feathers showed what dress had a century ago adorned their now baring heads. Many of the once beautiful creatures looked for all the world as though they had been scalped.

'The light is bad for them, that is why I keep them in the dark,' our hostess explained. 'Even then . . . '.

She opened the glass door, and an almost overpowering smell of dry decomposition flooded outwards. She picked up the little torso of a creature which, from its size and bill shape, I took to have been a hummingbird. It had fallen from its perch, the leg joints having rotted through. A head lay all alone on the floor of the show-case, a

large head which evidently belonged to a bittern, for a handsome
bird of that species leaned headless against the back wall, like some
fearful relic of the Revolution. The woman took up the skull and
pressed it over the dry vertebrae so that the bird was intact again,
if shrunken in height.

'It is a fine collection,' we said rather lamely, trying not to
breathe too deeply.

'Yes.' She shut the cabinet again. 'It decays, of course.'

'Of course.'

'The doctor had no family. The house was sold, and the new
owners were not interested in the museum. Not everyone is, you
know.'

'No.'

She pulled the shutters over the windows again and we groped
our way back towards the stairs.

'I do not have many visitors,' she said as we descended to the
hall. 'In a whole year perhaps there are none. You must see the
chapel of the house.'

The chapel had long lost its doors. Probably they had been used
for firewood. The windows were broken and boarded up, and
where once the priest had celebrated mass for the lords of Cucurrou
there was now only an untidy stack of wire-fronted hutches. From
within them great sleek rabbits twitched their noses at us, fat
fellows in robes of grey and brown, spotted white or agouti. Their
beady eyes surveyed us unblinking as though they were a council
of legates about to question us for heresy. On the floor below them
a few muscovy ducks and some hens were scraping in the accumu-
lated inches of dirt and dung, and at our approach they came
rushing out of the door with a babble of excited chatter. No doubt
the approach of the mistress of Cucurrou was usually accompanied
by food, and the first comers were best served. A young muscovy
was one of the first to reach us, and at once it was furiously
attacked by a bunch of hens. Our hostess took it up in her arms for
safety, explaining that hens would often gang up against a duck in
this way and would sometimes manage to assassinate the bird
before the din had brought her hurrying to the rescue.

We were not to depart from the château until we had taken a

glass of brandy with the mistress and the bailiff, whilst the old peasant and the hand took some watered red wine. We sat in what must once have been the servants' hall, and we had not long been there when the door creaked open and an aged woman came in, wrinkled and dressed in black, her tall body bent as though she was continually seeking something on the ground. This she indeed was, for she now carried two sticks, the result of an afternoon spent — like all other afternoons — gleaning firewood in the copse. Slowly she began to push them into the grate, and as she did so she gave an overwhelming impression of having done just that same thing for centuries past. Probably she was only in her late nineties, though she looked very much older. We stood up and wished her good evening but the mistress of Cucurrou told us to be seated.

'Pay no attention,' she said. 'She does not notice you. She has been like that for many years.'

Probably this aged woman had once been the nurse, we thought. She was part of the house and had a permanent place in it. Though she was no longer in possession of many faculties there was something superior about her and her presence made the place curiously unreal, like the stage set for a Russian play where everyone is linked either by service or blood relationship, or from long custom, and nothing ever happens except the snap of a twig broken by an old crone who has spent half the day in collecting it. Life at Cucurrou and a thousand other little manors had probably gone on in very much this way for many years, and would still be doing so centuries later, even if visitors from other lands were as rare as some of the birds mouldering in the upstairs darkness.

Back at the canal basin we noticed that beside the bridge across the top of the lock flight a signpost directed travellers to 'the Holy Places of the Dominicans'. These are in the Lauragais, the country situated south of the canal and having for its capital the diminutive little hill-top village with the grandiose name of Laurac-le-Grand.

Laurac was capital of the region in the days when Castelnaudary was nothing more than a *castellum novum*, and occupying its private pyramid mound it was a much safer place. But artillery made hill-top sites less advantageous, and so Laurac became displaced by the newer town in the wide agricultural plain below. Today it is no more than a forgotten village of humble houses clustered on the slope below a rather dilapidated fortified church, and there is not even the sound of a car in its few narrow and twisting streets. Old women and cats sun themselves in the roadway, and that is about the only sign of life in Laurac-le-Grand until the men return from working in the fields.

Yet Laurac was the home of the great Blanche de Laurac, one of the most famous of all the women *perfecti* of the Cathar Church. Her daughter Guirauda de Laurac was the *châtelaine* of Lavaur on the northern side of the plain now crossed by the canal, and no woman was more widely loved and respected than she. In an age of intolerance Guirauda gave home and food, charity and security to all who were persecuted, and within her town of Lavaur could be found Arab teacher and Jewish rabbi living in peace and tolerance and friendly disputation along with a population predominantly

Catholic. Coming as she did from a staunchly Cathar family, Guirauda also opened her gates to the Cathar *perfecti*. It was thus inevitable that such a haven of refuge should eventually excite the envy and fury of Simon de Montfort.

One day in the spring of 1211, there could be seen flocking towards Lavaur the peasants whose homesteads had been burned, the outlawed *seigneurs* who supported the Cathar cause, Catholics who could no longer tolerate the cruelties instituted by the crusade and the *perfecti* hounded from place to place ahead of the invading army of the northern knights. Guirauda took them all in to her town and her brother Aimery prepared to lead the defence.

Lavaur had not long to wait. Soon the forces of de Montfort were encamped around the hill, with the crowd of enthusiastic pilgrims in attendance. The Catholic canon went out to ask what it was that de Montfort wished with the place, and he received the straight answer that all non-Catholic fellow-citizens were to be surrendered. As at Béziers, the people of Lavaur rejected such an infamous suggestion, declaring that they would see themselves dead before they did any such thing.

And so the assault began. The town was well stocked with provisions and bravely defended. Week after week the garrison resisted, repelling attacks, burning the assault engines and the piles of timber in the moat, and making deadly sorties under the leadership of Guirauda's brother. But the town could not withstand for ever the impact of the rocks hurled by the catapults and trebuckets. At last the wall was breached, and the knights of the north and the mercenary rabble poured in.

The women and children and the Catholic priests were stripped and locked in the church. Of the male citizens many were murdered, and no quarter was given to Jews, or to any whom Guirauda had taken into the town out of her charity. Her brother Aimery who had so heroically led the defence was hanged, and eighty knights with him — until the gallows collapsed and de Montfort had their throats cut. Four hundred Cathar Christians, either *perfecti* or alleged to be so as an excuse to get rid of them, were led out to the meadow. Men and women alike, they were piled upon an enormous pyre and burned at night — a particularly pleasant touch, this —

whilst the zealous pilgrims who followed in de Montfort's wake celebrated around the fire by singing their familiar hymn with immense joy. *Cum ingenti gaudio* they burned their fellow men, the chronicler relates. Beneath the clear darkness of the Languedoc sky the frenzied strains of plainsong drowned the crackling of the branches flickering in the flames. *Come, Holy Ghost, our hearts inspire, And lighten with celestial fire* — and in the blaze the four hundred Cathars perishing without a sound.

As for the noble Guirauda, known through the Languedoc for her charity and her kindness to the poor, de Montfort's men stripped her, dragged her out of the gate and threw her down a dry well. Then they hurled stones on her until she died, and next morning they filled the well with rubble. The people of the plain still tell that on a night when the moon casts only a faint light, and the air is still, you may hear from somewhere beneath the ground the voice of the gentle Guirauda de Laurac singing a melody of long, long ago.

If the Lauragais was a Cathar stronghold, it is now a land venerated by the Dominicans for the simple reason that it was there that their order first sprang into being. Early in the thirteenth century the King of Castille decided upon a political marriage between his son and a Danish princess. The bishop of the Spanish diocese of Osma was requested to make the journey overland to Scandinavia to negotiate the contract, and taking with him a young monk named Dominic Guzman he crossed the Pyrénées on his way to the north in the company of a score or more of horsemen. The party stayed overnight at Toulouse, a city well stocked with adherents of the Cathar religion, and it is known that Dominic came to be boarded out with a heretic. This was a fateful encounter, for it determined the young sub-prior to spend his life in attempting to put down the heresy, and it was eventually to give rise to the Inquisition.

The Danish alliance was duly arranged, but the negotiations proved to have been a waste of time, for when the bishop of Osma again travelled north to fetch the princess for whose marriage the terms had been agreed, he found her dead. Rather than be sold off as a bargain lot she had killed herself — or perhaps had merely disappeared and left behind her a suitable rumour of death. The bishop and his sub-prior Dominic again returned to the south, arriving at Montpellier at the moment when the legates were gathered there to discuss the eradication of the heresy. One of these men was Arnald-Amalric, shortly to be the butcher of Béziers; another was Pierre de Castelnau, soon to be assassinated at St Gilles. As a result of this meeting it was decided that Dominic Guzman would be accompanied by two of the legates in an effort to deal with the heretics by sheer force of reason and argument. The Cathar Church had the support of the people of the Languedoc because of the sincerity and simple living of its ministers. These men, the *perfecti*, were poor, they tolerated no ostentation or extravagance, they preached. The deputation of the Church of Rome decided to try to beat them at their own game.

The two legates now sent home their attendants with the baggage, and with Dominic as their companion they set out to preach in poverty. In fact the legates soon tired of the effort of persuasion — or perhaps of the poverty — and the mission collapsed. Only Dominic remained to carry on with dogged determination, and there is no doubt that he was a very different type of man from his fellow missioners. Back in his student days he had sold his books and all his belongings in order to relieve suffering during a famine, and to match this sincerity he had a nature which positively welcomed hardship and suffering. But now, as he went his way alone from village to village and castle to castle, preaching to sceptical audiences, the founder of the Order of the Preaching Friars could certainly never have dreamed that seven and a half centuries later, in the mid-1960's, millions of teenagers on both sides of the Atlantic would be whistling or dancing to the tale of his missionary endeavours. Yet so it was to be, for one of the Top Ten discs was that of a nun in a Belgian convent ('*Sœur Sourire*') singing with herself the song of the encounter of St Dominic with the Albigensian heretics. And for that matter it is no more likely that very many of the millions of fans made by the simple voice of the singing nun ever listened carefully enough to the words to discover that this was no love song but a bit of ecclesiastical history.

Dominique — nique — nique
S'en allait tout simplement,
Au dieu, pauvré, chantant.
En tous chemins entre lieux
Il ne parle que du bon dieu,
Il ne parle que du bon dieu.

And just to set the tale squarely in its period one of the verses dates it precisely:

Á l'époque que Jean-sans-Terre
D'Angleterre était le roi,
Dominique notre père
Combattit les Albigeois.

Dominic did indeed walk from place to place in poverty, and perhaps chanting also, and it was in the Lauragais that his work was concentrated. With the approval of Rome he set about his uphill task of conversion by reasoning, and the house where he resided is still to be seen at Fanjeaux, south of the canal. It has a simple arched twelfth-century doorway in the village street, but the building has been remodelled inside as a Dominican retreat. At the back a beautiful little garden stretches to the edge of the hill and we almost envied the courteous Dominican friar who looked after the mesembryanthemums and carnations, the salvias and stocks and geraniums. We also appreciated his strict professional pride when he stood beside us to look down upon the rolling land of the Lauragais from the terrace at the end of the garden.

'You have been to Assisi?'

We said No, we had never been to the Holy Places of the Franciscans.

'Assisi is pleasant in its way,' he said casually. 'But of course the view from here is very much finer.'

The strategy by which St Dominic *combattit les Albigeois* did not consist merely in coming in simplicity and poverty. His object was to reason the people out of heresy by sheer debate. The Cathar clerics respected a man who came with neither scrip nor purse, travelling on foot, and they were often ready to mount a contest. A panel of local judges would be appointed, and the theological case for both sides would be debated in front of the whole local population. At the end of the argument the judges were expected to pronounce their verdict. But even a favourable verdict would not have converted the people themselves, and in fact the success of the mission was very slight. No doubt this was partly because the Cathar ministers were very able and sincere men, but it was galling to Dominic to find that he could debate for two weeks in a single protracted discussion and perhaps achieve not one single conversion. It is little wonder that the legates were so discouraged and all the more remarkable that Dominic himself carried on, drinking only water and eating nothing but bread, living in the open to outbid the piety of the Cathars, and always preaching, preaching, preaching. *Il ne parle que du bon dieu*, and if in the four years of quiet before the murder of Pierre de Castelnau he had only a handful of conversions to show for his efforts, this was perhaps because not even the sincerity of such a man could persuade people to rejoin a Church which was riddled with corruption and which threatened them with fire and sword if they thought for themselves.

But if the preaching of Dominic had little effect, his memorial was to be in the foundation a few years later of his Order of the Preaching Friars, the Dominicans — the followers of Dominic or perhaps the *domini canes* as they liked to think of themselves in medieval symbolism; the dogs of the Lord guarding the flock of sheep from the onslaughts of the devil. The first monastery was founded at Prouille, down the road from Fanjeaux.

If Castelnaudary is the place from which to explore the country of the Dominicans to the south, it is also the town closest to the Montagne Noire and the extraordinary works devised by the Baron of Bonrepos to supply his canal with water. Not everyone is an enthusiast either for inland waterways, or for civil engineering of any kind, but I would recommend any who think that canals are nothing more than dull ditches to spend a day or two in contemplation of the really astonishing works devised by the imaginative Riquet. The crew of the *Commodore* may be cranks, maniacs, rhapsodists, or nuts about canals, but here is something over which any person however landbound can be fanatical. And quite apart from the boldness of the concepts of the canal-minded tax-collector, to walk along the bankside paths of his feeder streams is sheer delight, always provided that one really hankers for a forty-mile walk — for that is the measure of these channels.

Forty miles of aqueduct — that is the almost incredible scale of what Riquet had to achieve before the canal itself was even a possibility. But once he had hit upon the simple fact that the feasibility of a coast-to-coast waterway depended upon whether a sufficient amount of water could be made to flow to the neighbour-hood of the Stones of Naurouze, he naturally turned his attention to the Montagne Noire, the nearest area of considerable rainfall.

> Riquet! le temps pour nous effaçait ta mémoire,
> C'est en vain que l'esprit de la Montagne Noire
> A grands cris, chaque jour, t'appelait dans ses bois.

So wrote one of the many poets who extolled the brilliance of his imagination. Riquet had by then been dead for a century and a half, but his name is even now inseparable from the group of hills which he milked so ingeniously in order to float the boats over the divide between sea and ocean.

After exploring the forest and conducting surveys which were remarkable for their accuracy, Riquet decided to concentrate first upon the River Sor. This stream was large enough to operate a number of mills in the plain of Revel, but it flowed away north-ward to join the larger River Agout and reach the Tarn below Albi. It thus headed in quite the wrong direction to be of direct use, but Riquet was not perturbed. He simply decided to divert the river, or as much of it as he needed, and he accordingly planned an artificial watercourse which would lead the Sor water round the western edge of the mountains to strike the course of the Laudot. Here the water from the southern slopes would be picked up also, and a feeder channel could conduct the combined amount all the way to Naurouze. This watercourse from the Sor to Naurouze is the Rigole de la Plaine It is no mere gutter either. Twenty-seven miles in length, it is twenty feet broad and nine deep, a channel which holds considerably more water than many an English canal.

M

And yet Riquet wanted still more water. Whereas many later engineers have been much too optimistic about the supply of water for their canals, Riquet realized that there could occasionally be a severe drought. In that event, he thought, the waters of the Sor and the Laudot might prove insufficient, so he would cut a second feeder on the south side of the mountains, his Rigole de la Montagne. This was to start from the Alzau brook, tucked deeply away in the recesses of the forest, and winding along the spurs of the hill at a slight gradient it would pick up several other streams on its way until after twelve miles it would be divided into two branches. One of these would discharge into the Sor, some miles upstream of the point where the first *rigole* left it, and in this way the supplies from the southern slopes would reach the Rigole de la Plaine. But the other branch was to dive by tunnel under the hill town of Les Cammazes (the tunnel was built by Vauban) and emerge into the valley of the Laudot. If this valley were then blocked with a dam it would provide an immense reservoir.

The intention — which was amply fulfilled — was that during the summer months the water of the Alzau and its neighbours would take the right-hand fork and swell the Sor during its period of least flow, whereas in winter the Sor could look after the whole canal and the Rigole de la Montagne would accumulate a store behind the dam and so provide a bank account of water to be drawn upon in case of drought. The notion was a brilliant one. Three centuries have now passed since Riquet cut his *rigoles* in the sheer granite of the slopes of the Montagne Noire, and throughout that time the canal has always been well provided with water, even when other waterways in less arid areas of the continent have been short of supplies. In fact, in three hundred years the only modification has been that in 1776 a second and smaller reservoir was added to cover the additional needs of the branch canal to Narbonne.

Having first planned the Rigole de la Plaine to his satisfaction, Riquet then thought of making it navigable. Around the market town of Revel, behind the Black Mountain, there was a rich plain from which surplus grain was exported to the surrounding areas. If the feeder were made large enough, this harvest could be carried down to Naurouze on the flow, and there loaded aboard the larger craft of the canal. To this end Riquet actually built the loading basin of Port-Louis near Revel, and added fourteen small locks between there and Naurouze. Special narrow craft of shallow draft were built, but before the main line of the Canal du Midi was opened Riquet wisely abandoned the scheme, realizing that the most important function of his feeders would be hard to maintain if the interests of local shipping conflicted with sudden demands for large quantities of water. The locks of the *rigole* were dismantled, and Revel's port remained without ships. This was a sad blow for the merchants of that town, and a century later they campaigned to have the navigation restored. But they were not successful, for the States of the Languedoc prudently refused to make the success of the whole canal depend upon the conditions for shipping at Revel.

I must confess that on our voyage across the country we did not actually walk the *rigoles* from source to mouth. Instead, we hired a small and bouncy car at Castelnaudary and set out for the Montagne Noire which for days past had stood away to our right, frowning across the plain to the Lauragais and the ridge of the Montagne d'Alaric. It was an interesting journey and one which took us into a land unbelievably lush and damp in comparison with the dry limestone plateau country to the north and the hot cactus land to the south-east.

In fact the Black Mountain is unexpectedly like a piece of German forest or a chunk of the Vosges set down in the middle of the Midi. The trees are not the tall and mysterious pines of the Black Forest but more like those of the mixed woodland of the Odenwald, with humbler conifers jostled together with beech and oak, ash and alder, the forest stretching up almost to the hilltops where the cattle graze in the open on green and rich pasture. The mountains are high enough to cause the air currents from the distant sea to lift and cool and drop their water, and the leaves of the trees condense the droplets from the airborne moisture drifting by.

There are few hamlets in the Montagne Noire, and altogether it is a beautiful, wild, and little known part of the Midi. Indeed, it is so little frequented that to find the source of Riquet's Rigole de la Montagne is not easy. It took us some time to track it down, but eventually we came to a cluster of houses forming the hamlet of La Galaube. Half a mile outside this village, and to the west of it, a minor road crosses a forest stream beside a mill, and here a pathway plunges down into the damp woodland to follow the Alzau as it tumbles along between mossy boulders and fallen tree trunks sprouting juicy clumps of fungi. We had gone perhaps half a mile when the disorder vanished and the brook emerged into a neat trough of masonry set in a piece of ornamental park with specimen trees and lawns and seats, quite the last thing one would expect to find tucked away in the forest but reflecting yet again the suave confidence of the Baron of Bonrepos.

A little bridge spanned the stream, and the *gardien* was adjusting the paddles which let some of the water run off into a channel at the

side, past a great slab of granite commemorating Riquet's solution
of the problem of water for the canal, a memorial put there by his
descendant General the Duke of Caraman — perhaps as a counter-
blast to the anti-Riquet propaganda of General Andreossy. The
unexpected dignity and beauty of the place reminded us of that
delightful corner of the London New River at Amwell in Hertford-
shire, for there also one can find monuments, and lawns, and
elegant trees nodding sagely over the wisdom of a watercourse
well planned and properly dug.

The Prise d'Alzau, with its memorials and waterfall, sluices and
trees and such grass as one rarely sees in France, is the departure
point of the Rigole de la Montagne, which immediately leads away
in a most determined fashion, its water rippling as clear as glass in
a channel perhaps ten feet broad and not very deep, to disappear
among the trees on its way to the parting of the waters and Les
Cammazes, beyond which it will emerge on the further side of the
ridge to join the Laudot. On this occasion we were content to let it
run its own course as far as Riquet's dam at St Ferréol, where we
would catch up with it again.

When we drove to St Ferréol we were already familiar with the
grand scale on which Riquet planned his hydraulic arrangements.
Nevertheless, the three-hundred-year-old barrage was more impressive than anything we had imagined, for it is more than half a
mile in length and one hundred and five feet high. The woman in
the house of the *gardien* informed us that it held up 250 million cubic
feet of water, and this we were quite prepared to believe when we
discovered that we had been a whole hour in walking round the reservoir, on which trip-boats were taking school parties for rides and a
score of sailing yachts were engaged in a serious race, their crews
leaning far out over the side and dipping the seats of their shorts in
the warm water. There were fishermen, too, and campers, for Riquet's
ingenuity has provided this part of France with a truly beautiful
lake of impressive dimensions, and one formed so long ago that it
now has a shoreline of its own instead of the uncouth plunge of
land into water which is more characteristic of a man-made
reservoir.

As usual, Riquet's detail matches up to the era of the *Roi Soleil*.

Handsome seats carved of granite are set along the top of the vast embankment of the dam, which at its foot reaches a thickness of some two hundred and fifty feet. Below it is a park landscaped into watercourses and cataracts fed by the overflow or Rigole de Cienture, which curves round the outside of the lake to sport and gambol among the glades, with stepping stones leading invitingly from point to point. As a splendid final touch the hydraulic engineers have not forgotten that the head of water provides an opportunity to do something even more spectacular with this surplus water, and by means of sluices it feeds a tall and graceful waterfall in the park below, and a powerful fountain jet which leaps sixty feet or more into the air to drench the ornamental trees with its drifting mist. Riquet, Colbert and Louis XIV — theirs were the days when a man might have a very definite object, such as building a canal from coast to coast, but yet would not fetter his imagination and neglect to give the care, and spend the extra money which was so hard to come by, in order to make a work not just of practical use but of grandeur and stately beauty.

Riquet's vast dam was built as three parallel walls. The space between them was filled with earth and rubble, and the result was something very solid. But the water from such a reservoir as it contained must, we realized, be drawn off at the lowest point, and seeking out again the woman whom we had found in the house of the *gardien* we asked to see the outlet. She was very willing to show us how the water was drawn off, if only we would not mind her first feeding her hens. When she had satisfied them she joined us down in the shrubbery and led us to an iron gate which opened into the darkness of a cavity set in the bottom of the bank, between creepers and roses and ornamental shrubs. As she unlocked it we seemed to be stepping into a mausoleum, perhaps the tomb of St Ferréol himself, or penetrating one of those fateful caverns in which the last of the Cathars had held out against their persecutors.

Our guide switched on a light, and we saw ahead of us a long and damp nave with stalactites several inches in length already formed upon the vaulting. Our steps echoed behind her, and the fact that she spoke in a kind of whisper enhanced the impression that this was some weird temple and that the great slab dimly seen at the further end was the altar at which victims would be offered in the course of a terrible ritual. Above the slab were three huge and richly ornamented objects, as difficult of description as the wheels that Ezekiel saw, but no doubt connected with hieromancy, or sortilege, or more probably with hydromancy. They were, we discovered, nothing more than three cocks of gigantic proportions, each of which was operated by a lever and ratchet arrangement. Through this trio of giant taps the whole of the waters of the reservoir could be released as a flood or as a trickle, to swell the Laudot stream and replenish the Rigole de la Plaine with ample supplies which would eventually surge into the canal at Naurouze and feed all the canal on either side of the summit, from Toulouse on the Garonne to Carcassonne upon the Aude. In fact we were now standing just behind the inner wall of the reservoir, and we were thankful that Riquet's work was too solid to slip and engulf us, or wash us all the way down to Naurouze on the front of a wave of inundation.

Having visited the places sacred to St Dominic and to Pierre-Paul Riquet respectively, we set out again towards the summit at Naurouze. We first cut a course straight down the length of the Castelnaudary basin, skirting at its western end the pretty island left by Riquet not just for sheer ornament but so that its dense screen of trees should shelter from the strong easterly winds the barges coming out from beneath the bridge leading out of the old port, and the bulk of the isle itself would serve to protect them from waves which otherwise might have driven the ships ashore. Beyond it a trio of wine ships and a fuel tanker were lying at the quay of the port, a pretty little harbour with a cobbled wharf and stacks of barrels and boxes, and women kneeling to dip their pails to rinse the soap from the washing lying on the stones. With the gay colours of the wooden craft, the sun-bleached tints of the houses and the intense hues of the flowers along the window ledges, the port of Castelnaudary might have been some little sea-harbour on the Mediterranean shore. All the boats stopped there on their passage, whether to do business with the shipping agents in the offices across the road, or to fuel, or that the captain's wife might shop for her supplies, or more probably just for the opportunity of spending a casual hour or two in bargeman's gossip over a glass of local wine at one of the pavement cafés just up the road.

Another bridge, and the *Commodore* had left the port astern. Now the canal turned and twisted as though none too anxious to get on with the journey, and after another two or three miles we were in sight of the first of the eight locks remaining before the summit pound, seventy-five steps up from the Mediterranean. Two locks further ahead we climbed a flight of three steps, and looking out over the plain with our binoculars we could see standing in a cornfield the grey stone memorial to the *Saintes Puelles* after which the nearby village took its name. The two girls were sculpted in clothes of flowing seventeenth-century style, but we were told that their tale lay much further back in history. The woman who helped us work the locks believed that they were contemporary with St Sernin of Toulouse, but more than that we could not discover.

It was late in the morning that we reached the seventy-fifth and final lock of the ascent, the *écluse Méditerranée*. Beyond it the summit pound meandered along in a carefree fashion towards the first of the twenty-five locks of the descent to Toulouse, and near the further end and on the starboard hand we could see a tall obelisk standing up above the flat land of the top of the pass. This, we knew, marked the Stones of Naurouze, and when we had drawn level we pulled in to the side, made fast to the trees, and found ourselves close to the point where the Rigole de la Plaine poured a great volume of water into the canal.

At Naurouze, as elsewhere, everything is majestic. The anglers may sit lethargic in the midday shade, but the waters of the Montagne Noire run past them fresh and clear after tripping through a mill and pausing to move more slowly through a stately basin, which was to serve as a port for the small ships of Revel which never came. There are alleys and seats, specimen trees, sluices and walks, and everywhere the crystal water rippling in its bed, splashing and laughing at its achievement in having found its way through forty miles of trough to the summit of the Canal Royal.

Behind the basin and across a meadow are the Stones of

Naurouze, a pile of blocks so strange and improbable that it is not surprising that they should be regarded as of mysterious origin. It seems that Naurouze was a giant, way back in the days between the culture of Aurignac and Lascaux and that of the Kingdom of Charlemagne. He was engaged in carrying a load of stones out of which it was hoped to build Toulouse, but the long ascent to the top of the pass so exhausted the poor fellow that he dropped his burden. The stones were broken in pieces, and the debris has remained there ever since, with the result that Toulouse had subsequently to be built of brick instead.

So striking is the pile of giant boulders, standing alone upon an open landscape, that they have always been associated with legend and prophecy. Even the great Nostradamus brought them into his catalogue, predicting that when they should piece themselves together the end of the world would be at hand — a safe enough forecast, one might think. More curiously, it was in these same fields that Marshal Soult signed an armistice with the Duke of Wellington, but that was before the monument to Riquet was erected, for it was not until after the Revolution that the site was acquired for a memorial. The descendants of Riquet, who included a number of titled gentry fortunate enough to have escaped the guillotine, banded together and bought the mound of rocks from the lady who owned the land. Ambassadors, officers, counts and gentlewomen, their names are all there on the monument, and on one face is a handsome medallion of the Baron of Bonrepos himself. Not that all this is very easy to discover. We found the gate locked, and unable to obtain at the nearby house any answer other than the savage growls of a hungry-eyed Alsatian, we found a part of the wall which offered possible footholds and climbed in.

To scramble over the sacred wall is probably *interdit*, but in the Languedoc prohibitions are not taken very seriously. Besides, the view from the base of the monument itself is worth the climb. To the north-east the forests of the Montagne Noire appear as dark and damp as indeed they are, and one can just make out the position of the pocket containing the lake of St Ferréol even if the water is necessarily at a higher level and so cannot be seen from Naurouze. More to the east the land falls away toward the valley of the Aude, with the Mountains of Alaric bald and smooth beyond it and the Pyrénées visible as a glimmer of hazy brightness in the brilliant blue. South-eastwards the hills around Fanjeaux and Laurac are not far away, the rich land where St Dominic strode on his dusty rounds, attempting in vain to divert the stubborn Cathar Christians from their ways. Westward the view is open across the broad neck of the pass where the lorries bump and jolt a dusty course past little villages and manors and prosperous farms set in the rich fields of grain.

It is a peaceful landscape, old and mellowed, and of the two visitations of the English foe little trace is left. In the nineteenth century came The Iron Duke. In the fourteenth the men of the Black Prince marched past the Stones of Naurouze to pillage the hamlets and sack Castelnaudary, whilst the Black Death was killing one in three of their people back home. But whatever terrors the Hundred Years War may have brought, this land between Toulouse and Castelnaudary had already seen the foundation of the system of terrorization by informers, by interrogation under solitary confinement, and by every means which in our own day we would associate with brainwashing and the torture techniques of a police state.

For followers are not always like their leaders. The mission of Dominic began as one of preaching, but he had not long been dead before two of the Brothers Dominican at Toulouse were appointed as the first Inquisitors.

There was to be no more of that gentle Dominic sung by *Sœur Sourire*. *Au Dieu, pauvré, chantant* had had its day, and the Dominicans Arnald and Seila were sent out to interrogate, to root out heresy by threat of sword and stake without reference to any authority of law, civil or ecclesiastical. At Rocamadour one can climb the famous steps to which a heretic was made to walk in penitent pilgrimage, wearing upon back and front a great cross and on his head a huge and ridiculous hat. At the foot of the rock he would be stripped, and wearing a hair shirt he then had to climb the two hundred steps of the cliff on his knees whilst the clergy beat him along with birches at every shuffle. Just to make it harder work, the heretic was loaded with chains until, reaching the summit at last, his irons were struck off whilst he grovelled before the priest at the altar of the Virgin.

And all this was for those lucky enough to be guilty only of lesser degrees of involvement in the Cathar Church. For the *perfectus* there was rarely such pardon. Not even death thirty years earlier could save his body from the insensate fury of the Dominicans, who would order his grave to be dug up, his coffin broken open, and the unresisting bones ceremonially burned upon a pyre whilst the people of the villages looked on in awestruck horror at the fate which was engulfing their land, and which within another decade was to draw the curtain for ever over the freedom and tolerance which once the troubadours of the Languedoc had sung, and for which Guirauda of Laurac and many others had met their death.

IX

Ten hours of plodding the pounds from one step to the next is enough to carry a vessel through the whole length of the western descent from Naurouze to Toulouse, and along all this course the canal is pleasant, though not spectacular, and the only very noticeable change is that the bridges of faded limestone, sometimes bearing dates of years when Riquet was still superintending the works of his army of navvies, now give way to others just as old but of a narrow brick almost as pink as the icing on a cake. Toulouse is known as the Rose City and this rosiness of the buildings extends as far as Albi, where the famous cathedral and the bishop's palace appear at first sight to be built of a very fine red sandstone. But it is brick just the same. In Toulouse itself, all the buildings before the skyscraper era are of the same material, and the mere colour of the place gives it a strange unreality.

Toulouse is said to be only a shadow of its former self, but it is a most attractive city none the less. It bids fair to be a real capital, and one cannot escape the impression that the people regard Paris and all its works of bureaucracy with the same sort of resigned contempt which the good people of Edinburgh show towards London. Scots know that the 'Flying Scotsman' disappearing down the track is said to reach London, but beyond that they are not greatly interested. In just the same way, a Tolosan is aware that the night express from the Matabiau station is bound for the Gare d'Austerlitz, and to this he has no objection so long as he does not have to accompany it.

Toulouse was already a large city when Riquet laid out his waterway, and he intended to connect the canal with the city moats so that the ships could load or deliver at many points. But the *capitouls* or city fathers objected, as city fathers nearly always do. They obliged him to keep his new-fangled system of simplified transport outside the confines of their great Tolosa, and he therefore had to skirt the place at a little distance, curving round its perimeter to reach the Garonne below the city itself. One and a half centuries later Toulouse was threatened by the allied armies, and the canal became the defensive line which served successfully to hold at bay for a while the English forces under Wellington. But the city continued to spread, with the result that Riquet's canal now courses through an outer and decidedly dingy part of Toulouse, an area of motor repair shops and small factories. Along the dirty quays lie the older wooden barges as well as some of their more modern successors. Dutch fashion, there is a road on either side, but the traverse of the city is sordidly commercial rather than beautiful. One may glimpse the curious cathedral of St Stephen, and a statue of Riquet near the end of one of the more imposing bridges, but mostly it is hustle and bustle and noise, with here and there a fine new steel-framed building looking down in curiosity upon the antique form of a wooden family barge chugging heavily round the bend from lock to lock. It is not until near the end of the descent that the factory walls and skyscraper office blocks give way to an avenue of trees once more, and the canal musters a final show of elegance before running to its end, emerging through a final arch of brick into the long sheet of water of the Port de l'Embouchure.

This port basin is an attractive place. It was originally the harbour where the barges handed over their cargoes to smaller craft of lesser draught which would pass down to the river through two locks now sealed off, to continue on their way to Bordeaux by a natural waterway. But so swift and shallow was the river course that twenty Garonne craft were needed for the cargo of a single canal barge. Riquet himself urged that the waterway should be continued all the way to the estuary, and Vauban repeated the suggestion, but it was not until 1838 that work was at last put in hand and the Canal Latéral à la Garonne began to take shape.

Except for millers, life at Toulouse has always been complicated by the weir of Bazacle which spans the river in the middle of its course round the further side of the city. This weir used to work seventeen mills, and it still exists to provide a head of water for a hydro-electric station. Riquet sensibly decided to build his port below the weir and far enough downstream to have a reasonable amount of water, but this meant that his canal was sited more than a mile from the wharves above the weir. At these quays the timber and produce of the Upper Garonne were landed, and it would have been of great advantage to the merchants if they could have transferred their wares directly to canal ships, but another century was to pass before the Canal de Brienne was cut through the town to join the upper river with Riquet's port. Today the upper reaches are no longer navigable, so this cut is only used as a feeder for the Garonne lateral canal, but it is a popular stretch for anglers. More than that, it greatly improved Riquet's port by entering at a bridge designed as a twin of his original. Side by side the two canals run in through the Ponts-Jumeaux or Twin Bridges, the graceful arches of which are separated only by an immense and flamboyant sculpture in Carrara marble, showing the Province of Languedoc as a seated woman ordering the sprites of the arts to join the Garonne waters to the Canal du Midi by a new canal. The cherubs are hard at work, digging locks with pick and shovel or fitting the lock-gates as though they were engineers of the *Ponts et Chaussées*, while the Mediterranean and Atlantic look on in puzzled surprise. This great piece of decoration serves also to remind one that Riquet's canal was not constructed as a barge waterway but as a ship canal, and that it is merely the case that the ships of the sea have now outgrown it. For caravels it was large enough, and the marble used in the Ponts-Jumeaux sculpture was shipped to the site direct from the Ligurian coast aboard Genoese trading vessels.

Although the bridges and their locality are still known as the Ponts-Jumeaux they are not twins but triplets, the third brother having been added later to span the entrance of the Garonne lateral canal. A better scene for collisions it would be impossible to devise, the craft from either waterway cutting across the entirely blind entry to the other. During the week we spent in this pretty basin we would often see a pair of barges converging, invisible to each other but with a member of the family leaning out from the bow as a look-out to peep round the corner. Twice we saw the craft approach simultaneously, so that the first warning either of the look-outs had was the head of the other craning out from under the arch. There followed wild shouts to the skippers and both craft would churn the water as they went astern, receding into their holes like frightened rabbits.

The *Commodore*'s safe arrival at Toulouse was a source of satisfaction to others besides ourselves, and we were asked if she would permit her deck to be used on the following day. With the matter explained to her in more detail she declared herself very willing, and the next evening some splendid champagne was discovered hidden away near the wheel as a reward for her gracious services. It so happened that the season was ripe for the fashion houses of Toulouse to present to the public a display of their summer creations, and the modistes saw the splendid opportunity of having the latest elegance in yachting wear modelled and photographed upon the only business-like boat of sea-going appearance which had turned up in the port of Toulouse for months past.

'*Soyez élégantes de bâbord à tribord*,' the *Dépêche du Midi* exhorted its feminine readers, and to show that it could really be done the attractive Karole and handsome Tony dressed in everything in turn which might prove that even aboard ship one could be a '*loup-de-mer-chic*' a dandy old sea-dog, male or female. Splendid tailored trousers of immaculate white were to be kept for the *ports chics* of the Costa Brava, and this we could readily believe. The photographs certainly showed a charming girl in spotless elegance with one finger delicately looped under the *Commodore*'s mooring line, but we wondered whether one would really look so beautifully turned out after a hundred locks of the Canal du Midi without ladders to climb, and a hundred scrambles up slippery walls to the lock sides above or down to the boat below. One might also have an attractive *thé schirt* for *le five-au-clock* on the open waves. Indeed, after a morning of seeing how smart we could really look if only we were to put our minds to it, we set off in humility towards the town, realising that our clean clothes were not quite as *élégante pour descendre à terre* as those displayed upon the *Commodore*'s foredeck before a startled gathering of bargemen.

Toulouse is rightly proud of those things which set it above Paris — its supremacy in aircraft pioneering, and the annual poetry contest of the *Jeux floraux*. Its natives are so pleasant and good-humoured a people that we never once heard that hostile sound which forms the background music to Parisian life, the crescendo of voices raised in anger over nothing at all. The city can also be proud of its many fine buildings in pink brick, and among them the great church of St Sernin, built on the place where the wild bull dragging him to death is said to have come to a halt. Its pink octagonal tower of five storeys rises high above the roofs, and somehow carries just a hint of the Kew Gardens pagoda in its ancestry, or perhaps a whiff of the leaning tower of Pisa, but in fact this splendid edifice was there in the days of the Cathars and the infamous Simon de Montfort is said to have had his skull crushed by a stone hurled from the roof by a catapult worked by some of the townswomen. 'It struck the Count Simon upon his helmet of iron in such fashion that his eyes, brains, teeth, skull and jaws flew quite to pieces, and he fell to the earth utterly dead and bloody.' Every church bell rang, the besieged danced with delight, and even today one can only wish that the incident had happened a few years earlier.

And there one should perhaps leave St Sernin's church and not venture inside. It was a stopping place on the road to St James of Compostella, and its whole arrangement is designed to accommo-date the long shuffling processions of pilgrims in their weird shell-decorated cloaks filing through the nave and from transept to transept. Already they had passed by way of St Martha's at

Tarascon, through St Gilles and by the abbey of Psalmody, chanting their pilgrim song:

> '*Voyez les beaux genêts,*
> *Le romarin qui branche*
> *Et d'où sort si grande odeur.*'

But the great odour awaiting them at St Sernin's was not that of rosemary. For their delectation there had been collected an all-time world-beating collection of relics.

In the centre of the nave is a sort of great cage of stone which surrounds the stairs down which one may walk to peer at the rows of priceless caskets with their glass panels revealing hunks of dried flesh, and hair, teeth and bones and bits of skulls. Once, on a voyage in Alsace, we had seen a tiny splinter of bone labelled *Les onze milles vierges de Cologne*. St Sernin's clerics would not have been satisfied with that token demonstration, I suspect. They would have had eleven thousand whole skeletons or nothing.

The relics of St Sernin's are quite frightful. If Charlemagne furnished bits of six apostles that is already something, but every other revered person is also there, it seems, in bits. The skull of Thomas Aquinas is a particular pride, and so are the pieces of St Edmund King and Martyr and Monsieur Vincent. I have forgotten the total of saints who are represented by parts of their bodies, but I think it was one hundred and eighty-six. Not surprisingly, from this great boneyard an indefinable but thick and musty atmosphere seems to steam upward into the nave, and if there is one feeling which it is almost impossible to experience it is any sense of reverence for the truly great men and women, here remembered not for what they were in their lives but as a source of molars and toenails. Just to add a final touch of the ludicrous there is no need even to have a living guide. One pays for a ticket, and a disembodied voice — that of St Tape — recites the whole catalogue of the chamber of horrors in an unearthly and metallic voice which rasps through the tracery to vanish in the dust of the vaulting above before completing the loop and beginning all over again.

Having come by water we had of course to make our pilgrimage

N

to the cathedral of St Stephen. Standing in a beautiful square in the older section of the town, this building is weird to say the least, and Monsieur Michelin decorously admits that it appears *curieusement disparate*. It looks very much as though a firm of ecclesiastical builders had a job lot of doors, windows, buttresses and bricks left in stock, and one of the brighter foremen hit on the idea that added together they were just about enough to make up a modest cathedral, provided nobody was fussy about symmetry, or style, or functional suitability, or whether there was enough glass to fill the windows. Inside — where the choir is not even remotely in line with the nave — the whole affair is sustained and held together by a single pillar of gigantic proportions from which spokes of vaulting radiate for various distances and on a variety of curves to wherever they are needed. Awestruck at such a curiosity, a visitor unaware of the nearby Canal du Midi might overlook the plaque of black marble let into the column, a memorial which briefly announces that at the foot of the pillar there lies buried *le génie bienfaisant qui a créé la prosperité du Languedoc*, Pierre-Paul Riquet, Baron of Bonrepos.

With its churches and museums, its great patrician houses and the splendid sweep of the Garonne, Toulouse is a city in which one may happily spend a week — particularly if one can return in the evenings to such a cool and pleasant place as the quayside of the canal basin at the Ponts-Jumeaux. We shared this pleasure with a variety of barges which came and went about their business, discharging oil by pipe-line or loading golden grain from tip-trucks. Our immediate neighbours for two days were a handsome and bronzed southerner and his dark-haired wife, aboard a wooden barge of beautiful lines and gay colours. We presented them with an old motor-tyre on a rope, a fender rather too large for our own use but which we had hesitated to throw away because it was a gift from a friend who had seen it floating past the august waterfront of the Quai d'Orsay in Paris and had immediately put out in a boat to recover it and place it in our hold. The skipper of the barge was delighted with it, and thus we fell into conversation.

From the cleanliness of the craft it was clear that *madame* must, like himself, have been born and bred on the canal, and we discovered that the great pride of his boat and the fact which made others instinctively treat it with the greatest respect was not just that his own family had been canal-carriers since 1870 but that *madame* came of a long line of progenitors who had the distinction of being afloat on the Canal du Midi ever since the days of Riquet. This was more than could be said of many skippers, the man remarked sardonically as we turned out heads and watched a steel boat grind awkwardly against the side of one of the handsome original twins among the bridges. That fellow there was a Spaniard, he added. Had we not suspected it from the way he could not steer through a bridge? No?

Tiens! Everyone could see that a Spaniard would not understand how to navigate a canal and steer a barge. Spaniards were right enough working on land, but not on the water. It stood to reason, and experience confirmed it, as we could see. As for himself, he had no desire to be rammed and sunk, so whenever he saw the Spaniard coming he made for the shore and stayed there until he had passed. Come to think of it, that stout new tyre-fender from the Seine might come in very handy the next time *l'Espagnol* should bear down upon them.

Toulouse is said to have had four wonders — *la Belle Paulo, Saint Sernin, le Bazacle, et Matoli*. Apart from the weir and the cathedral they were human. *Matoli* was a popular local violinist, but *la Belle Paulo* was a lady so beauteous that even Catherine de Médici 'remained stupefied at the sight of so many perfections united in one person'. She was the Baroness Paule de Fontenille, and in her day she created a considerable problem. So extraordinary was her beauty that she could not so much as appear on the street or in the parks without at once drawing such a crowd of awe-struck and admiring onlookers that the traffic of the city was brought to a halt. Indeed, her appearances so disrupted the orderly life of Toulouse that the *capitouls* passed a remarkable measure by which the number of times she might appear in the confines of the city was strictly limited.

The disruption of traffic during our stay in Toulouse was not, however, the result of any incomparable female face nor was it caused by the mere presence of the *Commodore*. It had to do with that extraordinary event which overtakes the French nation every summer and so disrupts its life that the newspapers and radio even of adjoining countries can speak of nothing but yellow vests. My wife was trying on a dress at one of the excellent *modistes* in the Boulevard Alsace-Lorraine when the tumult began. Three giant-sized Hoover vacuum-cleaners swept rapidly along the roadway with music blaring from their suction pipes.

As soon as the dress was selected and fitted we went out to the pavement and joined the onlookers, and at that moment a team of display vehicles surged down the roadway extolling the virtues of a butane cooking gas. In their wake followed some brobdignagian cigarette packets and a vehicle disguised as a bottle of beer. Far in their rear an immense cheese came motoring down the street, and close behind it a grinning cow with a loud mechanized and bovine laugh. There followed a car of tired-looking technicians of the Belgian Television, and some mobile wagons of the French Broadcasting service. Lorries of chocolate followed, then displays of tyres, kitchen sinks, ice-cream, lollypops, sewing machines, motor-cycles, gramophone discs, electric batteries, proprietary wines, soft drinks, ink, typewriters, radio sets, watches, coffee, brushes, cocoa, washing machines, toothpaste, hairdriers, deodorants, odorants, bath essence, crank-case oil and ready-mix cakes. Interspersed among them were police motor-cycles, reporters by the car-load, ambulances, referees, and a number of dusty vehicles full of hard-faced men, bronzed with their weeks of travel. Each of these cars had a rack of inverted cycles sitting on the roof, wheels in the air.

Not quite last, but forty-three minutes behind the vacuum-cleaner division, came a tired-looking and anxious man in tight shorts and a striped woollen vest. From cap to shoes every part of his clothing bore the name of a brake-maker, a tyre-manufacturer, a wine or an aperitif, and on his back was a number. Amid the din and hullaballoo he passed almost unnoticed — even when, like any ordinary traveller, he drew up by the policeman on point duty to ask him the way. Nobody waved or cheered as he passed, and the leader for the day's run of the *Tour de France* pedalled by with no more applause than would have greeted a clerk cycling home from work. He appeared very hot, we thought, and hungry. He needed a square meal and a good bath, and a rest for those bulging calf muscles which had already carried him from end to end of the country, over the Savoy Alps and through the Pyrénées.

In our childish way we had thought of the *Tour de France* as consisting of a covey of several dozen cyclists straggling along the roads in desperate wheeled competition, but we now realized that cycling was only an excuse for almost every sizeable firm and every French advertising agency to put all available members of staff into the field and cover the country in one long and protracted sales sweep. The riders might secretly be hankering for the honour or status of a *maillot jaune*, but that was purely incidental. The cyclists were no more than a minor accompaniment to the shows put on by their patrons, the great purveyors of consumer goods and *consommations*. Indeed, the hard-pedalling young heroes were the last to arrive on the scene, and when we walked through towards the market we discovered that the city had already been miraculously transformed into a great caravanserai. Down the side-streets were parked long blue trailer caravans like immense horseboxes, each containing several separate flatlets for race officials and engineers and maintenance crews. Neatly they were stationed so that each drainage pipe was immediately over a gutter drain, and the city fire-engines were touring the lines to replenish the roof tanks with water. But the most feverish activity of all was in the market-place in front of the long and stately Capitol itself.

Exactly where one succeeds in pitching a display may be as important as the precise staking of a claim in the Klondyke or the hills of Cripple Creek, and at least something of the same issues are involved. Indeed, the invasion of the Capitol square had something of a gold rush about it. When we arrived the claims had already been staked out and roped, and a team of spidermen in blue overalls was already thirty feet above the ground on the frame of scaffolding they were feverishly erecting to hold a gigantic movie screen on which, as a loudspeaker deafeningly informed all those within a mile, the good citizens of Toulouse would see the day's cycle racing brilliantly displayed at ten o'clock that night, entirely free of charge, this incomparable service being offered through the unbounded magnanimity of the makers of the world's greatest margarine, a substance so delectable that no housewife could dispute that it was absolutely indistinguishable from butter. The show would be in brilliant colour, magnificently photographed by the margarine's special camera team.

The screen was soon erected, and its vast and sparkling sheet shut out one end of the Capitol itself. The further end of the building was also rapidly disappearing as a white-overalled group of steeplejacks wrestled to complete the projection arrangements for another film of the racing, presented to the excellent citizens by the generosity of a heart-sparing coffee. This, too, was to be in colour, and the projection would be at the same time as the margarine film across the square, the second announcer told us. It was evident that any citizen with a sufficient squint might watch both films at once as well as having the excitement of hearing the commentaries shouting each other down.

In the middle of the market a soap-flake outfit was equipping the population with free traffic signs of cardboard — halt, no entry, or parking restricted. Another manufacturer was throwing bundles of paper hats in the air, to be scrambled for by children. Red-coated chocolate men lured willing children into a van, barred them inside it, presented them with all the chocolate they could eat, and then set off round the city with their excited cargo. And as each advertiser had to turn up still further the output of his amplifier to drown the increasing loudness of a score or more of competitors the shindy was soon so ear-splitting that we retired to the Ponts-Jumeaux to flop exhausted on the deck, just as though we ourselves had been straining every muscle to attain the honour of the yellow vest.

Soon after daybreak next morning we were awakened by the sound of heavy traffic streaming over the bridge. It was only six o'clock, but already the vanguard of the great sales column was on its way to the next city along the route. Three hours later the first of the cyclists set out, nose to handlebars, in their dusty wake. The *Tour de France* was on its way again, leaving the municipal street-washers and road-brushers to shovel away the debris of sales brochures and advertisements.

From the way she took to surging and tugging at her ropes we suspected that the *Commodore* wished to be done with Toulouse and start off down the Canal Latéral à la Garonne. But there still remained one visit we wished to make, and for this we could not use her services but would be obliged to go by car — a form of transport much too rapid if one wishes to see anything of the land along the way, but necessary where rivers are absent or nothing more than mountain streams. We wanted to aim southward, to a point some twenty miles north of the Andorran border, and to find the hill which towers above the forgotten little village of Mont-ségur among the foothills of the Pyrénées. For if Riquet's canal had led us to Toulouse, so the tragedy of the Cathars through whose land it had taken us once reached its climax upon that hilltop. There, in a position which was impregnable, they had built their own holy place — the Synagogue of Satan, as the Pope called it — and thither came the sick and the dying for the last rites of their religion. The church of Montségur was no cathedral but an immensely strong and thick-walled building of stone, built upon the site of a ruined fort, and in the final years of the struggle it was the place to which came the *perfecti*, establishing their own simple huts or cells against its wall, perched on the narrow ledge between church and precipice.

For thirty-five years Simon de Montfort and his successors, and finally the French crown, hunted the Cathar Christians with all the ferocity they could muster. Resistance was finally centred upon Montségur, and the forces of orthodoxy moved slowly in to reduce it. In 1243 the siege was begun, and as the new year opened the hill had already been beleaguered for many months. Yet so impregnable was the steep hill that within the church upon its top there lived many *perfecti* and their families, together with others who took their part. The top of the hill was defended by no more than three hundred armed men.

Over this community presided three men. The spiritual leader was the saintly Bishop Bertrand d'En Marti, and the defence was under the captaincy of Pierre-Roger de Mirepoix, aided by Raymond de Perella, the lord of Montségur. Against them were ranged the several thousand soldiers of the investing forces together with such military experts as the Bishop of Albi with his siege-catapult. Although the defenders might have been starved into submission it seems improbable that the top of the hill could ever have been captured except by treachery. After ten months of frustration the French bribed guides to show them a secret approach route, and with their enemies at the gates the defenders knew that they could no longer hold out. It was agreed that there should be a truce of fifteen days, at the end of which the fortress would be handed over. The soldiers would go free, or with only the lightest penances — though in fact they were mostly destined to die in chains in the gaol of Carcassonne. The heretics too, like the Christians at the time of the Roman persecutions, had merely to acknowledge their errors. Perhaps it was expected that the fortnight's reflection would enable them to do so without much difficulty.

On the fourteenth night a beacon light could be seen shining from the top of Mont St Barthélemy, a wild mountain nearly 8,000 feet high and only six miles distant from the battered church. The flaming signal must have mystified the victorious investing forces, but Bishop Bertrand and Pierre-Roger de Mirepoix knew that it meant that the four men detailed to make the dangerous descent of the cliff by ropes in the darkness of the night had reached safety, taking with them the great treasure of the Cathar Church to prevent its falling into the hands of the enemy. What this treasure can have been is still a mystery. It can hardly have consisted of gold or money, for the Cathars embraced poverty and despised possessions. Nor can it have been anything so vague as mere doctrine or articles of belief, as some have suggested, for there were plenty of Cathars in hiding in the mountain fastness who were already versed in these spiritual matters. Conceivably it might have been holy books, and it is sometimes thought that a manuscript copy of St John's gospel was among the treasure.

Romantic writers have convinced themselves that the mysterious treasure was none other than the Holy Grail — the cup which, in medieval legend, had been used for the Last Supper and had also been employed by Joseph of Arimathea to catch the blood of Christ dripping from the spear gash. The Occitan word for a vessel is *grazal*, and this similarity is enough to spark off a train of imagination. No doubt it did so in the mind of Richard Wagner, for it is on the high hill of 'Montsalvat' that the pure ones in *Parsifal* guard the treasure of the grail, and Wagner himself was sure that the mystery of the grail lay in the Pyrénées. A German writer has even identified the Albigensian Crusade as being a war against the Holy Grail.

All this is academic and literary, but extremely unlikely. If little of Cathar doctrine has come down to us the one thing we know for certain is that these people would have no truck with relics and they detested the symbolism of the cross. It is inconceivable that they could have venerated or treasured any cup, and least of all one identified with the Passion. Yet if it is clear that the treasure of the Cathar Church was no chalice or relic, nobody has yet discovered what it was. And there we can leave it, taken down the precipice seven centuries ago, safely hidden, and lost even to any real knowledge of its identity.

The flaming signal on the peak of St Barthélemy pierced the Pyrenean darkness on the night of March 15, 1244. The following night any watchers on the slopes of that wind-swept mountain-top might have seen another fire break the blackness of the lower hills to the north. That same day the truce had expired and the fortress of Montségur was now handed over to the possession of the Pope and his French servants. Disarmed, the soldiers went innocently on their way to betrayal. Of the Cathar Church, more than two hundred men and women were still alive, among them the ageing Bishop Bertrand and several deacons, and a number of volunteer defenders who had asked to be received into it within the period of the truce, although they had no illusions as to what this would mean.

Among the heretics were at least three women, of the family of Raymond de Perella. His daughter was one of them, the young and radiantly beautiful Esclarmonde, whose name alone is a reflection of the light she spread upon the world. Her own mother and her grandmother were with her, and these three staunch women were symbolic of the three generations which had lived through the tragedy until this day when the resistance of the Cathars and the existence of the Languedoc were finally extinguished.

This second and much larger outburst of flames confirmed that
the truce was at an end. Not one single member of that peaceful
community which abhorred violence had been prepared to recant.
All through the day the French soldiers had been busy hewing
trees to construct in the meadow at the foot of the rock a square of
stockade within which was piled an immense heap of brushwood
and branches. Unresisting, the Cathar Christians were fettered,
roped together, and dragged brutally down from the remains of
their fortress church. They laid themselves quietly upon the pyre,
and in one great blaze which flickered across the valleys they were
burned. Perhaps the scent of the resin helped to mask the smell,
and the roar of the fire to drown their groans. Meanwhile the friars
and clergy stood far enough upwind to be safe from the heat so that
they might chant their plainsong of holy devotion and piety, and
the French knights chafed at the irritating way these heretics had
of being so poor that there was no loot to be had.

The church of Montségur is still there today. Roofless, its
massive walls have stood since 1244 on the summit of a peak which
until recent years none could be bothered to visit. At the foot of
the precipitous rocks beneath it there is a meadow where for
centuries sheep have tolled their little bells as they have safely
grazed, or some hardy village peasant has sweatily scythed the
campanulas and gentians and anemones which spot the hay with
patches of vivid colour. This pleasant slope is none other than the
Champ de Cramatchs — the field of the cremated. It was a wish to
see this meadow and to climb up to the site of that protesting
Church long distant in time which drew us to follow the country
road which winds up through the pinewoods south of Lavelanet.
We were not lured merely by curiosity, nor by the morbid attrac-
tion which leads people to wish to stand on the site of a particularly
blood-drenched battlefield of long ago, but by some indefinable
desire to experience something of the place where these things had
happened. For if the men and women of Montségur were burned
and the Languedoc was crushed, the movement for freedom of
faith begun by the Cathars and so terribly repaid at Montségur had
not been destroyed in the flames.

The night that the glow flickered in the sky above the Champ de

Cramatchs there were still many hundreds of Cathars living alone or in small groups, hidden from their hunters in the remote valleys and fastnesses of the Pyrénées. Although Montségur was crushed the Church remained, and the people began secretly to organize themselves into local congregations. Still hunted, they took to the calcareous caverns, the very same caves in which their primitive ancestors had once eked out the life of hunters and had perhaps drawn the outlines of their prey upon the walls. In the cave of Lombrives the Cathar Bishop Loup de Foix preached from a great natural pulpit of rock, and for nearly a century this church and several others survived, its members drawn together for worship and study. Some lived in the recesses far inside the hill, others were scattered among the mountains.

In 1328, another expedition was mounted. French troops made their way doggedly up the mountain torrent of the Ariége, the great river which rises in Andorra, and smelling out three smaller cave-churches they raided and destroyed them. Driving the out-lawed heretics before them they at length reached the entrance to the great cavern of Lombrives. Venturing too close their com-mander was struck by a well-aimed arrow, and he prudently decided not to risk ordering his men to enter the cave. Very much simpler and less costly means of victory were at his disposal. The troops were ordered to carry up an adequate amount of stones and mortar, and before very long the last of the Cathar congregations was sealed up and left to die of suffocation and hunger in the damp darkness of the dripping cavity below the hill.

As time passed, the existence of the cave-cathedral was forgotten, and when its sealing wall began to crumble nobody seems to have been interested. And then one day, just 250 years after the congregation had been entombed, a party of hunters happened upon the cave when seeking shelter from a storm. By now the entrance was open, so the men lit some torches and went further inside to explore. To their astonishment they came upon ladders leaning up against shoulders of the rock, and climbing up to follow the route they found themselves in the upper galleries of the cavern. The sight that met their eyes must have been enough to unnerve the strongest, for in the flickering of the torches held aloft they saw spread out upon the floor a whole people. Men, women and children, they were lying as though asleep, yet their bodies were partly petrified in the stalagmitic deposit from the dripping water which encrusted them where they lay and covered them with a shining case as though of alabaster.

One of the men in the party was deeply moved, and he at once gave orders that the bodies should be removed to cemeteries in the valley villages. And this same individual scratched his name on the rock face, as so many visitors to caves are tempted to do. The title he scrawled was that of *Henri, Roi de Navarre, Comte de Foix* It was only a few years later that he was to mount the throne of France as Henry IV.

It was a strange coincidence that this king had behind him a long line of ancestors of the house of Foix, right back to those who had given protection and succour to the hard-pressed Cathars. Indeed, one of them had herself been a *perfecta*, and Montségur had been part of her inheritance. Perhaps it is less of a coincidence that it was the same King Henry IV who was to issue the famous Edict of Nantes which guaranteed freedom and safety to those who protested against the dogma and doctrine of the established church. Probably that sudden discovery of the sleeping people of Lombrives played its part in shaping that decision.

This second tragedy was to be the end of the Cathar Church, and with it the fugitive heretics pass out of history. And yet they were not extinct. Throughout the Languedoc they still existed, in hiding or in the mountains. But as no further organized Church was possible these men and women dispersed, some crossing into Spain, others heading northward into Germany and the Rhineland, a few reaching Britain. Still they treasured the independence and integrity for which their fellows and their families had been slain, and these things they handed on. The germ lay dormant, but within two hundred years it sent up vigorous new shoots and at last the Reformation broke over Europe. In this great and sweeping revolt against abuse and autocracy, and in the many subsequent murmurings of groups within the Protestant world itself, the heretics of the Languedoc have their more abiding memorial.

It was thoughts such as these which ran through our minds as we urged our small hired car to keep up its courage and carry us ever higher through the woods, rising from the valley of the Ariège to wind among the pines and skirt the shoulders projecting into the vale which sloped to the summit of the pass below the peak of Montségur. The day was sunlit but sultry, and further down the valley the heat of June had been oppressive. Yet the sky was reasonably clear and only the very lightest of fine-weather hazes overlay the sun. All of a sudden something strange occurred. We were no more than a hundred yards from the point where the path leads off from the road to wind up through the meadow, to and fro across the steep cliff until it reaches the bleached ruins of Montségur. As we drew in at the side of the road a cold mist came down, thick and wet as though it were weeping. Getting out of the car we could just make out the path where it climbed the bank, but ten yards further ahead it seemed to be obliterated in a formless whiteness of cold steam. The chill flowed over the slope so that even the sheep stopped munching and their bells were stilled. The grasshoppers had ceased to rasp their love songs, and not even the sound of a tit came from the woods now hidden from sight.

Somewhere within half a mile of us lay the Champ de Cramatchs and far, far above it the deserted walls of Montségur from which Bishop Bertrand d'En Marty, and Esclarmonde, and two hundred others had been dragged to their burning. But we were to see nothing. The cloud had swallowed up the meadow and the church, and left us in its greater wisdom to imagine them as they were on that terrible day of March in the year 1244, and to realize even more fully what they had done for the world.

X

*Wanted, a French Revolution — the Garonne lateral canal
— Cacor aqueduct — the glory of Moissac — disasters to
shipping — Castets-en-Dorthe — the ducks of St Luke —
down to Bordeaux — the rites of the bull — the* Commodore*'s last run*

Some miles to the north-east of Toulouse is the splendid city of
Albi, capital of the Albigensian lands. Its impressive and solid
fortress of rosy cathedral seems to state most emphatically that it
never had any intention of bowing to heretics and reformers,
though it would always be prepared if necessary to serve them as a
very efficient gaol. It rises proudly from the hillside above the
beautiful valley of the Tarn, and beside it is the stately Bishop's
Palace which now contains more than 150 pictures by the local
artist Toulouse-Lautrec, collected by one of his closest friends. All
this is a delight, and yet it is hardly likely to console a boatman
standing on the old bridge across the river. His attention will have
been diverted by the fact that the building just below the arch
nearest the left bank bears the faded inscription *Navigation du
Tarn*. He will hardly have recovered from his surprise when he
sees just beyond the bridge something which may cause him to
wish to end his life by throwing himself from the parapet, for what
he observes is a disused lock. And he can see that for mere peanuts
of expenditure this lock could be returned to use.

The French are admirable people, but if there is one thing they
lack it is a society such as the Inland Waterways Association, a
band of enthusiasts who will resist the corruption of official moth
and governmental rust and if necessary fight against all the
authorities in the country in order to restore to navigation a fine
waterway which has become derelict. Since the Second World War
the canals and rivers of England have sprung alive with boats, and

every year many thousands of people find upon them such holidays as they never dreamed of. Busy executives will fly the Atlantic by jet to glide for a week along such waterways as the Oxford Canal or the Shropshire Union, discovering a Britain of which they were quite unaware. France has a far more extensive system of water-ways than Britain — it has more locks in operation than any other country of the world. Yet the people are so landlubberly — if they will forgive my saying so — that between Paris and Toulouse we only met a single French boat other than barges, and at the time this book was written there was still only one fleet of hire cruisers in the whole country, that of the energetic Peter Zivy and his Saint Line at Poincy on the Marne. At the same date more than fifty firms were hiring out cruisers on the canals of England, and many of the fleets were fully booked a year ahead.

It is tragic that the French yachtsmen and boatowners should not appear to be even faintly interested in their waterways — with the notable exception of the Nautical Society of Toulouse, which we found energetically developing facilities in the basin. For the navigations which have been allowed to run to decay are enough to make one weep. In case we should enjoy ourselves too much aboard the *Commodore* we carry aboard her four navigation manuals of the French waterways, starting in 1888 and spread over seventy years. Anyone intoxicated with the delights of boating can quickly be sobered by reading a dose from these books. For example, he can discover that in 1888 the Tarn was classed as navigable from nine kilometres above Albi to its junction with the Garonne near Moissac, 147 kilometres downstream, through 31 locks. In 1903 traffic was already limited to the lower 62 kilometres; in 1921 it was almost totally absent. In the latest edition the Tarn is not even mentioned. It is defunct, derelict, stripped of its rights and regulations, shoaled, shingled and shallowed. As the French so neatly put it, the stream is *déclassé*.

In 1888 — and much later than that — the *Commodore* could have reached the river at either of two points. These locks are still in existence and intact, though padlocked, but even if a boatman were to secure a key or cut the chains he would get nowhere. On the Tarn itself the works have been blocked or destroyed. Nor is it only a matter of the Tarn. In earlier days we could have turned up into the Lot and navigated that magnificent river for 256 kilometres, passing through 76 locks and diving into three tunnels which, like those on the Meuse, were cut through necks of the hill to short-circuit large loops of river. The *Commodore* could even have passed under the glorious Pont Valentré at Cahors, a structure which not only has its three tall machicolated guard towers but under the southernmost arch a lock complete but for the fact that its rotted gates have been replaced by a concrete barrier dropped into slots. She might have turned into the Drot and explored its course with the aid of another 21 locks, or she could have elected instead to climb down from the canal into the Baise, with its 30 locks between St-Jean-Poutge and the Garonne. Gaillac and Albi, Cahors and Fumel, Puy l'Evêque and Montauban, these are only a few of the places to which a boatman could still penetrate on the waterways of southern France if only the works had not been allowed to decay.

There would be no finer cruising ground in Europe if the French would only wake up to the possessions that are theirs. Not even the Rhine and its tributaries could compete with the branching routes spread between the Rhône and the Gironde, yet apart from the canal route itself there is not one of these waterways which still remains navigable over even a single kilometre. *Allons, enfants de la patrie. Voyez* how the insular English have tackled the situation. Volunteers restored the Lower Avon. They dredged the Kennet too. Others rebuilt the 37 locks of the Stratford Canal so that in the year of Shakespeare's Quatercentenary the city was filled with colourful boats, and motor cycles from Japan were unloaded at the town quay as the first cargoes to reach the city since 1912 — at which date the rivers of the Languedoc were navigable also over much of their length.

The tributaries of the Garonne have particular characteristics which render them difficult to control — for example, the flow of the Lot can increase by a factor of one hundred, and in the sections where it runs between cliffs the flood may be penned up to raise the level forty feet above normal. But in spite of these troubles the rivers were navigable for many years, and the Lot since the first locks were built along its valley on the orders of Colbert. Is it really unthinkable that the French could rouse themselves and found a fighting organization, a *Societé des Voies Navigables Intérieures* pledged to undo the results of half a century of neglect?

We must leave the answer to the French themselves and resume

o

our voyage on the waters still open, allowing the *Commodore* to
blow a warning note across the Ponts-Jumeaux and disappear down
the Canal Latéral à la Garonne. This is not a particularly spectacular waterway in its upper reaches, for it runs hard beside the
main road and railway at least as far as Grisolles, four hours and
nine locks down the line. But at last the railway veers away as the
road has done, and the canal shakes off its matter-of-fact straight-
ness and adopts a more rural course with noticeable bends. At
Montech there is a junction where pretty canal craft are clustered
against the bank.

This side branch leads off to Montauban, seven miles distant,
and it is still navigable even if one can no longer steam proudly
through that city but must end the journey in a deserted but clean
canal basin tucked away out of sight behind the gasworks. This is
the same basin round which an excited crowd gathered on a
December night in 1843 to see the great marvel of water flowing in
to flood it to a depth of almost three feet. Little by little and week
by week the level was raised, and when it was evident that the
banks would stand the strain barges were allowed to use the waterway. In June a boat arrived from Sète, laden with wine, a fact
which demonstrated to any Montaubanais reluctant to credit such
rumours that their city really was in contact with the outside world
and even with the Mediterranean. An official opening was called
for, and no lesser person than the Minister of Public Works was
towed down the cut from Montech in a great barge pavilioned in
splendour and steered by sailors *en grand costume*. He arrived after
dark — it was November — and his ship was locked down into the
Tarn to steer through the city accompanied by a floating military
band. Flags, torches, a guard of honour and a banquet were laid
on, and the canal was well and truly opened.

The next step was to introduce a passenger service. The ship
Irma was built and launched at Montech, designed as a postboat for
the Montauban–Toulouse run. Of delicate lines and slim figure the
Irma was launched in sober fashion, with a religious service of
blessing at the Montech basin. She proved to be an extremely fast
runner, and with five relays of horses she could cover the distance
to Toulouse as fast as the stage-coaches and *diligences*, and for half

the price. Considering that she had to negotiate 21 locks she must have been swift indeed.

Montauban was now determined to become a centre of shipping. Another postboat was added, and the city campaigned successfully for locks into the Garonne at Moissac. Ships could then reach Bordeaux — even if the return journey up the Garonne was not so easy — and the city fathers next turned their minds to the idea of canalizing the Aveyron, which joined the Tarn below the city. The winding course of this beautiful stream with its castles set high on shoulders of rock was comparatively steep, for in the 140 kilometres above its junction with the Tarn it fell 300 feet and some 50 locks would have been necessary. The calculation of the costs was still in hand when the Grand Central Railway arrived and slew the navigation before it was born. Montauban's days as a great port were gone for ever.

We had gone no more than five miles beyond Montech when we saw a barge ahead of us, apparently stationary in the exit of a bridge. Coming up behind her we discovered her to be the *Lacourtensort*. She was jammed securely across the canal at an angle, her stern embedded in a shoal by the left bank and her bow similarly fast by the opposite shore. There was no question of passing round her, and this would in any case have been discourteous. The skipper was working the motor at full speed, his wife and daughter were winching a hawser attached to a tree, and grandmother was pushing vigorously with a barge-pole. Three farm labourers were straining at a rope. Yet all this effort was of no avail. The *Lacourtensort* was stuck fast.

The *Commodore* has always liked to play the gallant, and in the course of her life she has pulled a laden Thames steamer off a shoal, hauled home Thames cruisers broken down, dragged a boat out of Marlow weir, picked up an English yacht in trouble in the Channel and a Danish motorboat in the western Baltic, and separated a pair of Swedish schooners which had become a tangled mess of spars and rigging and mixed-up masts. On a Sunday afternoon she had once pulled a whole canoe rally up the Main in line astern to save them the mere bother of paddling. Splendidly manœuvreable to an inch she was just the ship for these occasions, so we now drew her back through the bridge to turn her, then let her run down again stern first towards the barge. We put two lines on the bulky craft and let the *Commodore* heave for all she was worth. The bargeman twirled his wheel, grandma poled, the women windlassed and the labourers lugged, but there was not half an inch of movement. Only the canal, churned by the propellers of the two craft, curled and slopped like milky coffee.

During a pause we asked the skipper how he came to be stuck in this strange position. He explained that it was not unusual to find that the supply of water running all the way down from the Ponts-Jumeaux thirty miles back was so great that where the canal narrowed for a bridge the flow came streaming through at quite a pace. The *Lacourtensort* had emerged from the bridge a few degrees off straight, and before her skipper could straighten her this jet-stream of water striking one side of the stern had shoved her round. The bow had struck, then the stern had been forced into the opposite shore and there she was.

Once again we essayed, and then again. We even tried taking up the slack of the lines less gradually, but in so doing we only managed to part both the ropes. By now it was clear that not even the combined engines of the barge and the *Commodore* were enough to pull the barge back against the power of the streaming, so a lad was sent cycling off to a farm. The farmer soon arrived with a powerful new tractor and he was obviously delighted to try to pull the barge across the canal. This his tractor did, with the greatest of ease, and we were as relieved as was the skipper. He invited everyone within sight to swallow a mouthful of the ordinary red wine he carried aboard, and then he beckoned us to pass him towards Lock 17, St Martin.

The canal was still unspectacular. Another half hour brought us to run under the bridges and past the *boules* pitch of the town of Castelsarrasin, but even from on board we could judge confidently that the best thing about the town was its misleadingly romantic name with an echo of wild warriors with scimitars. Perhaps it was indeed the site of a saracen castle, but not even the ruins remained and so we headed the *Commodore* on towards Moissac. Before she reached it she came to one of the most impressive of all the sights along the canal, the great long aqueduct of thirteen stone arches which spans the Tarn river and leads to the lock of Cacor. To the left the Tarn flows away towards a weir and a derelict river lock, but upstream and on the right of the canal the railway bridge is a reminder of one of the most curious adventures a canal aqueduct could ever have had.

The rivers of southern France are capricious, long dry periods being sometimes interspersed with powerful floods. Undoubtedly it was these floods and the shoals they brought with them that made navigation unusually difficult and costly to maintain, but first and foremost the waterways were broken by the railways, and by the lack of adequate industry. Yet the floods could cause great damage, and one of the most serious inundations in modern times occurred in 1930, when the flood-water surged down the Tarn with such force that the railway viaduct of Cacor was snapped off and swept away. Overnight, the main line from coast to coast was broken, and in place of the bridge there was now a gap of two or three hundred yards of swirling and sucking muddy turmoil. Surprisingly, the canal bridge — which offered much greater resistance to the stream, was left quite intact.

These circumstances provided the background for a piece of engineering unique in history. The railway bridge had gone but the canal still stood. The watercourse of the aqueduct happened to be broader than was necessary for the barges, so the canal was drained off and the towpath on the northern side broadened with blocks of concrete. Upon these a railway track was laid, and at either end of the aqueduct a mile of line led away to rejoin the railway. When the works were complete and the canal refilled with water six weeks after the interruption, the first pair of locomotives steamed along the towpath beside the canal to test the new track. They weighed 180 tons apiece, and hauled a further nine wagons loaded with earth and stone. The bridge held without a murmur or a crack, and for another two years all the trains passed over the canal bridge, their speed limited to five kilometres per hour. As the barges were sometimes making six, or even seven if unladen, there were occasionally some exciting races, with the ships only a foot or two from the wheels of the coaches to which they had given the hospitality of their private river-crossing.

Beyond the aqueduct the canal turns sharply toward the Tarn and opens out into the long and attractive canal port of Moissac. Perhaps we would have stayed some days at this place without further reason, but the lock-keeper informed us that a day's journey ahead the canal had been blocked by a freak wind, which had so effectively felled a number of trees across it that the engineering staff expected to have a week's work before the route was clear and the ships could pass. This happened to suit us well enough, for there could be no better place than Moissac at which to wait awhile, particularly when the enforced delay happened to coincide with the celebrations of the nine hundredth anniversary of the foundation — or rather, of the reconsecration — of the abbey.

The foundation is said in legend to go back to Clovis in the sixth century and in history more probably to the seventh. Certainly the abbey was sacked by the Vikings when they sailed up the Garonne, and after it had been rebuilt it was affiliated to the famous foundation of Cluny. It is this second building with its famous cloisters which has survived for nine centuries, in spite of the attacks upon the town of Simon de Montfort, the occupation by the English, and their expulsion a few years later by the Duke of Anjou. The next adventure was its pillaging by the revolutionaries, who would have destroyed the whole abbey if a public-spirited local official had not swiftly bought it at his own expense and later presented it to the town. It then became in turn a barracks, a gunpowder factory and a forage store. Thoroughly humiliated, the great court of cloisters was to be pulled down to make way for the Bordeaux-Sète railway line when reason began to assert itself again and the Fine Arts Commission intervened at the last moment to preserve from complete destruction what is confidently asserted to be the finest work of romanesque architecture in the whole of France.

Perhaps it is the Lancastrian in me, or maybe it is no more than the effect of free-churchmanship and a nonconformist ancestry, but if ever I am told that I am certain to like some particular object of art there arises within me a curious kind of rejection which is more likely to make me avoid seeing or hearing or experiencing the thing in any way whatsoever, or, if that is unavoidable, to dislike it intensely. I knew that Moissac had been awarded two of M.

Michelin's guide book stars and the gateway three, that bus tours
went to the abbey, and that it was said that the portal was something nobody should miss, so the scene might hardly have been
better set for me to approach Moissac with a mixture of hostility
and suspicion. And then I came upon Robert Payne's *The Splendour of France*. Here was a man of obvious sense, integrity, and
strong religious feeling, one who was as likely as myself to be
deterred by eulogies and recitals of architectural merit, and yet he
was so utterly carried away with the gateway of Moissac that one
could see that merely to be confronted by the Christ of the Second
Coming over the doorway had been a tremendous experience to
him, a spiritual adventure more than an excursion into the
criticism of art.

'If everything in France had to be destroyed and only one object
was allowed to remain, I would choose that gateway,' he concluded.
And one knew that he meant it, that it had done something to him
which was vital and indescribable. And it was perhaps because of
what Robert Payne had written of Moissac that I approached with
rather more humility the abbey church of St Peter, standing at the
end of a long curving small-town street of shops leading up from
the canal port.

Even if I had not been in a reasonable frame of mind the Christ
of Moissac would have shattered any opposition. He and his whole
vibrant entourage of seraphims and elders and evangelists come
from a century before the Inquisition burned two hundred
Albigensian Christians in the town. He is not a Christ of hatred,
nor is he a figure of passion or a mere man of sorrows exalted to
wear a saintly dressing-gown, but a person of utter authority and of
a power that would be terrifying were it not for the complete calm
and serenity with which he is opening the new age of justice and
right. There is a halo behind his head, made up of a formal cross
and a dozen thistles, but it is not the halo which makes the Christ
truly royal. Nor is it the grandeur of the kingly robe. It is the face,
of a Christ who is infinitely great. The twenty-four elders are
almost breaking their necks in the suddenness of their amazement
at his appearance and the rebecs on which they were about to play
a well-practised song of welcome dangle unplucked from their

hands. Only the two angels in attendance have an air of superior knowledge, as though they had known all along that it would be like this when time had come to an end and existence ran into a new dimension.

There is no anger in the face of the Christ regnant, no humility and yet no pride. He stares one straight in the face as he has done since 1130 — a fact which itself stresses the childish relativity of human dating beneath that gaze. He is a Christ who cannot be deceived, but who understands what it is to be human and bound within four dimensions. He forgives, but he will have no compromise with evil. Absolute justice and glory is portrayed above the door of the abbey church of Moissac, and it was done by a man unknown. Perhaps it is best that he cannot just be catalogued as a particular artist in stone, for what is more important than his identity is the certainty that this central figure of the parousia is not one that any man could have thought up. It is authentic, and can only have come from knowledge, from a genuine vision of the truth of eternity.

Nine hundred years before our arrival at Moissac the Abbot de Bredon had reconsecrated the church, but it was not until the year 1100 that the court of cloisters was completed in the reign of the Abbot Ansquitil whose stocky figure is seen on one of the pillars, looking cautiously sideways as though trying to catch one of the brethren whispering during the office. It was already dark when we took our seats on the lawn within them, beneath a cedar tree already five centuries old. The night was warm, and so still that the air did not stir the scented needles of the cedar or cause the least flicker of the candles. We were to have Vivaldi and Bach and Mozart, and if there had been nothing else to delight us at Moissac it would have been worth the journey merely to be introduced to Mozart's Double Concerto for Flute and Harp.

The concert began with Vivaldi, and the orchestra — which had come from the University of Tübingen — seemed to be ill at ease, not in their playing but over some matter which we in the audience could not guess. The first movement of the concerto was followed by only the swiftest break before the second began, and the piece had reached the third movement when it seemed to us that the conductor was definitely accelerating. The tempo increased still further, and we were surprised to see the maestro glance at his watch. The horns horned, the harpsichord tinkled as fast as its jacks would pluck, and the string-players sweated in the warmth of their energetic bowing. At last with a grand flourish the conductor brought the orchestra into the final chord, sustained it for a moment, then cut it off. And even as we began to applaud we realised why Vivaldi's *allegro* had had that night to be more *allegro* than ever. With a roar like an intercontinental ballistic missile the SNCF sent the Marseille night-mail thundering by.

When in the previous century the Fine Arts Commission had intervened to save the cloisters, the railway was cut through the town just the same and was merely moved a few yards further back towards the hill. Lesser abbey buildings were demolished, and a rock cutting was chopped in the stone immediately behind the corner of the cloisters. Trains from the west steal up unheard to approach through a tunnel, and there is almost complete silence until the locomotive bursts screaming into the open air, shaking even the confident Abbot Ansquitil where he stands with his hand raised in blessing.

By the end of the week barges were arriving from the west, a sign that the blockage had been cleared. Early in the morning we blew for the *pontier* to be so good as to swing back the town bridges, and the *Commodore* moved out of Moissac into the broad plain of the Garonne with its orchards and fields of grain and maize. The great stream itself was soon so close beside us that a bridge could span the railway, canal, towpath, bank and the river itself in one grand suspended span, but a few miles ahead the river cut off to the left and the railway to the right, leaving us to make a stately and unaccompanied entry into the town of Valence d'Agen, a place which provides an elegant course of lawns and trees and walks to please the bargeman, but nevertheless turns its own face the other way. Not that the town is particularly interesting. It has changed too much for the plan of an English *bastide* or fortified strong-point to be discernable any more, but it is said locally that hard by the old church English knights lie buried in all their armour.

The largest city on the Canal Latéral is Agen, five and a half hours and seven locks down the line. It is a centre of fruit-growing, but its appearance from the canal is hideous in the extreme, a large and grimy goods yard and a cathedral restored in the worst possible period giving the place an air of an industrial town of the Lille industrial basin rather than of a French Evesham. By far its most attractive feature is the aqueduct, for on the edge of the town the canal suddenly takes it into its head that the left bank of the Garonne is better than the right, and flying high over the shoals and the fleet water it crosses to the further shore by a canal bridge more than one third of a mile in length.

Beyond this the waterway runs for many miles with few locks and very little in the way of scenery. One long straight section follows another, the flat line broken only by very plain concrete bridges above and the plop of fishes teasing the anglers spread out in seated file along the banks. The towns lie away to the side, clustered by the river which was navigable for flat boats in the middle ages and in the time of Riquet. Indeed as late as the last century there were attempts to make use of it for transport, and an enterprising Monsieur Jollet of Toulouse built a passenger vessel, the *Clémence-Isaure*, with a draught of only eleven inches. She was to be able to navigate the river under all conditions, and in fact she worked up from Agen to Toulouse in about fifteen hours. When the river was reasonably high barges could float down it instead of using the canal, and for this reason locks were provided to connect with the stream at Moissac and Agen. The river trip saved time and money, but it was certainly dangerous.

Only occasionally does the navigation itself brush against the edge of a village of fruit and vegetables. Sérignac and Buzet, Damazan and le Mas d'Agenais, Fourques, Meilhan and Hure — each appears for a moment through a rift in the trees along the bank and is a pleasant enough place in which to take a simple lunch or supper at the village inn, but none of them is in any way famous. Watching the numbers on the kilometre stones along the bank we knew that we were approaching the scene of the recent blockage, and turning a slight bend beyond km. 147 we came upon an astonishing scene of destruction. The towpath was on the right,

and on that side the trees were set well back from the water, but on the left bank the giant planes perched rather more precariously with only the roots on the further side anchored in firm ground. Or rather, that was how they had stood until ten days earlier when the storm had struck, for now there was nothing but a slope scored by tractor treads and dotted with heaps of gigantic logs, neatly sawn. Within minutes the whole row of magnificent trees had been tipped over and felled, their massive trunks stretching right across the waterway and their branches mingling with those of their fellows on the further shore.

Upon one of the upended stumps was painted the inscription *J. Marie, 14 août 63*. Certainly it must have been an exciting moment for the skipper of the *Jane-Marie* when he found himself chugging along the wind-lashed water and saw the great plane tree abeam of his craft begin to crack and topple. He wound back the throttle to its full extent and the old engine panted its hardest, so that the wheelhouse and stern were just clear before the tree struck the water with a crash which shook the timbers of the craft from stem to stern. But the captain had no time even to offer up a prayer of thanks to St Nicholas — the patron saint of bargees throughout Europe — for ahead of the *Jane-Marie* another of the huge trees was tipping, bending and starting its slow plunge towards the water. Full speed astern the hot engine strained, and once again the barge avoided being taken to the bottom. She had had a remarkable escape, and she now had to wait a week before the two fallen trees could be dismantled which held her so neatly imprisoned between them.

One cannot pass along the unspectacular stretch of canal from Agen to Castets without noticing that disasters have more than once struck upon vessels using the waterway. Indeed, there is something unnerving about the little memorials along the towpath imploring prayers for the souls of bargemen who have lost their lives at various points. At km. 162 the monument to the victims of the steamer *Le Gascon* in 1908 induced me to jump ashore in the village of Fourques to buy a bottle of wine and some eggs, and to enquire what had happened to the vessel in question. Nobody seemed to know, but the grocer sent his small boy running to seek out an ancient sage of the village who would be sure to remember. And so he did. *Le Gascon*, he explained, tapping the ground with his stick for emphasis, was a steam barge. There had been a celebration, and the master was drunk. He omitted to pay attention to the pressure-gauge. Hardly had the ship passed under the village bridge when there was an explosion which shook the houses, dismantled *Le Gascon* into a number of pieces of steel of irregular shape, and hurled all five men aboard her into the air with such force that their shattered bodies descended on the further side of the trees beyond the towpath. It was foolish, the old man added, tapping his forehead significantly. Yes, it was extremely irresponsible to drink oneself stupid when steering a barge, particularly a steamer.

At km. 179 another explosion is commemorated, but a more recent one. The memorial is to the crew of a petrol tanker which was somehow sparked off at that point. How it happened was never known, for of the boat and its crew even less was left than of *Le Gascon*.

In spite of these fearful reminders we carried on, and only twelve kilometres further ahead we came in sight of Castets. Of all the places west of Moissac this is the most attractive, for though the village of Castets-en-Dorthe itself has no buildings or streets of any interest it has a real charm which derives from the presence of the water. A château and the village itself are perched on the top of a cliff, so close to the edge that they appear to be wondering whether

or not to fling themselves off in a suicide pact. Were they to do so
they would land in a narrow strip of meadow which flanks the
canal, here broadened out into a fine sheet of water which ends at a
pair of deep barge-locks leading out into a curve of the Garonne,
just above a bridge. The yellowish-brown water of the river comes
careering round the bend with tremendous force, swashing and
gurgling against the shoals and moving at such a pace that to
attempt to bathe in it would probably be disastrous. And if anything were needed to emphasize the might of the river it is there in
the lock-cottage, which is perched far above the level of the water
and yet has its accommodation and office on the first floor and
reached by an outside staircase which runs up beside a calibrated
measure. From this the keeper can occasionally read that the water
lapping against the walls is perhaps thirty feet above the normal
summer level, but the outside stair enables him to get into a boat
and row over to the hilltop village to buy provisions for his
beleaguered home.

Several Midi barges were lying along the shore on the village
side of the canal, waiting for the tide on the following day. We
drew in across the water from them and walked across the lock
gates to the pathway winding up towards the village. There were
sounds of a band from up on the cliff, but the music was almost lost
in the noise of breaking glass, and on reaching the summit we found
the villagers and bargemen celebrating the festival of St Luke —
who, it seemed, was the particular patron of Castets-en-Dorthe.
The sounds of wreckage came from the space behind the church,
where anyone who could break three empty wine-bottles with three
steel *boules* at a range of ten yards could win a full one. Heaps of
cullet of dark and light green were piled along the cliff edge and
shards were tinkling down to the path below.

A notice tacked to trees all through the village announced that
on the following morning there would be a *grande course de canards*
on the canal. French is a language almost as full of traps as English,
but we dismissed the possibility that the race could be one of
lumps of sugar dipped in brandy. Could the *canards* be of the hoax
variety? Over our wine we asked the innkeeper what species of
canards were to be raced. Were they real quack-quack ducks?

'*Pourquoi pas?*' he said. 'On the feast of St Luke one makes always the race of ducks. It is very amusing.'

Towards eleven next morning the younger members of the community began to congregate along the water's edge to either side of the *Commodore* and on both banks. Then a rowboat put out from the shore and took up a station in the middle of the broad water between ourselves and the waiting barges. In this boat were a boy who did the actual rowing, an old village father with a mysterious bulging sack, and the local constable, in his shirt sleeves and with trousers rolled up above his knees, but wearing his pill-box hat as a symbol of the law and order conferred upon the country of France by her police force.

A loudspeaker croaked over the water. 'The first duck is presented by the community of Castets to those born within the parish boundaries and not more than fourteen years of age.'

The older youths and girls stepped back and the younger ones crowded along the banks. A dozen or more dived into the canal and waited, afloat.

The old man in the boat was the duck-keeper, and untying the neck of his sack he pulled out a muscovy, holding it by the shoulders of its wings. He handed it to the constable, who stood up in the stern and heaved it high in the air, watching with arms out-stretched as the bird fluttered down to the water. Except for his cap and the fact that he had no beard he looked like the representations of Noah one sometimes sees in stained glass, his arms raised to heaven as he launches the dove on its fact-finding mission.

At once the boys and girls were racing for the duck, which sat on the water watching them out of the side of its head as though trying to remember everything its relations had told it about the St Luke celebrations. The leading boy was approaching swiftly with a crawl stroke and now he was near enough to shoot out a hand to grab. But the duck was not there. As he lunged, the bird rose to its feet and flapped splashing along the water to sit down a few yards further up the canal. Several boys were swiftly in pursuit and others plunged in from the further bank. The muscovy looked quickly, saw itself hemmed in, and upending its stern it dived neatly below the hunters to surface again close to the bank.

But with primaries trimmed to prevent it flying right away the duck could not escape for ever. After a chase up and down the reach it was at last seized by a boy, who conveyed it struggling to the bank. The duck was his — to carry home for dinner if it was a male, or to keep as a pet, or as a layer if a female.

Other ducks released were for girls only, or for the under eighteens, or open for general competition. One of them was quickly caught by a good swimmer who approached the mêlée along the canal bottom, reached up, and grabbed the astonished bird by the feet. The next was nearly landed on three occasions but always struggled free from its captor before the shore, and raced away to start all over again. The sixth duck had just been thrown aloft when we moved up to the lock to start dropping down to the tideway an hour before the ebb, so that we should be sure of plenty of water over the shallows at Langon, five miles down the river.

We dropped slowly down between the wet walls with the strange smell of summer water all around us. It was a deep lock and some of the local people leaned over the edge to wave to us and wish us *bon voyage*. But we ourselves were just a bit solemn, and if we were more silent than usual this was because each of us knew that this was the last lock through which the *Commodore* would ever take us. She had carried us up the Thames to Gloucestershire and by the Grand Union Canal to Warwickshire. In Sweden she had climbed uphill and down dale through locks large and small until she crossed into Norway. Five years before she reached Castets I had counted up her lockage and discovered from her collection of toll-tickets that she had then passed through more than one thousand. Since then she had crossed France to Alsace, explored the German rivers, nosed her way through the grimy locks of the Ruhr area, swept round through Holland, and set out again from the Scheldt on this last voyage which alone had involved more than five hundred locks before she reached the Garonne. If ever a boat was at home in a lock, or *écluse*, a *Schleuse* or *sas*, a *sluis* or *slus* or *sluss*, that boat was the *Commodore*. But it was no use deceiving ourselves. She was ageing fast, both in her timbers and in her machinery, and however affectionately we might regard her as a

friend who had opened up for us one country after another it was
time for her to be pensioned off. She would not have the stamina
to reach Prague, or Moscow or Odessa, or to find her way to the
meres of Finland or the fast reaches of the Danube, or wherever
else the waterways of Europe might take us. She would have to
hand over to a young successor and disappear gracefully into
retirement, just as though she were a human parent.

The Castets lock drained slowly, but at last the lower gates were
cranked open to let her out. We did not at once start off, but
waited for the wooden barge *Alcyon*, hidden in the deep pen of the
twin lock beside us. Her skipper had told us that we would do well
to follow astern of him until beyond the Langon bridge, after
which we could run straight down the river without worry.
Eventually we heard the chug-chug of his motor increase to a
furious hum as he thrust the barge out into the current, and then
her handsome curving stem came sweeping past the opening
where we were waiting. We gave him a start of a hundred yards or
more and then surged out into the turbulence of the Garonne.

Skipper Ferrand beckoned us alongside and insisted on lashing
the *Commodore* to his own craft, suggesting that we should go
below and have lunch instead of bothering to steer. But it was
difficult to accept the kind offer, for we were on the last run we
should ever make aboard our ship, and we wanted to enjoy it to
the full. We shared a bottle of wine with him whilst other vintages
went gliding by on either hand — Sauternes behind the hill to
port, Barsac facing across the valley to Loupiac, and somewhere
in the haze over the starboard bow the land of Entre Deux Mers.

Off Cadillac we cast adrift and left the friendly *Alcyon* astern,
wallowing behind us down a river which was neither ugly nor
beautiful. The course ran all the way between belts of trees and we
saw little of the places we passed. None of the little towns spread
down to the water, for they knew too much about the capricious
floods of the Garonne to venture too close to its banks. It was more
than three hours before we made out the outline of the first of the
Bordeaux chimneys, and just four hours down from Castets that
the *Commodore* shot an arch of the long stone bridge at the
entrance to the city. Astern, the colourful barges of the Midi

canals lay lashed like a raft of huge logs beside the loading wharf. Ahead the stream swept round a fine curve where the liners and cargo-vessels lay along the broad quays, with the cranes poking down into their holds. We spun the wheel, circled over our wash and let the *Commodore* slide in on the current.

'Finished with engines,' a liner's captain would have signalled on the engine-room telegraph. We only had one engine, and I had spent several evenings crouching over its works to persuade it to persevere as far as Bordeaux without a hiccup. For the last hundred miles it had been propped up with blocks of wood culled from a building site, for the starboard bearers had given way and I had found the engine still turning merrily but supported on its own shaft. It was the *Commodore*'s fourth engine since she had set out under our command fifteen years earlier, and now she was nearly finished with it. Its last job a day or two later would be to take her to the shipyard.

If the end of this voyage had meant for us an end to all such explorations I think none of us could have borne it. We would rather she had sunk and we had gone down with her — though no doubt we would have rowed very lustily for the shore if she had really shown any likelihood of foundering. But on our way across the Languedoc we had accepted that the old *Commodore* had reached that point where the refits and repairs became too time-consuming and too costly to be worth while. We had already been planning a *Commodore II* to take her place, and we soon realized that this craft would be better built specially, ideally fitted to carry on where her predecessor had left off. She would be an unpretentious ship but strong and sturdy, capable of breasting the fast rivers, striking occasionally on shoals, and resisting firmly the unintentional squeezes and pinches given her by two-thousand-ton Rhine barges in the locks of the larger canals of Europe. She would be. . . . But her story belongs to the future. This book is about the elder *Commodore* and her young sister must wait.

Packing up the contents of a ship and filling one's folded shirts and trousers with plates and cutlery is a time-consuming business and one which the reader need not share. The *Commodore* was beginning to look extremely bare inside, and rather than stay aboard her in her reproachful and stripped state we took ourselves off into the Landes, the area south of Bordeaux where the Atlantic is edged with giant dunes behind which stretch the forests of terebinth trees, each with a gash above a little pot hung on the trunk to catch the resin from which is produced the turpentine for which the Landes is famous. Here in a small village by the coast we came once again upon the cult of the bull, and on our final night we were initiated into new varieties of ritual — though only as spectators.

It may be that the game of bull jumping is played exactly as it was in Crete long ago. However, that may be, a strong-armed individual stands at one end of the arena, braced against a barrier. In front and facing away from him is an amiable bull, probably of Basque origin, and round its horns is a noose of rope. The bull moves forward a foot or two, and at once the man hauls the rope to pull it back. The bull pushes out more strongly and is tugged back again. At each successive check the bull's muscles become more tensed, and when at last the man slips the noose the creature shoots down the arena like a rocket fired horizontally.

At the same moment the jumper starts his run from the further end of the pitch. Bull rushes at man, man charges bull. It seems that nothing can prevent the most fearful collision, but at the last instant the young man hurdles, passing right over the horns of the creature, all down the length of its steaming body, and landing lightly on the ground behind its tail. We found it a beautiful skill to watch but we wondered how one began. Did one start with a cat and gradually work upwards?

Perhaps the most diverting form of the bull cult is le Tauroball. I have never enjoyed watching ordinary soccer, but there can be no doubt that the mere addition of a loose bull on the pitch transforms it into a game with great possibilities. The teams on this particular evening were volunteers from the crowd, and we ourselves were quite willing to stand down and let the local lads have the fun. The game was played according to the ordinary rules of association football, but it is a curious thing how difficult it is for a player to give his undivided attention to a long dribble up the edge of the field when he finds that the moment he starts to run the bull runs too, converging upon him sharply and with obvious intent. Even goalkeeping is not so simple if one has to dodge behind the post just when an attacking forward is well placed to shoot.

The bull was well used to the game and he had an endearing habit of standing right over the ball, pawing the ground and snorting. Considerable ingenuity was needed to put the ball into play again, and in the course of the match there were some ripped trousers and a few successful knock-downs by the bull. But the better players among the young men knew that if no other escape was possible from a real charge it was best to fling themselves prostrate on the ground. The bull would go thundering overhead and there was a chance of being trodden upon rather heavily in the course of its repeated and clumsy charges, but with the hands held over the neck and back of the head there was nothing worse than a slight bruising to fear. Certainly the bull had formidable horns, but it could not stand on its head sufficiently to gore a person on the ground or skewer them to the earth. Getting up again might be a dangerous moment, but we noticed that another player would assist by courteously having himself chased to distract the creature whilst the other scrambled quickly to his feet.

Tauroball was a more violent sport than boating, and we were well content to enjoy it from the ringside. Then we returned to the Garonne and to the *Commodore*, now ready to offer herself to any other owner who would be less exacting than ourselves. Thirty-five minutes on the tide was enough to take her up from her temporary mooring to the shipyard where she was to lie. We each steered her part of the way, remembering among ourselves some of the adventures we had had with her in fifteen years of companionship. How she had assaulted the half-derelict Kennet and Avon Navigation and battled her way to Newbury. The friends she had made for us in Friesland and Bavaria. The skill with which she rode up a Dutch dyke in the darkness, and her nineteen hours on a shoal in a wild Swedish river. The city of Linköping dismantling a bridge to let her pass. Aubry with his '*ici graviers, là rochers*'. The whole glorious voyage across the Languedoc, one worthy to be her last.

We had reached the shipyard pontoon, and we stopped the engine and closed the sea-cocks. It was an evening of soft sunshine and the *Commodore* looked very beautiful. We brought up the champagne she had won for helping the *modistes* of Toulouse to show their new fashions, and we drank it on deck. Then we hauled down her flag and walked away through the lumber of the shipyard. I think we were really very close to tears, but we never looked back. And when the night train for Paris clanked across the wide Garonne to carry us home, she was hidden from us by the warehouses down the quay.

INDEX OF PEOPLE AND PLACES

(For ease of reference people are listed in italics)

PRINTED IN GREAT BRITAIN
BY ROBERT MACLEHOSE AND CO. LTD
THE UNIVERSITY PRESS, GLASGOW